The Hidden Door

Mark A. Burch

THE HIDDEN DOOR: MINDFUL SUFFICIENCY AS AN
ALTERNATIVE TO EXTINCTION

First published by the Simplicity Institute, Melbourne, 2013
www.simplicityinstitute.org

ISBN-13: 978-0-9875884-7-0

WHAT OTHERS ARE SAYING ABOUT *THE HIDDEN DOOR*:

"Mark Burch's anthology is part of a new generation of literature that has begun to foreground the ethos and practices of voluntary simplicity and sufficiency within our understanding of the technology of social change. Surfing the zeitgeist with great personal insight, Mark addresses many current and latent questions about the tools and concepts that will be essential aids on the journey to the great transition."

Dr. Peter Doran
School of Law, Queen's University Belfast Northern Ireland

"In this book, Mark Burch confronts lurking inconsistencies between the economics of sustainability and the practices of everyday life. This provocative exploration transcends shallow fixes, breaks down the consumer walls that confine us, and inspires the transformation of consciousness our society so urgently needs."

James Magnus-Johnston
Canadian Director, Centre for the Advancement of the Steady-State Economy (CASSE)

"I have been a big fan of Mark Burch and his writings on mindfulness and voluntary simplicity for years. *The Hidden Door* brings fresh perspective to the subject with wisdom, insight and compassion. A must read for anyone who cares about the planet and the direction of human destiny."

Dr. Randall Hardy
Wellness Author, Speaker and Consultant

"Humanity is demonstrating a remarkable capacity to ignore the very real likelihood that involuntary simplicity will be thrust upon billions of people in the not-so-distant future if we do not do a better job of preventing environmental catastrophes caused by short-sighted political, social and economic policies and behaviour. Mark Burch's comprehensive and *deep* essays argue that *voluntary* simplicity is good for what ails us, individually and collectively. He rightly acknowledges that the grip of consumerism is tight on oh so many of us, but he makes it clear that we need not fear change, and that it would be so much better to do it sooner and voluntarily, rather than later and involuntarily."

Dr. Danny Blair,
Geography / Climatology, Principal, Richardson College for the Environment, University of Winnipeg, Canada

CONTENTS

Acknowledgements

1. The Door Hidden in the Wall   1

2. Mindfulness: The Doorway to Simple Living   9

3. Sufficiency: Enough for Everyone Forever   49

4. Communicating Simplicity   79

5. Educating for Simple Living   103

6. Simplicity and Economy   151

7. Twenty Questions: Technology and Simple Living   187

8. Simplicity, Sustainability, and Human Rights   231

References   251
About the Author   271

Acknowledgements

I wish to extend my utmost gratitude first to my spouse Charlotte for her patient support and unfailing encouragement during the writing of these essays.

I also want to thank Dr. Samuel Alexander for his personal and professional encouragement and for his role in assisting in the preparation of the manuscript for publication. Thanks also are due to Dr. Simon Ussher of The Simplicity Institute for his contributions to Institute projects.

There are many others who have assisted in one way or another to make this book possible. Thanks to Carrie Walker-Jones for assistance with copy editing, Tracey O'Neil of SimpleLife Designs for her brilliant work on the book cover, to Peter Globensky, Dr. Peter Doran, Dr. Samuel Alexander, Dr. Randall Hardy, Dr. Danny Blair and James Magnus-Johnston for their reviews, comments and kind endorsements of this work.

1

THE DOOR HIDDEN IN THE WALL

A few years ago, I participated in a practice called *kirtan*. Kirtan is a form of call and response singing conducted as a meditative practice. Its primary purpose is to generate joy. One evening the lead singer introduced a chant in English, instead of the customary Sanskrit, with the words: "I can see a door hidden in the wall."

The image of a door hidden in a wall is one that has stayed with me ever since. For me, it's a metaphor for the survival challenge humanity now faces. It expresses a sense of the forcible confinement into which consumer culture has brought us. But it also expresses the hope that an exit exists—if only we can find it.

In my imagination, the confining wall is the whole of consumer culture. It is not an individual person, or a specific institution, or a particular corporation per se, but rather the worldview, customs, and ideology that shapes all of these. It is a *culture*, even though individuals sometimes speak in its defense, institutions implement its practices and policies, and individuals teach their children its songs and stories so that it can replicate itself for generations. But consumer culture is also a cell, the walls of which are closing in on us. The constriction of the walls is driven forward by many forces, the most important of which are psychological. Now they are crushing many beings including us.

I believe the door in the wall to be voluntary simplicity, or what, in this particular collection of essays, I will sometimes refer to as *mindful sufficiency*. I'm not the discoverer of this way of life. Neither did I author its perspective of the good life. But I've been its avid student for half a century, and in that time and through personal experience I have come to believe that it represents a doorway to life flourishing in a situation that otherwise promises our extinction.

Some people find voluntary simplicity mysterious, even opaque. The door leading from extinction to renewed life is hidden in the same sense in which some Buddhist's describe their doctrines as "self-secret." They are truths hidden in plain sight because seeing them requires a change in the seer. When we change, then the way to the exit is obvious. Until we change, however, it remains hidden.

Over the last thirty years or so, a considerable literature has appeared about voluntary simplicity. A great deal of it recycles the same common sense advice about how individuals can simplify how they live. This literature has its place. Some of it is very useful. Some is trivial. Some is completely personal and anecdotal. Some is downright bizarre.

Far less common are works that penetrate the deeper structure of values and meaning that I believe constitutes the DNA of voluntary simplicity. What might happen if, beginning from a place of sympathy and admiration for this way of life, we were to dream it forward? What sort of culture might appear if we took seriously the essential values and principles that constitute simple living and let them shape a new perspective of the good life? What might happen if we extended this outlook from the realm of individual lifestyle choice to that of an agenda for cultural renaissance? This book aims to make a contribution to such a process by exploring topics not usually addressed in the simplicity literature.

This collection of essays is not a primer on simple living. The discussions we undertake here assume that readers are already familiar with the concepts and values of voluntary simplicity and perhaps even some of its history. I will offer a very brief overview here by way of introduction, but if this is a new topic for you, I recommend that you consult one of the very good introductions to be found elsewhere, which will certainly help in navigating the regions we will explore below.[1]

---

[1] For an introductory discussion of voluntary simplicity see: Mark A. Burch, *Stepping Lightly: Simplicity for People and the Planet* (Gabriola Island, BC.: New Society, 2000). For an excellent history of simple living in North America, see: David E. Shi, *The Simple Life: Plain Living and High Thinking in American Culture* (New York, NY: Oxford University Press, 1985). For a truly inspiring anthology of quotations from many cultures and historical periods respecting simple living, see: VandenBroeck & Goldian, eds., *Less Is More: An Anthology of Ancient & Modern Voices Raised in Praise of Simplicity* (Rochester, VT: Inner Traditions, 1996). For an unsurpassed

Voluntary simplicity is a way of life. It is a philosophical outlook as well as an aesthetic and a spiritual sensibility. Some might say it's also a direction for cultural and technical development that calls for its own politics, its own economic institutions, and its own creative process.

Voluntary simplicity is rooted in the practices of mindfulness and material sufficiency. Through bringing mindfulness to our daily routines, we seek the *maximum of well-being* achievable through the *minimum* of material consumption. Well-being applies to all life on Earth, not just human beings. It is about enough, for everyone, forever.

In addition to mindfulness and material sufficiency, voluntary simplicity includes the practice of ecological trusteeship, nonviolence, individual and local economic self-reliance, and community solidarity. It prefers sufficiency to affluence. It values leisure, relationships, and community involvement more than profit. It values spiritual development without endorsing a particular doctrine or tradition. It seeks ways of *integrating* meeting human needs with those of the natural world rather than merely balancing them as if they stood in opposition. Many people who share this perspective have experienced how a good life, rich in meaning, love, community, and reward, can flourish on very modest material resources. They have discovered that it is the single-minded pursuit of luxury affluence that undermines the long-term sustainability and well-being of both human societies and Earth's natural communities.

Voluntary simplicity is *not* new, not a celebration of poverty, not a religion, not exclusively rural, and not at all opposed to beauty or artistic expression. It affirms the value of technology when selectively developed and employed to serve purposes worthy of humanity. While the frugal use of money and resources certainly has its role, voluntary simplicity is not primarily about living cheaply. Most of all, it is certainly not about going back to any previous period in history. I believe that only by pursuing

---

anthology of contemporary writing about simple living see: Samuel Alexander, ed., *Voluntary Simplicity: The Poetic Alternative to Consumer Culture*. Whanganui, New Zealand: Stead & Daughters, 2009). For a classic anthem to simple living and an account of a personal experiment with this way of life see: Henry David Thoreau, *Walden* (Rev. ed. New York, NY: Alfred A. Knopf., 1992). And finally, for what has become another North American classic, see: Duane Elgin, *Voluntary Simplicity: Toward a Way of Life that is Outwardly Simple, Inwardly Rich*.(2nd rev. ed. New York, NY: Harper, 1993).

sufficiency can both the injustice of poverty and the unsustainability of affluence be resolved without harm. Discerning sufficiency requires mindfulness.

Another way to describe voluntary simplicity is to contrast some of its key elements with their counterparts in consumer culture:

- In consumer culture, people want to go as fast as possible, wield as much power as possible, and amass as many material goods as possible. This leads to a rushed, inattentive, and unappreciative way of life. Voluntary simplicity cultivates a slower, more *mindful* approach to life, less cluttered with stuff and more appreciative of the present moment.

- In consumer culture, people want to increase their consumption of everything because they think this makes them better off. For practitioners of voluntary simplicity, the goal is *sufficiency* of consumption. Both under-consumption (poverty) and over-consumption (affluence) are viewed as harmful.

- In consumer culture, people pursue external sources of reward such as social status, material possessions, money, and power over others. Simple living promotes cultivation of internal sources of reward such as friendship, *strong families and healthy communities*, expansion of knowledge, aesthetic values, and spiritual insight.

- In consumer culture, the main engine of production is the corporation. For voluntary simplicity, the main engine of production is symbiotic relationships between the ecosphere and human communities. Therefore, *environmental stewardship* is basic to simple living.

- Consumer culture is structurally violent, whereas practitioners of simple living strive to *minimize structural violence* by changing their consumption choices, especially for luxury goods.

- In consumer culture, we meet all important life needs through earning income and spending the income in markets that supply goods and services. In simple living, there is more of a do-it-yourself ethic, more production occurs at or near home, or outside money exchange markets.

- Consumer culture requires far-flung global markets and resource supplies. Living simply values local production, working with and for one's neighbours, and keeping social and economic relations close to home and under local control.

- Consumer culture focuses on production and consumption of luxuries, while simple living focuses on production of leisure and well-being provided by sufficiency of necessities.

- In consumer culture, technology is an end in itself, a profit centre, and the main measure of progress. For simple living, technology is a means to an end and only one factor contributing to a good life.

Voluntary simplicity is a highly progressive socio-cultural development. It aims to take us beyond the obvious failures of consumer culture to deliver a healthy, environmentally and socially sustainable, way of life. Voluntary simplicity is about qualitative deepening, not quantitative growth. It therefore implies a steady-state economics with a focus on qualitative development as a barometer of progress—not mere expansion of the gross domestic product (GDP) per capita.

To date, voluntary simplicity has been mostly an individual choice. But over the last fifteen years, it has become obvious that social and economic structures play a significant role in making it easier or more difficult to choose a simple life. A politics of simple living is beginning to emerge, which will someday address these issues.

I've come to believe that both the source and the destination of simple living is the cultivation of *mindfulness*—a more mindful way of life. I see it as the first strand in the DNA of simplicity. Accordingly, mindfulness is the topic of the first essay in this anthology. Others who write about simple living may have differing views on the matter or may give mindfulness a different priority in their hierarchy of values. But my own study and experience continues to reveal mindfulness (known by many different names) as a perennial theme in the history of simple living, in the accounts of those who love simple living, and a mental discipline, the development of which is central to a good life.

The second strand in the DNA of simplicity is the principle of *sufficiency*. Both in individual livelihood and a culture of simple living, sufficiency is the value that replaces consumer culture's obsession with avarice and affluence. The value of sufficiency arises from a radically different understanding of what material consumption contributes to a good life. Also embedded in the value of sufficiency is a sense of proportion and sensitivity to limits that are both essential to fashioning meaning and sustaining well-being for all, forever. It would be difficult to deny that in its pursuit of luxury comfort and material affluence, consumer culture offers many pleasures. But what is mostly missing from its menus are the longer term costs incurred by luxury indulgences. A rational culture needs also to take these into account if it aims to live long in the land.

Mindfulness and *sufficiency* together form the essential braid of voluntary simplicity's DNA. They spiral around each other lending this way of life its dynamic, structure, and direction. All the other essays in this anthology explore how the perspective offered by mindfulness and sufficiency can be brought to bear on a number of considerations central to a culture of simple living. Staying with the metaphor of DNA, we might think of these other topics as base-pairs that bridge between the spiral strands of *mindfulness* and *sufficiency*, relating them to each other in specific ways, enabling their synergy, and offering at least a partial anatomy of an alternative to consumer culture.

I can imagine a great many such bridges. We should explore them all. In what follows, I make a beginning by discussing five of them:

"Communicating Simplicity" begins from the observation that once we discover the value of mindfulness and sufficiency, a natural impulse is to share this experience with others. This process is inherently relational and implies community. It also implies opting for certain ways of communicating and leaving aside others. Every mode of communication known to humanity brings the parties into a relationship, which is partly structured by the mode of communication itself. Bringing mindfulness to these relationships is necessary to choosing wisely how we behave in them.

Discussion of communication evolves naturally toward the subject of "Educating for Simple Living." There is a myth prevalent in popular culture that simplicity is somehow natural to human beings—that we begin from simplicity and develop toward complexity and sophistication. But the thesis of this essay is that while development from simplicity to complexity characterizes the early stages of human growth, the story doesn't and shouldn't end there. What comes naturally to human beings are the same things that come naturally to other species with whom we share the Earth: To feed and breed to the limits of the available resource base, while often overshooting them. To manifest a way of life which is materially simple but culturally and spiritually rich is profoundly *unnatural* and requires deliberate attention to learning what exactly it is that empowers people to secure an ever greater measure of well-being on an ever more modest expenditure of energy, resources, and labour. It is what the great twentieth-century historian Arnold Toynbee called the "Law of Progressive Simplification" that characterized great civilizations. We need to teach each other how to do this with at least as much dedication and discipline as we once gave to achieving success in consumer culture.

Another important dimension along which we relate to each other and to the natural world is the economy. "Simplicity and Economy" takes up the question of what an economy might look like if it was oriented around the values of mindfulness and sufficiency rather than the oppressive promotion of consumerism and economic growth. Our economic behavior—the things we do that transform matter and energy into the goods and services we need for a good life—have threads leading back into the education that prepares us for our economic roles and the part played by communication in economic relationships. But deeper still, it leads back to the role played by mindfulness in guiding our choices and behavior, and how the value of sufficiency brings a sense of proportion and limits to our economic activities.

Today, it is almost impossible to discuss economics without also considering technology. "Technology and Simplicity" explores what role technology might play in a culture of simple living. The benefits that scientific discovery and technical innovation have brought to people are obvious. But under regimes of capitalism, consumerism, and paranoid institutions of governance, technological hypertrophy and misapplication are equally obvious. Bringing mindfulness to our use of technology leads to insights about how the role of technology in society in general, and the economy in particular, might change if technology was oriented to serve simple living rather than consumerism and private profit. In this essay, I also hope to dispel the stereotype that simple living is anti-technological, when instead it calls for a reorientation of the technological project to serve different values.

Finally, if there is one goal we might all agree on, it is that the good life aims to increase human well-being. We often differ, sometimes violently, about exactly what constitutes well-being and how to achieve it. We also differ as to whether achieving well-being for people is even possible apart from assuring the well-being of the whole community of life on Earth. But it seems to me that the concept of well-being is inextricably linked with that of human rights, since human rights are declarations about the conditions of livelihood we believe are necessary for a minimum of well-being. In "Simplicity, Sustainability, and Human Rights," I take up this discussion and I argue that consumer culture—traditionally portrayed as the most successful pathway to increasing well-being and protecting human rights— is in fact the single greatest threat to them and that conserving our rights and promoting well-being is highly unlikely apart from a culture of simple living.

I hope this book becomes one seed in a landscape planted by many hands. Indeed, the planting is already started. The landscape is that of the heart, and the imagination, and of culture. As this new land is tended and flourishes, so will humanity flourish. Voluntary simplicity is the door hidden in the impregnable wall of our cultural blindness and inertia. I believe it is our single best hope for thriving into the deep future.

2

MINDFULNESS: THE DOORWAY TO SIMPLE LIVING

1. Introduction

Words contain no awareness.
They can only trigger awareness.
It does no good to try to impress a man
        with some thought he can't relate to.
But if you can make him realize the obvious,
that might change his life.

(Williams 1973, 21)

The term *mindfulness* has a specific meaning and has only recently been incorporated into narratives about simple living as such. It is clear, however, that for those passionate about voluntary simplicity, there has always been more involved than mere material minimalism—though reducing material baggage is certainly an important aspect of the practice. Some contemporary writers about simplicity seem to think of it as little more than a spate of Spring house cleaning. But in the lives of those inclined to drill deep and suck out all of simplicity's sweetness, a transformation of consciousness is also involved. The physical changes that come into our lives are often preceded and organized by some prior psychological, and sometimes spiritual, change of perspective. Charles Wagner (Wagner 1903, 16-17), a nineteenth-century Alsatian writer about simple living described it this way:

No class has the prerogative of simplicity; no dress, however humble in appearance, is its unfailing badge. Its dwelling need not be a garret, a hut, the cell of the ascetic, nor the lowliest fisherman's bark. Under all the forms in which life vests itself. . . there are people who live simply, and others who do not. We do not mean by

> this that simplicity betrays itself in no visible signs, has
> not its own habits, its distinguishing tastes and ways; but
> this outward show, which may now and then be
> counterfeited, must not be confounded with its essence
> and its deep and wholly inward source. *Simplicity is a
> state of mind.* (emphasis in original)

In consumer culture, people can bring good humor and a spirit of camaraderie to parting with material possessions, especially if this arises from some sort of trauma or catastrophe. But such events are viewed as temporary setbacks from which we hope soon to return to the pursuit of a consumerist way of life. Enduring loss because we must is quite different from deliberately cultivating a shift in how we see the world, what we desire for ourselves, how we feel about our relationships, and how we live our daily lives. This shift in worldview is something I think is fundamental to living a joyful, fulfilling simplicity in some approximation to a life-sustaining symbiosis with the rest of nature. We don't arrive at this point of view simply by choosing to change our minds. We can choose, however, to cultivate practices which effectively change our minds for us.

Richard Gregg, the originator of the phrase *voluntary simplicity*, writing in 1936, went so far as to suggest that an inner transformation of consciousness is both prior to and essential for making progress toward simple living. It is from a transformed awareness that new social forms and institutions evolve to change the course of history:

> . . . the way to master the increasing complexity of life
> is not through more complexity. The way is to turn
> inward to that which unifies all—not the intellect but
> the spirit, and then to devise and put into operation
> new forms and modes of economic and social life that
> will truly and vigorously express that spirit. As an aid
> to that and as a corrective to our feverish over-
> mechanization, simplicity is not outmoded but greatly
> needed. (Gregg 1936, 17)

Many other similar examples could be cited from the simplicity literatures of several centuries and a diversity of cultures, but these examples should suffice to illustrate an important connection between simple living and a transformation of consciousness, which for many is both its driver and its effect. But what is this transformation exactly and what role does it play in voluntary simplicity?

2. Mindfulness

All human evil comes from a single cause, man's inability to sit still in a room. (Pascal, date unknown)

Lest our discussion of mindfulness start off by sounding too esoteric, it is well to remember that all of us have ready access to several different states of awareness every day. There is nothing mysterious about this. Everyone can distinguish between sleeping and being awake, and perhaps even between sleep dreaming and dreamless sleep. We may also recall moments when intense danger or excitement seemed to make us hyper-awake, very much present in the moment and to the activity at hand. So these four states of consciousness are more or less familiar to everyone: dreamless sleep, sleep dreaming, waking awareness, and hyper-wakefulness under stress. Mindfulness is just another state of awareness no more mysterious and just as accessible as these.

When I was a boy of five or so, my father took me fishing for the first time. Besides learning how to put a worm on a hook, he told me to sit very still in the boat because banging my feet around could scare away the fish. I dropped my line over the side with a float attached. I should watch the float closely for any sign of its being pulled under water. Then I should pull up on my fishing rod and hook the fish. These few instructions—sit still, be quiet, watch for the invisible—introduced me to many hours of fishing. Also, without my knowing it at the time, learning to fish became my first doorway into a state of consciousness I would later discover is called *mindfulness*. For the first time in my life, I was being challenged to both pay attention to what a fish might be doing with my bait, but also to myself as motionless, vigilant, awake. The sort of mindfulness I experienced while fishing was spontaneous and natural. As such, it was also unpredictable and unstable. To sustain longer periods of mindfulness more or less on purpose, however, requires more regular and deliberate practice.

There are several ways of thinking about mindfulness. It can be a heightened state of concern and due diligence in decision-making; a particularly lucid awareness of everyday experience; a clear awareness of subtler processes of one's own mind such as distinguishing thoughts from feelings from desires, etc.; a clear awareness of being aware, i.e., self-reflective consciousness; and a continuous and precise awareness of the process of being aware itself (witness consciousness) (Goddard 1938; Tart 1994; Thera 1967). Exploring these in detail would take us beyond the scope of this writing. For now I will adopt John Kabat-Zinn's (1994, 4) definition of mindfulness as "a state of awareness consisting of unhurried, non-judgmental attention to one thing at a time." Mindfulness involves concentration—but without strain or tension. This concentration is akin to the feeling of being absorbed in some activity or experience, when time is forgotten and our whole awareness is filled with the business at hand. It involves paying attention to whatever we are experiencing in the moment, without being distracted by memory, expectations, or imagination. It is the very opposite of multi-tasking, rushed impulsiveness, or just zoning out in a daydream. It involves a readiness to look beneath the surface appearance of things and to open ourselves to the inner meaning they have for us.

3. Mindfulness in Ethical Context

Before discussing mindfulness in more detail, I want to say something about the ethical context of the practice. We in the West are sometimes tempted to cherry pick bits of other people's cultures to suit our whims or enhance our commercial prospects. Writing ad copy that sounds like Taoist philosophy can apparently help you sell luxury cars. Doing yoga can be a lifestyle statement if you're wearing gear from the right store. Similarly, there are now situations in which mindfulness practice is being treated as a handy technique for achieving goals that otherwise contradict the ethical context of which it was traditionally a part. This is not a trivial matter.

Mindfulness, or *Right Mindfulness*, is one precept drawn from a set of interdependent precepts called the Noble Eightfold Path of Buddhism. Within this tradition, it is assumed that practitioners of mindfulness are also going to be practicing the other seven precepts of the Path, plus participating in many other aspects of a disciplined and highly inner self-managed life. The tenets of the Path mutually reinforce and balance each other in such a way as to protect practitioners from harm they may cause themselves or others by misunderstanding or misapplying any single precept taken by itself. Thus we come to true Right Mindfulness only and also by cultivating Right Knowledge, Right Intention, Right Speech, Right Action, Right Livelihood, Right Effort, and Right Contemplation. It's a package deal. Practicing mindfulness in absence of harbouring Right Intention, applying it through Right Action, or lacking Right Knowledge of its meaning and value, can lead to some truly bizarre results.

It is deliriously misguided to think that mindfulness should be used as a gimmick to shield oneself from the suffering of other beings. Mindfulness is not a tool for taking advantage of others in their suffering or to anesthetize ourselves against injustice and fraud. To placidly pursue one's personal advantage, indifferent to the moral and systemic atrocities such as those that were committed in the 2008 global financial crisis, can strengthen the very ego-dominated thinking that the right practice of mindfulness is supposed to uproot. Right understanding of mindfulness practice helps nourish in us both the ethical sensitivity and spiritual capacity to act in solidarity with others to care for each other and the Earth. While I don't think it's necessary to become a professed Buddhist in order to cultivate mindfulness, I think it is imperative to be aware of the context of ethical precepts which have always surrounded the practice and which help define its meaning. Failing to do this can leave us in possession of too little knowledge, and what little knowledge we have, we apply like moral imbeciles.

4. Mindfulness Practice

Mindfulness *practice* has both a general meaning and also denotes specific activities. In the general sense, mindfulness practice can mean learning and repeating any skill or routine that helps intensify, steady, and focus mindful awareness. Like leaning how to dance or play a musical instrument, mindfulness practice is something that can be learned and then strengthened through repetition.

Formal mindfulness practice consists of sitting meditation with attention focused on one's breathing, either by counting breaths or by silently witnessing the act of breathing, to the exclusion of all other internal or external distractions. While basic mindfulness practice can be learned in an hour or two (more advanced practices demanding more time), mastering it takes considerably longer and often represents a time and energy commitment that few in consumer culture are willing to make. Persisting in practice is essential to discovering what it has to offer, and many mindfulness practices aim to become continuous. This quality of continuous practice is illuminated by the seventeenth-century Samurai warrior Yamamoto Tsunetomo:

> In one's life, there are levels in the pursuit of study. In the lowest level, a person studies but nothing comes of it and he feels that both he and others are unskillful. At this point he is worthless. In the middle level he is still useless but is aware of his own insufficiencies and can also see the insufficiencies of others. In a higher level he has pride concerning his own ability, rejoices in praise from others and laments the lack of ability in his fellows. This man has worth. In the highest level, a man has the look of knowing nothing.
>
> These are the levels in general. But there is one transcending level, and this is the most excellent of all. This person is aware of the endlessness of entering deeply into a certain Way and never thinks of himself as having finished. He truly knows his own in-sufficiencies and never in his whole life thinks that he has succeeded. He has no thoughts of pride but with self-abasement knows the Way to the end. . . .
>
> Throughout your life advance daily, becoming more skillful than yesterday, more skillful than today. This is never-ending. (Tsunetomo 1716, 26-27)

There are many specific practices that can cultivate mindfulness. My fishing story is an example of an activity, the primary purpose of which was recreational. Secondarily, we intended to catch some fish. Only incidentally did it also begin to establish mental habits which could heighten mindful awareness. Nearly anything which is repetitive and requires enough concentration that its effect is to still and focus the conscious mind, e.g., long distance running, swimming, many forms of repetitive work, paddling a canoe or kayak, can work like a mindfulness practice if we bring to it the appropriate intention. During such activities, people sometimes experience glimpses of the lucid-consciousness-in-stillness which is mindful awareness. However, the effect is usually sporadic and unstable unless a deliberate regime is in place to develop these fleeting moments of awakening toward a stable state of awareness.

Practices that specifically develop stable states of mindful awareness often entail formal meditation or contemplation. In Buddhist *Vipassana* (mindfulness of breathing) practice, for example, attention is focused on the breath with the intention of slowly developing concentration, cultivating inner stillness and eventually an ever deepening insight into the activities and dynamics of one's own conscious awareness. The practice itself is not very hard to understand but is challenging to maintain.

> Meditation means learning how to get out of this current [the incessant stream of thoughts], sit by its bank and listen to it, learn from it, and then use its energies to guide us rather than to tyrannize us. This process doesn't magically happen by itself. It takes energy. We call the effort to cultivate our ability to be in the present moment 'practice' or 'meditation practice'. (Kabat-Zinn 1994, 9)

Christian *Centering Prayer*, while differing from Buddhist Vipassana in its intention, is nearly indistinguishable in its method. The Buddhist is intent on liberation from suffering and growing in compassion whereas the Christian practitioner of centering prayer is intent on cultivating a state of inner stillness and spiritual receptivity to the action of the Holy Spirit. The Buddhist anchors attention on the breath while the Christian anchors it on a prayer word, not unlike a mantra, expressing the contemplative's intention to open themselves to intimacy with God (Keating 1998). But otherwise, all the physical postures, preparation, attitudes and activities that one brings to the practice are nearly identical.

I'm convinced that a sustainable culture will be one that voluntarily and consciously embraces both *simple living* and *mindful living* as its core values of the good life. The role mindfulness plays in sparking a taste for a simpler, more sustainable livelihood has always been of major interest to me. At first, I thought people choose a simpler life because they decide rationally that it is the best thing for them. Maybe they arrive at this choice because of reading or conversations with others, or maybe because some trauma has touched their lives, which forces them to rethink their priorities. But however it was that individuals got to their personal tipping points, I thought that eventually the decision was taken and the choice to simplify just unfolded from there.

One benefit of simple living is more leisure time. A common theme in the simplicity literature is the observation that about 70% of people who are practicing simple living also practice formal meditation or some similar activity. It's seldom clear from these stories, however, whether meditation came before the decision to live more simply and therefore may have been a contributing factor, or whether it was one choice among many of how to spend one's new found leisure time. After all, what *do* people do instead of go shopping? Well, among other things, maybe they meditate. On the other hand, maybe it is the accumulating effects of meditation itself that motivates us to leave off shopping and adopt a more sustainable way of life.

Over years of studying voluntary simplicity in the life stories of others, and after decades of personal practice, I've come to think the causal arrow more often points from mindfulness to simple living than vice versa. I will review below the variety of ways I think the practice of mindfulness also develops in us a desire for simple living. I'm not as certain that the choice to live simply, when springing from other motivations such as reducing debt, or choosing to live in solidarity with the poor, or even to reduce one's ecological footprint, leads as regularly toward the formal practice of mindfulness.

Lest this sound like a course in spiritual practices rather than an essay on voluntary simplicity, we only need to note that some such practices as these—and there are a great variety of them—have consistently appeared in the writings and memoirs of historical figures who have sung the praises of simplicity, as well as being frequently mentioned in modern surveys of people who identify themselves as practitioners of strong forms of voluntary simplicity. In an extensive study of over 200 practitioners of simple living, Linda Breen Pierce (2000) reported:

> Many of the participants talk about mindfulness. They feel that simplicity is about living mindfully and consciously. Some of them believe that it is through the practice of daily, mindful living that we come to experience our spiritual selves. Mindful living is developed through the conscious awareness and appreciation of the tasks we do each day, of the people with whom we interact, and of the natural beauty that surrounds us. (Pierce 2000, 305)

And elsewhere Pierce notes:

> Approximately 70 percent of the survey participants indicated that their religious or spiritual practices and experience are a high priority in their lives. In fact, the vast majority reported that living simply had enhanced their spirituality if, for no other reason, by giving them

more time to participate in spiritual and religious practices. . . .

Many study participants believe there is a strong relationship between spirituality and simplicity. Indeed, some feel that it is impossible to separate the two experiences. It is not always clear which comes first, but simplicity appears to reinforce spirituality and vice versa. (Pierce 2000, 302)

In the third edition of his book, *Voluntary Simplicity*, Duane Elgin (Elgin 2010, 73-89) offers more explicit and detailed discussion of *embedded consciousness* as contrasted with *self-reflective consciousness*, his terms for less and more mindful states of awareness respectively, than in previous editions of his book. Elgin argues that making a *voluntary* choice to live simply implies both that we are making a conscious choice, and also that we are conscious of ourselves as choosers. In consumer culture, we run on automatic, not making fully voluntary choices because our choices are often not fully conscious. We choose based on habit, conformity, impulse, expediency, short-term necessity, but rarely do we make choices in lucid self-awareness. We run on automatic in a constant state of mental distraction. Mental distraction was not invented by consumer culture, to be sure, but it is greatly amplified and exploited by it. Today, it's popular to call this distracted state *multi-tasking*, but which elsewhere has been more accurately called *chronic partial attention*. Remedy for this affliction can be found by learning the skills necessary to sustain conscious self-awareness. Learning to pay attention to ourselves, Elgin says, liberates us from the embedded consciousness which would otherwise make truly voluntary choice impossible.

The development of self-reflective consciousness is only a doorway into something much more profound for Elgin. The practice of conscious self-remembering gradually dissolves our delusion that we are separate, self-sufficient beings. As the boundaries between self and other soften and gradually disappear, far from falling into an abyss of nothingness, we discover instead that we're aware of ourselves in our inter-existence with everything else, a state of awareness that Buddhist teacher Thich Nhat Hanh has termed *inter-being* (Macy & Brown 1998, 52). This shift in self-consciousness in turn helps foster a number of what Elgin calls "enabling qualities" for a way of life which is both materially simpler and also environmentally and socially more sustainable. Above all, it is also freer and more joyous for the person living it.

Elgin's portrayal of the relation between cultivating self-reflective consciousness and more sustainable living is insightful, though largely philosophical and speculative. An empirical approach has been taken by psychologist Tim Kasser working at Knox College in Galesburg, Illinois (Kasser & Brown 2009). Kasser and research collaborator Kirk Warren Brown gathered survey information from 400 Americans, 200 of whom identified as voluntary simplifiers, and 200 matched controls who identified with the American mainstream consumerist lifestyle. Respondents were asked questions about their level of well-being and personal happiness, the size of their ecological footprint, their values, and mindfulness practice. Kasser and Brown found that, (a) respondents who reported performing more ecologically responsible behaviors also reported higher levels of happiness and personal well-being and smaller ecological footprints; and (b) mindfulness practice and being oriented toward intrinsic values (non-material, inner rewards) was a stronger predictor of happiness than just identifying oneself as a voluntary simplifier (as contrasted to identifying as a mainstream American). Kasser and Brown (2009, 40) concluded:

> A primary take-home message of the findings of this study is that living more happily and more lightly on the Earth is not as much about whether people think of themselves as voluntary simplifiers, but instead is more about their inner life—that is, whether they are living in a conscious, mindful way and with a set of values organized around intrinsic fulfillment. . . .
>
> In sum, then, [in promoting a happier, more sustainable way of life] a more productive approach may be to cultivate a way of life that encourages mindfulness and intrinsic values.

There is a growing literature about links between mindfulness practice and well-being. Reviewing all of it is beyond the scope of this essay. I hope we now have some basis for the idea that cultivating mindfulness is a necessary condition for an orientation of consciousness needed for a more sustainable livelihood. Below, we will take a closer look at what we mean by mindfulness as a state of consciousness, as contrasted with mindfulness *practice*, how mindfulness can be deliberately cultivated, what practical effects the practice of mindfulness can produce, and what contribution these might make to simple living.

5. Mindful Awareness

As we practice mindfulness, a mindful consciousness grows in us. We slow down and pay attention. We take time to look *into* things rather than just *at* them. We let ourselves be absorbed in the experience of this moment. What happens is something like the difference between eating an ice cream cone while talking with a friend, and going away to sit on a park bench with only the ice cream cone for company. In the first case, our attention is divided between the ice cream and our friend, and is constantly switching from one to the other and therefore not likely to get deeply absorbed in either one. In the second case, we are free enough from distractions to focus entirely on the experience of eating the ice cream. We may discover that the ice cream is really delicious or really terrible: Mindfulness will reveal both. The point is that we are mentally *present* to notice.

Mindfulness *in* the environment means becoming conscious through mindfulness of how we live all the time—even though often we are not paying attention. Mindfulness in the environment means waking up to the beauty all around us and enjoying it. It also means waking up to the ugliness all around us and perhaps choosing to do something about it. It means *noticing* noise, and odors, and dangers and then noticing *ourselves* and what decisions and actions we take in response to these things. Do we run and hide? Do we buy bottled water? Do we plug in iPods and zone out? Do we start working with others to change what offends our new awareness?

When we discover beauty, sometimes we find it in the most unlikely places—i.e., in places we weren't paying attention to before. Perhaps, for the first time, we begin to realize that beauty and value aren't confined to special wilderness areas, ecological reserves, or private collections. The whole Earth is full of the possibility of undiscovered beauty, and therefore worth protecting. Why do we surround a Picasso or Rembrandt with video cameras and security guards while wild flowers go unguarded? Because wildflowers are more common? Because we didn't make them? Or because we didn't notice them before?

If mindfulness practice is pursued with diligence, discipline, and regularity for some time, it reliably produces a number of changes in our worldviews, values, and consciousness of life. I believe these changes constitute the primary colour pallet of a worldview of simple and sustainable living. These trans-formations don't have to be forced and they aren't a new list of laws coming from a self-appointed moral authority. They emerge gradually and organically along with mindful awareness, once the decision is made to cultivate mindfulness in the first place. What is required of us is to stay loyal to the practice.

To help describe these changes in awareness, I'm arbitrarily grouping them under two broad headings: (a) transformations of thinking and perceiving, and (b) transformations of feeling and desire.

6. Transformations of Thinking and Perceiving

Helpful in visualizing what happens to thinking and perception as mindfulness practice starts to take hold is an old gimmick from the field of perceptual psychology called the Necker Cube. It is usually used to illustrate figure-ground reversal:

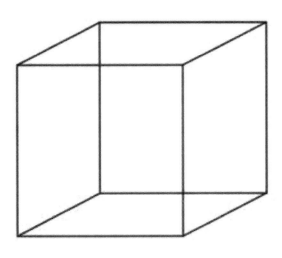

A

In the illustration above, corner "A" of the cube can be either the front or the back surface, depending on one's perspective. If you see it as part of the front, see if you can make the perspective shift so that it now appears to be the back and vice-versa. Can you make it shift from one place to the other as often as you like? How do you feel when you do so? Some people find it impossible to shift perspective but most can make the switch, which also sometimes comes with a subtle inner sensation of shift. The shifty feeling and perhaps our complete inability to make the perspective shift are both signs of attachment to our customary way of perceiving the world. Prising it loose, even in this very minor example, takes effort, concentration, and can be a little disorienting at first.

Also noteworthy is the fact that the physical sensation of making this shift means that the perceptual habit is embedded in the body as well as the psyche. Recognition that our state of mind is partly grounded in the body may be one reason so many Eastern spiritual practices include more physical elements such as yoga, t'ai-chi, kundalini, etc., than has traditionally been the case in Western practice, which tends to draw a sharper boundary between the body and the mind/spirit.

The transformations of perceiving and thinking that can result from mindfulness practice can have this quality of arising as sudden little jerks in our consciousness. They reveal a whole new perspective that we realize was staring us in the face all along, just as both sides of the Necker Cube are visible from the very beginning. Suddenly we are seeing or thinking differently. Sometimes, these transformations occur much more slowly, as if an image is coming into focus. Perhaps we have been dimly aware of the image for some time, but little by little it comes into view until one day, we recognize it for what it is. As the opening quote for this essay observes: We are realizing something obvious that can change our lives.

Following below are some of the transformations of thinking and perceiving that appear in conjunction with mindfulness practice that I think are also central to living a rich simplicity. In my experience they arise more or less together as an organic whole—a new *gestalt* for consciousness itself. But this doesn't happen suddenly and certainly not quickly.

6.1 *Shifting from experiencing oneself as the subject of awareness to oneself as both the subject and the object of awareness*

Our habitual state of awareness is usually that we experience ourselves as simple observers of the objects comprising an outside world. But during mindfulness practice, attention is turned inward so that it is ourselves which become the focus of attention. In this way, we become both the subjects and the objects of our own awareness. This shift from being the subject of our own awareness to become both the subject and object of awareness is pretty much synonymous with mindfulness practice as such. Anyone incapable of making their own thoughts, feelings, and inner states the object of their awareness is probably also incapable of meditation itself because this is the essence of where ordinary daily awareness leaves off and meditation begins.

The practice of mindfulness strengthens our inclination to make ourselves the objects of our own self-knowledge. It also increases our capacity to do so. Our own thinking, feeling and acting thus become not just *outputs* from an unreflective consciousness, but inputs to conscious reflection itself. We become self-aware. This shift in where we focus attention, at least part of the time, is the essential foundation for the other transformations of consciousness made possible by mindfulness practice.

We may all be capable of self-reflective awareness, but that's not to say that many of us spend very much time in this frame of mind. After all, consumer culture is not a way of life that encourages us to do so. Even though Socrates cautioned that the unexamined life isn't worth living, consumer culture uses all manner of attention-getting strategies to keep our awareness focused outward on the products it wants to sell, the work it wants us doing, the dangers we should be avoiding, the opportunities we should be seizing. Consumer culture offers very little encouragement for directing attention inward to strengthen self-awareness or to discover our inner (intrinsic) sources of joy and well-being. Because it takes attention, energy and commitment away from consumer culture, mindfulness practice is the ultimate subversive act.

Cultivating a more introspective (contemplative, meditative) approach to life is essential to sustainability and human well-being because it's unimaginable that habit-driven, semi-self-aware people can successfully meet the challenges that lie ahead. We will need to notice and respect everything both within us and outside us in order to fashion a more skillful way of life. Mindfulness practice requires that we slow down, pay attention, take things to heart, notice the full range of experience presenting itself to us, and open ourselves to the spontaneous moral sense necessary for important decisions. Mindfulness practice helps us know our place, respecting both our capacities and our limits. Such fundamental lessons in humility are essential to living in harmony with both our human and non-human neighbours.

6.2 Shift in consciousness from foreground-only awareness to foreground + background awareness

The consciousness dominant in consumer culture is strongly foreground oriented. It attends closely to what most strongly stands out in present moment experience. What stands out is action, movement, change, novelty, the shock and awe cultivated by advertising, the media, and the military. Even more important, what usually dominates our foreground awareness of things is their surface appearance. That's why so much time and energy are spent in consumer culture on cosmetic activities, image management, issue "spin," while so little energy is invested in finding out and engaging the essence of a thing. Consumer culture also does this at the expense of noticing what is *not* present, apparently stationary, apparently silent, invisible, or entirely absent. There is probably even an evolutionary bias toward this foreground-dominant orientation of perception since it would have been important to human survival that we pay attention to the moving lion rather than the background of motionless grass against which the lion was moving.

The practice of mindfulness makes possible a shift between foreground and background perspectives such that the background is taken more into account. It's possible even to cultivate an awareness that integrates them—being able to see the Necker Cube vibrate back and forth between its two possible orientations, or even fuse them together in a single perceptual experience. Less abstractly, it's easy for us to see some human actions as environmental threats (mining tar sands) and different human actions as conserving of the environment (planting trees). What we find nearly impossible is fully appreciating what the Earth can do for itself when human meddling is entirely *absent*. It is easier for us to notice pollution (a bad odor, gunk pouring into a stream, etc.) than it is to register the *absence* of these as positive evidence of health. Correspondingly, we find it hard to properly value things that don't exist or that shouldn't exist. A young mother being interviewed recently for a television program on organic foods had the idea, however, when she told the interviewer that her main reason for buying organic food was for what was *not* in the food—pesticide/herbicide residues, hormones, antibiotics, modified genes, etc. It's easy to see the validity of this perspective when it's pointed out this way, but it's an altogether different thing to sustain a continuous awareness of both the foreground and background, visible and invisible, acting and non-acting aspects of our experience.

Mindfulness practice teaches us literally to perceive more clearly and then to value more highly stillness (the absence of motion); solitude (the absence of intrusions); letting go (the absence of clinging); simplicity (the absence of clutter and distraction). We start to sound more like Taoists who know the value of the absence of a thing as well as the possession of it. Two particularly important instances of this principle can be found in leisure and non-action.

It is sometimes observed that living simply can both increase leisure and is also a form of the life of leisure itself. Consumer culture has difficulty differentiating leisure from idleness even though they are very different psychological experiences. Some would say idleness is even the opposite of leisure. But if simple living might sometimes be a synonym for leisurely living, then the twentieth-century German ethicist and social philosopher Josef Pieper also gives us some insight into the connection between leisure and a mindful orientation of consciousness:

> Leisure, it must be clearly understood, is a mental and spiritual attitude—it is not simply the result of external factors, it is not the inevitable result of spare time. . .
>
> Compared with the exclusive ideal of work as activity, leisure implies an attitude of non-activity, of inward calm, of silence; it means not being 'busy', but letting things happen.
>
> Leisure is a form of silence, of that silence which is the prerequisite of the apprehension of reality. . . For leisure is a receptive attitude of mind, a contemplative attitude, and it is not only the occasion but also the capacity for steeping oneself in the whole of creation.
>
> Leisure, like contemplation, is of a higher order than the *vita activa*. (It) is the power of stepping beyond the workaday world, and in doing so, touching upon the superhuman life-giving powers which, incidentally almost, renew and quicken us for our everyday tasks. It is only in and through leisure that the 'gate of freedom' is opened and man can escape from

the closed circle of that 'latent dread and anxiety'. . .the mark of the world of work. (Pieper 1952, 189-190)

One of history's greatest poets of simplicity was Henry David Thoreau. In *Walden*, his journal of country living, Thoreau offered many descriptions of how he was occupied in his leisure. Clearly, he used his simplicity to deepen his mystical and philosophical perception, another way of understanding the cultivation of mindfulness:

> Time is but the stream I go a-fishing in. I drink at it; but while I drink I see the sandy bottom and detect how shallow it is. Its thin current slides away, but eternity remains. I would drink deeper; fish in the sky, whose bottom is pebbly with stars. I cannot count one. I know not the first letter of the alphabet. I have always been regretting that I was not as wise as the day I was born. The intellect is a cleaver; it discerns and rifts its way into the secret of things. I do not wish to be any more busy with my hands than is necessary. My head is hands and feet. I feel all my best faculties concentrated in it. My instinct tells me that my head is an organ for burrowing, as some creatures use their snout and forepaws, and with it I would mine and burrow my way through these hills. I think that the richest vein is somewhere hereabouts; so by the divining rod and thin rising vapors I judge; and here I will begin to mine. (Thoreau 1854, 87)

A second example of this more inclusive orientation of consciousness is appreciating the value of non-action. The narcissistic West has always lionized the man of action. He's always in motion, always on the attack. His best defense is a good offense. He's the early bird after the worm. Such people are deeply puzzled by the Eastern view that just as often as we want to act, it is sometimes wiser not to act—to actively practice non-action. The Western consciousness confuses *non-action* with *inaction*, which it interprets as lack of strength, nerve, or capacity. Yet, far from lacking the ability to act, a person operating from a different sort of awareness might discern circumstances in which the greater wisdom is not to act at all.

For example, two generations ago, it was heroic to tame the howling wilderness and force nature to surrender her riches. Nearly everyone agreed with Descartes that nature must be vexed to give up her secrets. Now that nature lies battered and bleeding at our feet, we think it is heroic to save her. So we invade wilderness trying to count every species on Earth. We net them, weigh them, tag them, sample their blood, collect their DNA, halter them with radio tracking devices, stress them nearly to death, and then release them again thinking we're doing nature a favour. What we seem utterly incapable of doing is living simply, desist from meddling, and allow nature space and time to heal itself.

6.3 *Shift of consciousness to perceive and value interdependence*

We are represented in everyday awareness as discrete observers of a world of objects which seem separate from us. They are jumbled together in the same physical space, "out there," and the space itself appears to be a inert background upon which the action of life happens. The boundaries between *me* and *that* seem sharply drawn and distinct. This way of experiencing helps promote physical survival in nature because a too mystical, touchy-feely attitude toward a potential predator could delete one's genes from the evolutionary pool in short order. But as we have evolved, we've also discovered that there are unseen forces and relationships that play a major role in our survival and well-being. We ignore radiation and some bacteria at our peril, even though we can't see them. The winds and oceans and nutrient cycles of nature move energy around and recombine materials in ways that sustain our lives, even though they are mostly invisible. If we take the time to become mindful of these relationships, we eventually discover that we are literally constituted by them.

Entanglement is a term used in quantum physics to describe a relationship between two subatomic particles such that any change in one particle is accompanied instantly by a change in its counterpart (Arntz & Chase, *What the Bleep! Down the Rabbit Hole* 2004). Taken as a metaphor, quantum entanglement is a specific instance of a more general principle of relatedness and interdependence in nature. Again we meet Thich Nhat Hanh's idea of *inter-being*, itself a rendering of the ancient Buddhist doctrine of *codependent arising*.

Entanglement can be empirically demonstrated for quantum level particles by means of physical experiments. I don't intend to generalize a quantum phenomenon too literally to non-quantum levels of nature. But the concept of entanglement is a powerful metaphor for the interdependence of all beings at many different levels.

For example, there's lots of evidence for what might be called *ecological interdependence*. The cycles of weather, ocean currents, nutrients passing through food webs, energy exchanges, and genetic diffusion all link physically distant members, even of different species, in relationships of mutual influence.[2] Not only are nutrients and energy cycled through these relationships, but also pollution, toxins and mutations. Everything each of us does from breathing, eating, excreting and reproducing has consequences for other species and physical and biological systems elsewhere on Earth. These impacts are proportional to the amounts of matter and energy appropriated by human beings for our own uses, as well as to the toxicity of these activities. A consumer culture that preaches that maximizing consumption of matter and energy literally constitutes well-being is also a culture that will create maximum impacts on nature. Growing in mindfulness of how our lives inter-depend on the lives and health of others opens to us a different basis for making our decisions about how to live.

At yet another level, we can discern various forms of *psycho-social interdependence* which can be both beneficial and pathological. From conception onwards, we are profoundly social

---

[2] The possibility of viewing the universe as a connected whole rather than an assemblage of un-related bits and pieces has been with us at least since the 19th century, as discussed in Paul Hawken, *Blessed Unrest*, (New York, NY: Penguin, 2007), 34ff. Ralph Waldo Emerson's (1836) book *Nature*. (Corvallis, OR: Oregon State University, 1836), developed from a vision of holistic interdependence of plants and animals, which resonated with the English Romantic vision of nature and later went on to influence the life and thought of Henry David Thoreau and many others. The holistic vision of nature would again appear in the work of the South African statesman and scholar Jan Christian Smuts, *Holism and Evolution*, (New York, NY: Macmillan, 1926), in Julian Huxley's (1953) *Evolution in Action* (New York, NY: Signet Books), in the eminent botanist Edmund Sinnott's *Mind, Matter and Man*, (New York, NY: Harper and Bros., 1957), in Arthur Koestler's development of the idea of holons (*The Ghost in the Machine*, [London, UK: Arkana, 1967]), and in a continuing line of thought running through Ludwig VonBertallanffry's (1968) *General System Theory: Foundations, Development, Applications*. (New York, NY: George Braziller, 1976), and the theories of complex living systems as discussed by Gregory Bateson and writers like Myron J. Wheatley and Margaret Kellner-Rogers in *A Simpler Way*, (San Francisco, CA: Berrett-Koehler, 1996).

beings. We are conceived *in* relationships. We are raised and educated through interactions with other people and life forms. Power is exercised through social and physical relationships. The whole construction of the ego and our mental universe of learned knowledge and skill is built up and maintained through interactions with others with whom we are interdependent. This reality of connection also makes us vulnerable as individuals to strong cultural influences on the development of our values, attitudes and behavior and also vulnerable to mass social hysterias, delusions and mob thinking. Some thinkers have even proposed that the human species as a whole is psychologically entangled at an archetypal level—the level of heritable psychic structures that determine characteristically human ways of behaving (Jung 1969; Progoff 1969).[3] In light of our profound psycho-social interdependence, the neo-conservative ideology that views people as isolated individuals pitted in competitions for personal advantage in an indifferent and inanimate world seems positively delusional.

Many spiritual traditions teach that we are spiritually interdependent as well. We sense that we live in a universe that has a moral dimension that implies larger than personal connections and responsibilities. It is expressed in such metaphors as everyone being children of the same God (Judeo-Christian); or of a people who receives its identity from a common source or heritage (Judaic, Muslim); or of diverse peoples who nevertheless comprise a single whole by virtue of their connection within the sacred dimension of the universe (Medicine Wheel). Evidence of spiritual interdependence is difficult to verify publicly but it is often authoritative for individuals who experience it subjectively. In any case, for many spiritual teachers, the essence of spiritual experience is liberation from the delusion of being a separate Self and coming to experience oneself as at home or belonging, i.e., embedded, in

---

[3] Ralph Waldo Emerson's book *Nature*, deeply impressed Henry David Thoreau, but Thoreau extended Emerson's vision of the connectedness of nature to include human beings and issues of human rights and justice (see Paul Hawken, *Blessed Unrest: How the Largest Social Movement in History is Restoring Grace, Justice, and Beauty to the World*, (New York, NY: Penguin Books, 2007), 76. The vision of an interconnected humanity is probably as old as history itself, but most visibly present in modern times in the lives and work of people like American poet Walt Whitman, novelist Leo Tolstoy, spiritual-political leaders like Mohandas Gandhi and Martin Luther King, Jr., as well as the work of psychologists such as C. G. Jung and Ira Progoff.

the universe rather than a stranger in it (James 1958; Progoff 1973; Walters 2001). Thus, our deepest spiritual experiences may not be theistic at all, but simply awakening to, or perhaps remembering, our birthright of relatedness to every Other.

This intuitive apprehension of connection to everything else also includes a moral dimension which is eloquently described by Mildred Binns Young (Young 1939, 5-7). Note that her attention is absorbed not in supplying her own desires or aggrandizing her ego in some way, but rather, finding that way of life by which she can be most serviceable for a new world:

> My thesis is that some of the means for freeing our lives lie in drastic limiting of material possessions and processes, in a discipline which paradoxically has its reward in extension of our strength and insight to use them to the full. But we cannot grasp these means for freeing our lives until the necessity is made plain in our hearts and we want it completely.
>
> When the necessity becomes plain, when the longing to set ourselves free is past denying, we begin to open into a realization of personal responsibility, of the oneness of human life, or what has been called *unlimited liability*. **We feel the obligation and the privilege to live as if we each had many lives to live and could afford to hold loosely our little footholds in this one. This opening out is the great release.**
>
> Now, frankly, most of us have our hands so full of baubles that we haven't even a finger free with which to reach out and satisfy the claim of *unlimited liability*. Poverty, or some approximation to it, willingly assumed, would set us free both for finding our responsibility and for fulfilling it when found. That is why I have called it *functional* poverty. It is to be embraced not as an ideal of beauty, our Lady Poverty of the Middle Ages, though it may wear her features. It is to be embraced not as a penance for the benefit we have long had from a society that starves our brothers, though it may be partly that. It is to be taken up not as a shirking of the responsibility of wealth or privilege, but as acceptance of wider responsibility. **It is to be taken up as a way to freedom, and as a practical method for finding the time and strength to answer one's deepest need to be serviceable for a new world.**

Functional poverty means an adjustment of the mechanics of living by clearing off the rubble. This is a clearing off that opens the way for new growth in wisdom, love and function. It means a discipline that tempers the tools by which we work, and scours clean the glass of self through which we see at best but darkly. (emphasis added)

As we simplify focal awareness through mindfulness cultivation practices, we discover that we are carried within a larger Life that is layered and complex. This lends to life a certain precious charm and mystery. This is easy to overlook if we are too much in a hurry or our awareness is too distracted to notice such things. It is one thing to just gobble down an orange. It is another thing to hold it, feel it, smell it; to look deeply into it to see the blossom it came from; the tree that sustained the blossom; the earth that supported the tree; the air and rain that fed the tree; the harvester who picked the fruit; and the whole chain of hands through which it passed to arrive on our table. When the sun and the seasons, and the bees and the rains, and the clouds and the human labour are all present in our awareness—because we have deliberately taught ourselves to take time and pay attention until they *are* present—then the experience of eating an orange, or consuming anything for that matter, is replete with relationships and responsibilities we didn't notice before. Consciousness of how interdependent everything is increases appreciation and respect. We also become more aware of how our action, or non-action, has consequences no matter what. It therefore becomes important that both our actions and non-action have life-giving effects.

Another effect of consciousness of interdependence is to break down our sense of isolation and excessive individuality. While we are responsible for each other, we are also supported and strengthened by the relationships we are responsible to. This support can be literal and material as when the Earth literally feeds us from itself or friends help support us in times of loss or distress. But the support can also be extremely subtle as when we experience moments of being linked into and sustained by some vast, intuitive communion of spiritual energies that hugely surpass in power and extent anything we know at the material level of our lives. This reality has been given many names like the *Communion of Saints* in Christianity, *Indra's Net* in Hinduism, *the Tao* of Taoism, *the Cosmic Body* of the Buddha. It is this knowledge that increasingly claims our loyalty.

Appreciating our place in a connected universe can also increase our appreciation for our own fallibility and thereby promote humility. Individuality is relativized rather than being the absolute measure of all other values. Since the rational functions of the ego are what virtually constitute individuality, the compass of what the ego can grasp appears from the perspective of mindfulness to be very limited compared to the vastness of an entangled universe. We are only *apparently* individuals and our egos exist, relatively speaking, for only a very short time. Because our individuality is at every level limited, contingent, and transient, we can *never*, as individuals, grasp the whole. Therefore our perceptions, thoughts, decisions and actions relative to the whole will *always* be more or less fallible because they are always based on incomplete information. Then, the way to happiness and harmony, if that's what we want, is: (a) counterbalancing the ego delusion by cultivating consciousness and remembrance of our interdependence with everything else; (b) cultivating humility in recognition of our limitations and fallibility, and; (c) living simply and modestly so that the consequences of our relative ignorance and proneness to err are minimized. Humility is something that consumer culture doesn't do very well since hubris and blind self-assertion are mistakenly viewed as signs of ego strength.

The gradually ripening awareness of interdependence at many levels also has many implications. We start caring about community again. Because everyone is linked, caring for others becomes an important way of caring for oneself. Not only humans, but all life is part of this web of being. So our caring naturally extends to the Earth and all its beings. It also extends to past and future generations because we recognize a relationship with them as well. All that we do starts to seek nonviolent expression because, obviously, violence toward any is violence towards all—including violence toward ourselves as well. Since it is impossible to care for that which we do not know, we become interested again in what is local, what is *here*. Focusing on what is local helps keep us grounded and mindful. So we begin to think about rebuilding local economies and local communities of self-reliance and more conscious inter-dependence. This keeps life in view. It makes it possible for us to be responsible as well as awake to our responsibilities. All of this really starts to add up to a different way of living. And it turns out to be vibrantly luminous, loving, and rich.

To arrive at the unshakable, you must befriend the Tao.
To do this, quiet your thinking.
Stop analyzing, dividing, making distinctions between
    one thing and another.
Simply see that you are at the center of the universe,
    and accept all things and beings as parts of your
    infinite body.
When you perceive that an act done to another is done
    to yourself, you have understood the great truth. (Walker
1995, n.p.)

6.4 Shift of consciousness from scarcity and craving to perceive plenitude and gratitude

Just as during formal mindfulness training we may focus attention on breathing and exclude both inner and outer distractions, so later can we focus attention on different aspects of our inner experience. Sometimes it isn't until we discover mindfulness practice that we begin to appreciate how consumer culture's incessantly repeated siren songs of advertising, government propaganda, corporate branding, etc., subtly directs our attention in certain ways and distracts it in others.

In the class I teach about voluntary simplicity, I invite my students to begin by recalling three moments in their lives when they felt very well, happy, and fully in touch with the meaning of their lives. They write these down, at first just as phrases or single sentences. Then we expand these one-line recollections into more detailed descriptions of these life experiences. Finally, we share the stories. I then invite everyone to create a gratitude log, a log book like a ship's log, but dedicated to the practice of remembering and compiling a record of events from previous times in our lives for which we feel gratitude. We also aim to build this into a daily practice of noticing events and experiences for which we feel grateful and establishing the discipline of writing them down. This practice has recently been popularized in a number of different modern renditions (Ban Breathnach 1995), but it also has an ancient pedigree in formal spiritual practice and secular philosophy (Ignatius of Loyola 1521; Irvine 2009, 68). What is happening here is another version of the Necker Cube juxtaposition. We aim to shift attention away from the noise of consumer culture which is continually focusing our awareness on what we lack, what is scarce, what we must fear will happen, or what we might fear to lose. Instead, we focus attention on the signal from our *Lifeworld* that sufficiency is already present in our daily experience and our past experiences of well-being. We also develop, based on this history, rational confidence in our own ability to learn to *want what we* have regardless of what the universe provides in the future, rather than wanting what we *don't have*, thus multiplying our suffering by intensifying desire.

6.5 *Shifting goals from pursuing the extrinsic reward of material possessions more toward intrinsic and non-material sources of well-being*

The cultivation of mindfulness can also shift where we focus our effort in life and where we look for sources of well-being. Kasser & Brown's (2009) research mentioned above suggests that people who focus attention on intrinsic, non-material sources of reward tend to be both happier and better environmental citizens than people who look outside to material things for the good life. Mindfulness can help foster this shift by helping us appreciate more fully the absolutely pivotal role that inner states, inner monologues, and the orientation of consciousness play in relation to personal well-being. We appreciate it more because we are paying more attention to it. We learn to leave off asking how many *things* we need to provide for our many desires, and start asking instead how many *desires* we are willing to provide for.

The work of cognitive psychologist Timothy Miller (1995) is very helpful in this respect. Miller argues that human beings evolved to crave more and more because this helped early hominids acquire larger territories and more mates, which in turn increased reproductive success. We humans have certainly succeeded in this mission—so much so that our population and our consumption habits threaten most other species. The survival challenge for humans now is not to amass ever larger territories and harems. Instead, we should aim to use the capacity of consciousness to subordinate desires which are completely natural to what mindful self-awareness now tells us is necessary for the well-being of the whole, interdependent life system of the Earth. In other words, the boundaries of our consciousness are being challenged to expand yet further to construct our personal identities around the whole interdependent community of life, rather than the pursuit of our individual consumption prerogatives.

Despite the differences between cognitive therapy and mindfulness practice per se, Miller makes a convincing case that it is not material consumption itself which contributes most to well-being, but the orientation of consciousness that we bring to our life experience. If we want to, we can orient consciousness toward paying close, non-judgmental attention to daily experience. We can teach ourselves to practice gratitude. We can teach ourselves to extend compassion to others growing from mindful awareness of our own experiences of suffering and knowledge of our connectedness. If we do these things, then we give ourselves the best possible chance for mortal beings living in uncertain times to experience contentment.

7. **Transformations of Feeling and Desire**

Mindfulness practice can also affect shifts in how we feel and what we want out of life. I believe this is absolutely crucial to a culture of simplicity and sustainability. It's one thing to know what we need to do to live more sustainably. It's an altogether different matter to actually want to do it. Complicating this process is what I will call a *confusion of desire* that I think is an artifact of consumer culture. This takes a bit of explaining.

I was once giving a workshop about voluntary simplicity when, close to the end, one of the workshop participants commented: "I don't feel like you're trying to convince us that simple living is a good thing. I feel instead that you believe this is what comes naturally to people and what is healthy for us. We're just here trying to remember that." This was a revelatory moment for me.

A simpler, more sustainable way of life is often portrayed in popular culture as requiring many sacrifices and deprivations. But the key word is *portrayed*. Like any other portrayal, a great deal depends on the biases and agendas of the portrayers. Because it is so close to us, we scarcely appreciate how thoroughgoing is the influence of consumer culture. It is very challenging to parse how much of what we desire is spontaneously present in our human nature, and how much of it has been drummed into us from infancy by consumer culture. Furthermore, even supposing that a destructive desire such as greed may be innately present, we seldom explore to what extent we might reduce the influence of such destructive desires through routines of psychological hygiene that we might learn as we grow up. Mindfulness practice can help us distinguish the innate desires present in human nature, the desires that help assure our survival, from the blooming confusion of learned wants we accumulate during our passage through consumer culture. Thus mindfulness practice is not changing what we want so much as offering insight into the origin of what we want. Given this insight, we then enjoy a greater measure of freedom in deciding which of our desires serves well-being and which do not. In this way, mindfulness practice can change both what we want in life, and the emotional basis from which we work for it.

7.1 *The transformation of the emotional basis of working for change*

All discussions about the sustainability crisis we face include some sort of emotional subtext. Between the lines of all but the driest academic reports, we can pick up a specific feeling tone, and sometimes more than one. In nearly every case, I usually hear one or more of three possibilities:

Fear—We should be concerned about the sustainability challenge because absolutely terrible things will happen if we don't act right away. Appeals to fear of environmental catastrophe have been the common motivational currency for environmentalists for two generations now. Even David Suzuki, the lion of Canadian environmentalists, has softened his doom and gloom warnings lately, choosing to focus instead on all the benefits we could enjoy by conserving ecosystems and species. Environmental activists have their neo-con (neoconservative) counterparts who threaten us with economic collapse, comp-romised national security, and deterioration of our standard of living, if the warnings of environmentalists are heeded. Recent experience seems to teach us, however, that greed is a closer threat to the economy than the dire warnings of environ-mentalists.

Guilt—We should be concerned about sustainability because what we have done to the planet is morally wrong, selfish, and a betrayal of our divine mandate to be good stewards of the Earth. Evidently, at least the Vatican thinks guilt is still a good motivator because it recently decided to issue a new list of mortal sins, most of them relating to acts of environmental abuse or violations of human rights (Pullela, 2008). Guilt, it should be noted, is another form of fear—fear that we stand condemned before a moral authority or a supreme being, or that we have betrayed our own values.

Greed—We should be concerned about sustainability because it represents unparalleled opportunities to invent new technologies, develop new services, create investment opportunities, do well by doing right, in short, to get rich. Failing to act on the sustainability file is to be economically irrational and to fail to take advantage of the paradoxical opportunity to make money cleaning up the mess created by our earlier pursuit of making money. What's not to like? Greed is also another form of fear--fear that I may live in deprivation if I don't amass surpluses; fear that others will take advantage of me unless I take advantage first; fear of scarcity.

As understandable as these feelings might be, we are left to ask if they are appropriate or even effective motivations for wise action? Fear can be a short-term motivator to be sure. But psychological studies of the effects of fear and stress on human beings show that it narrows attention rather than opening the mind. Fear is not conducive to the play and experimentation essential to discovering creative solutions to difficult problems. Fear focuses attention on the feared object or situation, which may not be the best focus in order to resolve what causes the fear. Finally, fear is not a stable motivator. As soon as the feared object is removed or the situation resolved, motivation drops to zero. When there are multiple, interacting, long-term threats, as in the sustainability challenge, this tactic simply won't do.

Guilt is an aversive feeling that motivates us to escape the situation or the company in which we feel guilty. Guilt aims to fix blame rather than fixing the problem. We can seek short-term stop-gap solutions or even magical remedies like confession/atonement rituals. I wreck the Earth, feel guilty, confess my sin, find absolution, then go out to wreck the Earth again. Most problematic is that guilt is essentially a self-indulgent sentiment. The focus is on me and the moral condition of my soul from which presumably I cannot change or be redeemed except by supernatural intervention, when the focus of attention could instead be on my behavior or structural characteristics of my society that I can change.

Greed is an inappropriate motivator for several reasons. First, greed is violent in so far as greed necessarily deprives others of access to whatever I am greedy for. Second, because greed is violent, it sows a psychology of division and competition within society at a time when cooperation would be more useful to solve our problems. Third, and most important, greed derives from a lack of awareness of our interdependence. Greed assumes that my individual welfare can be improved independently of the welfare of others. This is a metaphysical, ethical, and practical mistake.

An alternative to fear, greed, and guilt has been suggested by Cheri Huber (1990, 117-124), a Zen roshi living in California. Through her own practice of mindfulness, she brings wonderful insight to this question. Having witnessed some sheep being slaughtered on a farm near her practice centre, she brought this experience back into her practice of mindfulness. She wondered how we all become hardened to the suffering of animals, other sentient beings, and thereby also hardened to each others' suffering? She found that many of the reasons we might give ourselves for acting differently toward animals, such as guilt, amount to new forms of self-inflicted violence. Within the ambit of mindfulness practice, violence can never be used to reduce violence, precisely because we are all entangled and any violence toward the self, no matter how positive the intention (in this case in service of reducing the suffering of animals) merely propagates more violence. But since this violence is self-inflicted, it's avoidable. Huber points out to us the power of mindfulness practice to reveal a completely clean, nonviolent, wholesome basis for action in service of sustainability. We act not because we frighten ourselves with visions of what might happen if we fail to act (even though this might be justified); nor do we impose guilt on ourselves because of our moral failings (real as they may be); nor do we give free reign to our greed (even though "opportunities" may indeed appear because of the misery of other species and people). We act because the practice of mindfulness empowers us to perceive ourselves differently and feel ourselves to subsist in a different relationship with other people and with the Earth. From this new orientation of consciousness, we do the right thing—the nonviolent thing, the life-giving and life-sustaining thing. We behave differently because we see life differently now, and feel differently about it, not because we are frightened, guilty or greedy. It's that simple.

7.2 *Transformation in how we understand desire*

The view of human nature that prevails in consumer culture sees human desires as more or less innate, limitless, insatiable, and non-negotiable. Consumer culture says it's human nature to want things without limit. The main problem of life is finding the right things to satiate one's desire—the perfect car, house, spouse, vacation spot, deodorant. Little effort is spent on distinguishing desire itself from the objects that we desire, or whether desires really are insatiable or not. Instead, considerable effort and money are invested in trying to teach people to desire more things, more often, and more insatiably than ever, because this drives demand for consumption and hence profits.

Aristotle thought that indulging desires tends to strengthen them. So there is something about desire which is like an addictive narcotic. The more we indulge ourselves, the more we want to indulge ourselves. Modern researchers who study neuro-chemical activation of the brain have discovered that shopping releases dopamine, a brain chemical with effects similar to morphine, and also prone to be addictive (Lovitt 2010; Parker-Pope 2005). While there is certainly nothing wrong with pleasure, some of us would rather that our pleasures not lead us into addictions or become compulsive rituals that limit our freedom and ultimately reduce well-being by threatening the planet.

Dedicated practice of mindfulness involves witnessing the arising and dissolving of all sorts of mental events, including desires. Practice helps us discover several things about desire. First, desires arise spontaneously and continually. But they also go away spontaneously and continually, unless they are indulged, in which case they tend to stick around. Some take longer than others to dissipate, but unless a desire is directly linked to a basic physical need like thirst or hunger, it comes and goes like any other thought. Thus we discover that indulging our desires is actually our voluntary choice to form an attachment to them. In effect, we are choosing to allow an addiction to develop in us, and often we even encourage the process. Stated differently, we are indulging a way of living that binds us to our past, to habit, to inertia—which is another way of thinking of *karma*. Jon Kabat-Zinn (1994, 21ff) expresses this well:

> Here's how mindfulness changes karma. When you sit, you are not allowing your impulses to translate into

action. For the time being, at least, you are just watching them. Looking at them, you quickly see that all impulses in the mind arise and pass away, that they have a life of their own, that they are not you but just thinking, and that you do not have to be ruled by them. Not feeding or reacting to impulses, you come to understand their nature as thoughts directly. This process actually burns up destructive impulses in the fires of concentration and equanimity and non-doing. At the same time, creative insights and creative impulses are no longer squeezed out so much by the more turbulent, destructive ones. They are nourished as they are perceived and held in awareness. Mindfulness can thereby refashion the links in the chain of actions and consequences, and in doing so, it unchains us, frees us, and opens up new directions for us through the moments we call life. Without mindfulness, we are all too easily stuck in the momentum coming out of the past, with no clue to our own imprisonment, and no way out. Our dilemma always seems to be the other person's fault, or the world's fault, so our own views and feelings are always justified. The present moment is never a new beginning because we keep it from becoming one.

If we hope to change our karma, it means we have to stop making those things happen that cloud mind and body and color our every action. It doesn't mean doing good deeds. It means knowing who you are and that you are not your karma, whatever it may be at this moment. It means aligning yourself with the way things actually are. It means seeing clearly. . .When you stop outward activity for some time and practice being still, right there, in that moment, with that decision to sit, you are already breaking the flow of old karma and creating an entirely new and healthier karma.

Second, in being mindful of our desires, we discover that acquiring some object (car, house, backyard pool) never makes desire itself go away. The desire as associated with some specific object may cease to preoccupy us, but desire itself is right back vexing us with more demands, regardless of how many objects we accumulate.

Third, sooner or later, we begin to wonder if endlessly repeating cycles of craving things, obtaining the things we crave, only to discover that craving just returns to start the cycle all over again, is the best way of promoting well-being? The lessons of our own self-observation reveal that obtaining desired objects does not satisfy desire. The core premise of consumer culture is therefore a lie. We are slaves to the lie every day that we continue to indulge it. It's life in a hamster cage endlessly turning, but going nowhere.

When we really take this lesson to heart, usually by watching it in operation over and over again, and by suffering its consequences day in and day out, we begin to see that it is desire itself that is problematic. We stop worrying about how to get the objects we want and we start thinking about where wanting itself comes from and what to do about *that*. Happily, the answer is quite simple: Treat desire just like any other thought or feeling arising during practice. See it arise. Note that it is a desire arising. Then simply let it go—unless it is something arising from authentic physical or psychological needs. Our ability to do this becomes more efficient with more practice. Timothy Miller (1990, 203) summarizes this insight nicely:

> You achieve self-realization when you really understand—not just in your mind, but also in your heart and in your bones—that your desires are not important. Not only are they not important, but satisfying them will not bring you happiness or even contentment. Not only that, but satisfying them might actually do harm and bring you pain. Not only that, but your desires are actually the source of your suffering. When you completely understand these things—in such a way that you can never forget them—then it becomes possible to perceive yourself, the people around you, the world, and all that's in it in an entirely new way.

7.3 *Transformation of what we desire*

Not only can the practice of mindfulness change how we understand the dynamics of desire and their impact on our lives, in my experience, it can also change what we desire. The reasons I have to offer for this are more speculative than empirical.

As we cultivate mindfulness, a taste for simpler surroundings, fewer possessions, less clutter, a more spacious and tranquil way of life, can spontaneously accompany the development of our practice. The material de-cluttering of our lives then becomes a slowly and organically evolving process of reshaping the whole of our lives. It is not a forced agenda for personal improvement that we impose on ourselves. Instead, it grows up from the sweetness of mindfulness practice itself. It feels, and is, completely natural. We begin to discover in our human nature not only the instincts and drives that served us well as we were evolving up to this point, but also that which now draws us forward toward awakening. We are waking up to our true place in the universe and our role within the living world of the Earth.

These realizations set in motion a gradual development in what we are prepared to pursue in life and what we now feel free to leave off pursuing. Creating a more tranquil, less violent, more cooperative lifestyle that is more involved with others, more committed to our local place, becomes a priority. We cease needing to be somewhere else, doing something else, with someone else, because we know that everything we need for a good life is ready-at-hand. We cease struggling to be somebody because we realize deep down we already are somebody.

As mindfulness deepens, other things happen. Sometimes they can be very unpleasant and even painful. This is surprising to those who assume that mindfulness is a blissed-out state of awareness. We are now sensitized to the beauty but also to the ugliness that surrounds us much of the time. We notice the intrusiveness and discourtesy of consumer culture and greedy lust that powers it. We are sensitized to the danger, the haste, and the mostly avoidable violence which is so common a part of daily life in consumer culture. We notice how often we are motivated by fear, or habitual craving, and how often we suffer because of them. We start to feel caught in a badly scripted reality TV show, where all the rules require deceit, back-stabbing, and finally tossing others overboard. We start wanting something different, something better.

I think this transformation in what we desire may be energized in three ways:

First, the practice of mindfulness, if generalized beyond our formal practice periods to become our general way of approaching life, can greatly increase the quality and depth of our ordinary daily experiences. All we are doing is learning to pay attention to what was there all along. But now we do so with more regularity, more concentration, and a greater appreciation for what the daily round may hold. Since we are paying closer attention to what we already have and to what is intrinsically available to us, maybe we are less inclined to hanker for more. In a classic passage from Henry David Thoreau's *Walden* (1854, 78-

80), even the flight of a mosquito through his cabin is replete with metaphysical significance:

> Every morning was a cheerful invitation to make my life of equal simplicity, and I may say innocence, with Nature herself. . . I got up early and bathed in the pond: that was a religious exercise, and one of the best things which I did. . . I was as much affected by the faint hum of a mosquito making its invisible and unimaginable tour through my apartment at earliest dawn, when I was sitting with door and widows open, as I could be by any trumpet that ever sang of fame. . . There was something cosmical about it; a standing advertisement, till forbidden, of the everlasting vigor and fertility of the world. The morning, which is the most memorable season of the day, is the awakening hour. Then some part of us awakes which slumbers all the rest of the day and night. Little is to be expected of that day, if it can be called a day, to which we are not awakened by our Genius, but by the mechanical nudgings of some servitor, are not awakened by our own newly acquired force and aspirations from within, accompanied by the undulations of celestial music, instead of factory bells, and a fragrance filling the air— to a higher life than we fell asleep from; and thus the darkness bear its fruit, no less than the light. That man who does not believe that each day contains an earlier, more sacred, and auroral hour than he has yet profaned, had despair of life, and is pursuing a descending and darkening way. After a partial cessation of his sensuous life, the soul of man, or its organs rather, are reinvigorated each day, and his Genius tries again what noble life it can make. All memorable events, I should say, transpire in morning time and in a morning atmosphere. . . It matters not what the clocks say or the attitudes and labors of men. Morning is when I am awake and there is a dawn in me. Moral reform is the effort to throw off sleep. . . **The millions are awake enough for physical labor; but only one in a million is awake enough for effective intellectual exertion, only one in a hundred million to a poetic or divine life. To be awake is to be alive. I have never yet met a man who was quite awake. How could I have looked him in the face?** (emphasis added)

Second, I think through mindfulness practice to enhance our

ordinary experiences, we are introduced by direct experience to intrinsic sources of well-being. We discover personally and directly, not by hearsay on someone else's authority, how much we are the architects of both our own pleasure and our suffering. Well-being really does originate substantially inside us, arising from intentions and choices we ourselves can make. This discovery is empowering and joyous. We learn that there are inner and outer forms of possession, and inner and outer goods to be possessed. Those which are inner are inherently more accessible, secure and abundant than those which are outer. This causes our psychological center of identity to shift in an inward direction. It's like the Necker Cube shift of perspective again. Why would we, after discovering this new world, return to the anxiety and insecurity of well-being that depends on material possession? As the twelfth-century Islamic spiritual and legal philosopher Al-Ghazali once observed: "You possess only whatever will not be lost in a shipwreck."

Third, mindfulness practice helps us perceive directly how futile can be the cycle of pursuing desires, especially material ones, and how much suffering this brings into our individual lives, our relationships, and with the Earth. Thus it is merely common sense to exercise more discernment over what we want and give more attention to stilling desires as they arise.

Finally, mindfulness practice itself can be increasingly sweet as we make progress (Goddard 1938, 76). This is not always the case, but very regularly it is. It's quite natural then to desire to return to practices and states of mind that help us experience positive feelings rather than awaken every morning to gird ourselves for the general scramble for more. Having found a door in the wall, why would we not walk through it?

8. Why Cultivate Mindfulness?

> The evolution of man is the evolution of his consciousness, and 'consciousness' cannot evolve unconsciously. The evolution of man is the evolution of his will, and 'will' cannot evolve involuntarily. (Gender exclusive language in original.) (G. I. Gurdjieff)

Many benefits are claimed for the practice of mindfulness through formal sitting practices designed to help us learn it, even though paradoxically, one cannot practice mindfulness preoccupied by the conscious agenda of self-improvement and still be practicing mindfulness. I don't know whether all the same effects are found among people who practice mindfulness more or less unconsciously as I did as a child when fishing, or whether a formal practice under instruction is necessary to discover all its potentials. In any case, mindfulness practice improves our powers of concentration, fosters equanimity and calm in moments of stress, heightens self-awareness of inner psychic processes, relieves stress and refreshes the body, and contributes to a more grounded and connected sense of self. In its loftier reaches, it enables insights into the causes of suffering, it is a stimulus to compassion, generates understanding of the sources, causes, and consequences of all operations of the mind and emotions, and sometimes confers paranormal abilities. In the context of a theistic belief, generations of practitioners of contemplative prayer have claimed that such practices are essential to disposing oneself inwardly to a deeper and more transformative relationship with God.

I would like to propose another reason why one might take up the practice of mindfulness, which is linked to what I take to be the purpose of human existence. If there is anything singular about human beings that may distinguish us from other species— at least in degree, if not in kind—it is that we have somehow come to embody a self-reflective consciousness. All species feed and breed and sleep. However, when we make these our ethical norms and our main purpose in life, we fall far short of our potential. We're doing just exactly what comes naturally to all species. There are even many species that make tools, or in some other ways modify their environments to make them more congenial to their own interests. James Lovelock (1990) has proposed that the whole thrust of evolution itself has been life making the Earth a more congenial home for more life. And to be sure, there are species with complex signaling systems, which are only a step or two away from language if they do not already qualify. So what is left?

I think a great deal can be said for the great Swiss depth psychologist Carl Jung's hypothesis that the evolutionary purpose of human life appears to be the development and extension of consciousness itself (Jung 1961, 338). Of all the creatures we find in nature, humanity appears to be, at least so far, the species which is most conscious of itself, and most capable of reflecting back an image of nature to itself. We might say that we are nature waking up to have a look at itself, and perhaps even evolve beyond its own innate competitive instincts to adopt instead a consciously caring posture toward itself. This is a remarkable evolutionary achievement which is also a spiritual achievement and a Divine gift. *Everything* can be found represented in consciousness, or just beneath the surface as the unconscious. Together, consciousness and the unconscious contain, in one form or another, all that nature has been and all that nature strives to become. So the psyche contains both fact and aspiration—both history and many potential futures. I have come to believe that the practice of mindfulness can become one method of deliberately cooperating in the development of consciousness, both through the discovery and integration of unconscious contents, but also by manifesting the evolutionary and developmental possibilities present in consciousness.

Humanity is life on Earth thrusting itself toward whatever it is next capable of becoming. I don't believe this implies leaving behind our organic nature to develop some sort of silicon intelligence. Nor do I think what is well for us is to return to some dimly remembered or wishfully imagined primeval harmony.[4] Becoming conscious involves an increasingly deliberate cooperation with the natural developmental energies that already strive to carry nature beyond itself. It requires somehow resolving a paradox, namely, that the process of evolution builds on and includes exactly what it seeks to transcend. We are nature's offspring and therefore are heir to all the impulses,

---

[4] The tendency to idealize the past is a common characteristic of all atavist and naturist movements and finds its psychological counterpart in the belief that actualizing our development potentials merely amounts to returning to a developmentally prior stage. The eminent philosopher Ken Wilber has described all such notions as instances of the Pre-Trans Fallacy. This fallacy occurs when pre-rational states of consciousness such as those present in infancy and childhood are confused with transrational states such as those characteristic of spiritual and psychological maturity. This can have two consequences: First, all transrational states can be reduced to mere pre-rational states (the reductionist perspective), e.g., Freud's notion that religious experience was merely a regression to infantile narcissism and oceanic consciousness, or, for those who are sympathetic to higher or mystical states and confuse pre- and trans-, then there will be a tendency to elevate all pre-rational states and ascribe to them transrational significance (the elevationist perspective). Wilber argues that what we mean by the spiritual includes and transcends reason, but does not regress from or exclude it. It is neither reductionist nor elevationist in perspective (Ken Wilber, *The Essential Ken Wilber: An Introductory Reader*, [Boston, MA: Shambhala, 1998], 88–91).

tendencies, conflicts and behavior patterns that in past evolutionary epochs served us so well, and which are now obsolete and often threaten the next steps in our transformation. We acquire possessions like squirrels mindlessly storing nuts. We haggle over mates as if our reproductive success still depended on it while crowding the earth with seven billion of ourselves. We wage the most savage conflicts over the most sublime of our ideas and the most trivial of offenses.

I have come to think, however, that it is not the *contents* of consciousness we need to develop (ideas, philosophies, religious creeds), but consciousness itself—one pathway being the cultivation of mindfulness. With Jung, I think that this is also partly achieved through making conscious what is currently unconscious. This process largely engages the internalized world of the past. We also need a forward-looking program for the development of human consciousness and practices such as the cultivation of mindfulness which seem to have much to offer in this respect. As Jung also observed, what is most interesting about the psyche is not where it has come from, but where it is trying to go. Simplicity of living is a great help in this enterprise, and as the celebrated historian Arnold Toynbee also once observed, simplicity is evidence that we are making progress (Toynbee 1947, 198). He even assigned it the honour of making it a historical law: *The Law of Progressive Simplification*. It is not the society with the most military or economic power which is necessarily the most highly evolved. Greatness, he believed, consisted in the progressive simplification and dematerialization of culture—what he called *etherealization*. This occurred when a civilization could shift more and more of its economic and social resources away from dominance and manipulation of the material world and apply them instead to creative cultural pursuits and care of its members. Thus perhaps we can see mindfulness and simplicity as a process of co-evolution—a pair of dance partners who between them both facilitate and express the evolution of people toward what we are destined to become.

I have tried to illustrate that the practice of mindfulness changes the texture of consciousness in several specific ways. The decision even to take up formal meditation is already a decision to cultivate a more introspective, more intrinsically oriented way of living. Mindfulness practice amplifies and deepens this experience considerably. Our awareness shifts from simply being the subjects of our own awareness to also being objects of that awareness. The outputs of consciousness (thoughts, feelings, sensations, behavior) become objects for conscious inspection and insight. This sets in place a feedback loop of awareness that in turn nurtures other changes in awareness. We begin to notice both foreground action and figure, but also background causes and contexts. We begin to appreciate that we don't have to be lonely, isolated egos struggling with other egos for affluence, but that we are part of an interdependent community that implies both new sources of strength and new responsibilities. From this shift in focus, scarcity is transformed into plenitude and fearful clinging into gratitude. After securing material sufficiency for our authentic material and emotional needs, we're encouraged to pursue what are inner and non-material sources of well-being. We discover how to work for change not because of fear or greed or guilt, but from a newly emerging spontaneous awareness of the solidarity and love we feel for the whole community of life. This is sufficient. No other commandments are necessary. Mindfulness helps us understand that much of our suffering arises from desire and that desire itself must become an object of meditation if we are to discover insight that helps liberate us from this suffering. We learn to distinguish desires that serve life from those that serve profit. This insight transforms what we desire. For these many reasons, I see the practice of mindfulness and the changes it can bring into our lives as the source and essential foundation of a worldview which is actually capable of sustaining human and planetary well-being into the deep future. It is also the fundamental praxis of simple living.

MARK A. BURCH

3

SUFFICIENCY: ENOUGH FOR EVERYONE FOREVER

1. Introduction

The name of the mean is sufficiency.

—Roman de la Rosa, 13th cent.

Vision

Consciousness blossoms forth from mindfulness. We feel growing within us a great peace and sense of security. We thrill as we recognize how little indeed is needful and from this recognition we claim our freedom. We no longer subject ourselves to overwork to acquire the merely perishable things that offer only perishable pleasures. Our homes are modest and easily cared for. This has removed from our lives all manner of hurry and unwanted stress. Our possessions are well-made, beautiful, and capable of being remade when necessary. Everywhere there is light and all this world now consciously runs on light—the light of the sun. The grimy, smoking machines of consumer culture have passed away along with the fear and drudgery they demanded. No one slaves for more when all know how much is enough. In the practice of moderation we discover security and justice because scarcity disappears along with mindless craving and the forces that drive mindless craving. We learned that security cannot be found by hoarding up material things, but only in peaceable relationships with each other and with the Earth. We're secure when the Earth is well. We trust the Earth now to provide for us as she has for four billion years and we help her do so; but we no longer torment her for her riches. Her riches are safest when in safekeeping by her. The most admired among us is the one capable of the greatest happiness on the slenderest material means. We no longer ask our Elders the secret of a long life, or of how to procure affluence. We ask them: "How did it come to pass that you were so very happy and left so much love, but such a small mark on the world? Teach us how to be remembered and to leave no traces."

Ever since the Sophists of ancient Greece started teaching their followers how language could be skillfully manipulated to persuade their listeners, the meanings of words have been molded to serve the agendas of their speakers. George Orwell's political satire *Nineteen Eighty-Four* imagined a world in which the meanings of words had been turned inside out to buttress a totalitarian state. In modern times, this practice has evolved into a science used by both propagandists and advertisers—the latter merely being the propagandists of consumption. One effect of this takeover of language in service of the consumerist agenda is that it makes any proposals in favour of reducing consumption sound negative by comparison.

For example, the word *frugal* means "careful, sparing, economical, avoiding excess." These seem sensible enough practices, but in consumer culture frugality mostly denotes a sort of stingy selfishness, a lack of generosity. *Austerity* means "sternness of manner, severity of judgment, severe self-discipline, and severe simplicity," but is commonly used today to refer to any measure of self-discipline that a government or public authority might impose on itself to avoid operating deficits and debt. The implication is clearly that any gesture of self-control is an exercise in severity. *Prudence* is scarcely ever used today, probably because it sounds too close to *prude* or *prudish*, but it means "sound judgment, circumspection, sensibleness, wisdom, discernment, knowledgeable, and skillful." *Temperance*, which today implies a joyless, rigid self-denial, actually means "rational self-restraint, self-control, moderation, due proportion, mildness, forbearance, dispassion." But what is wrong with such values apart from their potential to moderate consumption and hence profits? If we had all learned to practice these a little more, would we have had to endure the far harsher medicine of the economic train wreck of 2008? Yet, in consumer culture, people who pay their entire credit card balance every month are known in the industry not as frugal or temperate, but rather as *deadbeats*—a term formerly applied to those who were "worthless, sponging idlers; loafers." One CNN economic commentator referred to people trying to save more and reduce their debts as misers, the actual definition of which is "a person who hoards wealth and lives miserably in order to do so." Yet it has been widely recognized that consumption enabled by excessive spending and easy credit was a major factor contributing to economic hardship following the 2008 financial collapse.

What we might call *definition creep* also afflicts the voluntary simplicity movement as it strives to help its various audiences understand the paradox that less can be more. Centuries ago the wisdom of moderation was expressed in phrases like *holy poverty, austerity,* and *asceticism.* In later centuries, these words were softened to frugality, temperance, and prudence until lately we prefer *balance, simplicity,* and *sufficiency.* Since consumer culture has had a century in which to reframe public narratives about the good life, and these have all been cast in terms that make ever increasing consumption sound like something wired into the human genome, any other point of view must make way against stiff headwinds. Education consultant Alan AtKisson (in Andrews & Urbanska 2010, 101-106) has even proposed the Swedish word *lagom* which he defines as "somewhere north of sufficiency but still south of excess" because any other synonym for moderation, e.g., enough, sufficiency, etc., still just sounds too dirge-like when compared to all the peppy tunes churned out by consumer culture. *Lagom* is preferable, AtKisson argues, ". . . because it speaks more to what people actually want." And what people actually want is *more.*

Note the trend line revealed by the changes in these words. It's the trend that is our challenge, not the specific words. Every attempt to soften the language of moderation in order to increase one's audience ratings seems to ratchet in the direction of "just a little more." But it's precisely this incessant desire for just a little more that forms the pivot upon which our survival now turns. We lose sight of this as individuals, and as a society especially, when the progression from less to more happens gradually over several generations. But Earth's memory is long and every one of our excesses leaves a mark in her body, some of them indelible. Neither the importance nor the magnitude of this challenge can be underestimated. Somewhere it is written that toward the end of his life Mahatma Gandhi observed that of all the vows he took, the most demanding was that of "voluntary meager eating." Self-control is the most extreme of all sports.

It's only fair then to unpack some of consumer culture's own claims about itself. Today, consumption is considered an economic virtue, if not a public duty. Former President of the United States, George W. Bush, urged us all to go shopping to fight terrorism, of all things! But only a century ago, *consumption* was a synonym for tuberculosis, not a national security strategy. Our modern term *credit* came into vogue when consumer culture just couldn't shake the negative connotations of debt. People, it seems, enjoy being given credit more than they do being given debts. The very goal of consumer culture, which is universal affluence, ignores the definition of affluence, which is "more than enough; abundance; excess beyond need." If we think about it, that which is beyond what is needed can only be one thing—waste. So to the extent that our governments and corporations turn all their thought toward the one goal of promoting an affluent society, they promote a society of profligate wastrels, of which we have abundant evidence.

Only for a society afflicted with affluence does the question of how much is enough become urgent. Once we evolve past the boundaries of bare subsistence, we come upon a much broader territory haunted everywhere by another threat to our survival just as lethal as poverty. Our most pressing challenge is no longer how to alleviate poverty, but rather how to consume appropriately so as to conserve our humanity and the ecosphere. So unlike the challenge of privation is the challenge of affluence, that it catches us unawares. We are ill-equipped to meet it because our economy was developed initially to resolve the problem of poverty, and then later to generate wealth for its own sake. No one worried about addictive consumerism. We can scarcely perceive what is happening. Our traditional discourses are useless. The times require that we see and respond differently.

This need is especially acute in the field of politics where nearly all the debates, and all the reportage, continues to be mired in language and worldviews that are no longer relevant. From the perspective of mindfulness, simplicity and sustainability, the traditional divide between right and left politics mostly misses the point. Through the 19th and 20th centuries, political debate turned on whether a laissez-faire market capitalist or centrally managed economy was the best means to a goal both sides shared—an affluent society. Whether we call it "democratic consumerism" or a "workers' paradise" makes no difference. Today, it happens that the laissez-faire capitalist system made a larger number of us affluent before the centrally managed economies did, but both were blind to the dysutilities of over-consumption. Now the debate should not continue to be about the best means to achieve the goal of affluence, but rather about the wisdom and sustainability of affluence itself.

If we are not aiming to build an affluent society, what are we aiming to build? I propose that we want an off-ramp that takes us to a different road than the one we are currently traveling. Consumer culture frightens people into thinking that life is a highway with only one lane and no off-ramps. Behind us lies poverty, primitivity, superstition, and suffering. Ahead of us lies the promised land of—well, of what? More of what we already have. More affluence; more things; more speed and power and noise; more competition and overwork; more pollution and more conflict; more booms and recessions and depressions. What consumer culture cannot imagine is that there might be an off-ramp leading neither back to poverty nor onward to more of this. Such thoughts would come from a different paradigm, a different consciousness, something that consumer culture doesn't understand and can't control. But the truth we have discovered is that neither poverty nor affluence is sustainable. We need an alternative to both.

2. An Alternative to the Familiar Catastrophe: Mindfulness and Sufficiency

In the essay about mindfulness, I argued that the practice of mindfulness can foster the growth in us of a desire for a materially simpler way of life. This comes about partly because mindful awareness is sweet and once having tasted it, we're inclined to want more of it. Living amidst many distractions makes this more difficult. So we simplify to help maintain mindful awareness. Also, mindfulness awakens in us a sensibility for the many ways we are interdependent with other beings. Attending responsibly to these relationships is made easier by simplifying the outer baggage of our lives. We've become sensitized to the potential for violence inherent in owning things and are beginning to desire a less violent way of life, which thus implies owning fewer things, especially luxuries.[5] Our search for

---

[5] The link between affluence and violence is not always obvious. Suffice it here to note that nearly all economic production and consumption activities

well-being is shifting from extrinsic to more intrinsic, non-material sources. We're developing insight into the dynamics of desire and how futile is the pursuit of goods to try to satiate desires which cannot, by their nature, be satiated. Finally, mindfulness practice helps us discover the experience of things in their depth rather than only in their number or superficial appearance. We take time to look more deeply into the ordinary experiences of our lives with the result that we see and appreciate them more. This deep experiencing and appreciation evolves naturally away from the need for many material possessions, and toward more attentive care for what we do have, and more sensitive awareness of when we have too much.

Since almost everywhere production and consumption of material things incurs environmental impacts (extraction of resources, expenditure of energy, generation of waste, and release of toxins), it's obvious that consuming less results in a smaller ecological footprint, which amounts to a more sustainable way of life (Robert 2002). The eco-logic of simple living is very straightforward: Less stuff = less environmental impact. I therefore argue that *any future sustainable culture will have mindfulness practice as one of its tap roots, and voluntary simplicity as another—a freely chosen lifestyle, one aim of which is obtaining a maximum of well-being on the minimum of material consumption.* While we can certainly commit to simple living just by choosing it, this choice seems to be deeper and more tenacious when rooted in mindfulness practice. It's only through such a mindfulness practice that we come to know, profoundly and personally, why we are adopting simplicity. Upon these two, then, rests everything else.

I want to nuance a bit this idea of simple living guided by mindfulness of sufficiency. First, we will get confused if we equate consuming less with spending less. Money and consumption are only very loosely related. Earth really doesn't care how much or how little money we spend. What matters to her is the mass of resources we harvest, the energy we liberate in the process, and the toxicity of what we make and discharge into the

---

incur violence of one sort or another, most of it structural rather than direct. This violence is especially egregious when luxury consumption is involved, because the consumption serves no inherent need other than status display and profit. Note also in Hawken (2007, 84) how many of the major historical figures who promoted nonviolence were also advocates of simple living (Gandhi, Thoreau, Gregg).

world. Neither does Earth care much whether we are Christians or Muslims or Buddhists, or whether or not we appreciate art, or can run a marathon, or spend our holidays playing Scrabble. The non-material aspects of human cultures are relevant to the sustainability challenge in so far as they influence our decisions about how we use the resources, energy, and toxic materials our economy produces. These are what have real effects on the ecosphere. Islamic fundamentalism, for example, is of no consequence to the sustainability of the Earth until we start launching aircraft carriers and depleted uranium munitions, or we start burning oil wells, that have direct environmental impacts. It's always the translation of our beliefs into material effects that contributes to or detracts from our longevity on Earth, not the beliefs themselves, which are psychological not biophysical in nature.[6]

Second, whether I use the term *simple living* or *sufficiency* (as I plan to use both), the associations that these words have in pop culture with a sense of limits, of restraint, etc., are inescapable. I really have searched without much success for alternative words that have more positive connotations in the dominant culture. I think this has also been true for others who are working on this subject. So stated tersely, if you have an issue with the idea of any sort of restraint, discipline or limit applying to your behavior for any reason whatever, that's something you will just have to deal with. Our oldest wisdom traditions have consistently recognized that restraint is required in some areas of life in order to secure maximum well-being in the whole of one's life. The exercise of self-control, of moderation, and the capacity to recognize and respect limits does not drain the joy or pleasure

---

[6] There are certainly some perspectives that suggest a tighter relationship between what we think and how those thoughts are manifested at the level of physical reality that should not be entirely dismissed. Rupert Sheldrake's theories about morphogenetic fields (Rupert Sheldrake, *The Presence of the Past: Morphic Resonance and the Habits of Nature*, [New York, NY: Times Books, 1988]) more recent extensions of quantum entanglement to the realm of how observer effects might influence the outcome of events at the day-to-day level of reality (See: W.Arntz & B. Chase (producers), *Down The Rabbit Hole (What the Bleep Do We Know?)* DVD, Lord of the Wind Films, 2004, www.whatthebleep.com.). Also, the perennial teachings of many spiritual traditions respecting the relationship between the microcosm and macrocosm all represent intriguing strands of inquiry, which nevertheless exceed the scope of this book.

out of life; on the contrary, it is an essential requirement for joy and pleasure. I'm more than open to contrary arguments that striving for sufficiency as contrasted with either poverty or affluence is a bad idea. I'm less sympathetic to those who just feel uncomfortable with any talk of limits, or those who rabidly oppose them on ideological grounds, without first examining the merits of a more moderate way of life or without offering any tangible reasons for their discomfort. Extinction will be uncomfortable too.

I've already suggested that the consistent practice of mindfulness can grow in us an awareness of our desire for a simpler way of living. This desire is not something that is put there by mindfulness practice, but rather something already in us that mindfulness practice reveals. The aim of a more sustainable culture, at the material level of things, is *sufficiency in the provision of material needs.* Sufficiency stands between destitution on the one hand, and wasteful affluence on the other, but it is probably much lower on the food chain than is our current level of affluence. Affluence seems to have no psychological limit at all, even though pursuing affluence clearly has environmental and resource limits. A synonym for sufficiency is enough. Not barely enough or barely sufficient but something that has a bit wider margin than the bare minimum required. This is the case because the wisdom granted by experience reveals that life includes variation and change. It sends us ups and downs. Our individual lives need some margins for the sake of resilience and flexibility. While mere survival may be possible on barely sufficient resources, flourishing requires something more than the bare minimum of consumption. Therefore, sufficiency is not synonymous with a bare minimum. It is our very concern that present and future generations be able to flourish that partly motivates our present practice of sufficiency. Moreover, individual consumption is only part of the sustainability equation. At least as important are how many individuals are consuming, and the ecological efficiency of the technology being used to produce consumer goods.[7] We should

---

[7] The relationship among these variables is described in Merkel (2003). Total environmental Impact (I) equals Population (P) times Affluence (A) times Technology (T), or $I = P \times A \times T$. This concept is useful because it transcends the debate about population control, technical development, or consumption reduction being silver bullets if applied individually or ideologically to the sustainability challenge. The equation clearly illustrates that even if population

also note that valuing sufficiency includes valuing beauty. There is no reason why the goods, services, and dwellings that provide sufficiently for our lives cannot also be beautifully made and comfortable to live in. Making something beautiful and making it well may take more time and forethought, but it certainly doesn't necessarily require greater expenditure of resources, energy, or use of toxic materials. In fact, we will discover that making things well includes making them to last, which will have the effect of reducing material consumption even as we increase beauty and well-being in our lives.

3. What is Sufficient?

What exactly is sufficient material consumption?

At the physical level, sufficiency is fairly easy to describe. Here we are in the realm of what twentieth-century psychologist Abraham Maslow called *deficiency needs*—or those things without which physical survival is threatened.[8] The average human adult requires about 11,000 liters of clean air per day. Lacking air, we die in five or six minutes. We also require about 2 liters of clean water for drinking, and perhaps 100 liters more per day for bathing, cooking, washing clothes, and other essential

---

was limited or reduced, we might still overshoot planetary carrying capacity if our expectations for consumption are unrealistic or if our technology is inefficient or environmentally toxic. Correspondingly, even Earth's present human population might be supportable if our consumption expectations are modest and we do all within our power to make technology more efficient and environmentally benign. Technical development by itself will not likely be sufficient to meet the sustainability challenge if population continues to grow and consumption expectations remain unlimited. Current public policy discourses, however, tend almost exclusively to focus on promoting technical development—because that is where most profit can be made—or to a lesser degree on population control, which is seen as a developing country issue by commentators who live in developed countries. More or less entirely taboo is any analysis of over-consumption and the desire for affluence and how to address them. Even scholars and diplomats from developing countries who point out over-consumption in developed countries as an environmental threat, continue to promote economic growth in their own countries and demand assistance from the North to continue to do so.

[8] All statistics found at:
http://www.canadaimmigrants.com/Winnipegliving.asp

personal uses.[9] Deprived of water, most people die in less than seven days. An average adult also requires about 2,200 calories per day of food which includes all minerals, vitamins and trace nutrients necessary for health.[10] Healthy adults can live without food for a month or two provided water is available. Obese adults can live far longer provided vitamins, minerals, and electrolytes are available. In North America today, it is excessive caloric intake, not starvation, which poses the greatest risks to our physical well-being. In addition to these, we also require access to technology that can moderate variations in temperature and exposure to the elements. For most of us, this need is met by either clothing or shelter or a combination of them. A naked human adult has difficulty surviving over the long term in temperatures hotter than about 35 C° or cooler than about 15 C°. Clothing needn't be stylish to serve its purpose, as we witness every day in the garb of the homeless.[11] But authorities do suggest that a minimum of about 25-square meters of living space be available per person within a building to avoid conditions of crowding that otherwise contribute to the spread of diseases like TB and influenza.[12] All of these needs can currently be provided at very low cost, even through a market system without supplementing them by foraging, production for own consumption, hunting and gathering, or dumpster diving. In Winnipeg, Manitoba, Canada—not a place known for its mild climate!—basic survival needs in 2010 could be met for about

---

[9] Water—cost -- $ 0.0018 at current (2009) Winnipeg water rates. Adding another 100 liters per day for hygienic purposes (NOT essential for survival), increases cost to $ 0.09 per day. Dasani Water, $1.80 / 600ml; daily requirement would cost $5.40 for drinking alone.

[10] Food—On a vegetarian diet, all nutritional requirements could be met for about $3.00 per day. Average food expenditure for Winnipeg household for 2009 was $6,553; assuming 3.5 persons per household, annual per capita food expenditure would be $1,872 or $ 5.17/day.

[11] Clothing to allow adaptation to a greater range of temperatures and activities can be procured for about $360 per year, or $1.00 per day. [Average value is 6% of household income, for Winnipeg for 2009, $68,642, assuming 3.5 persons per household, annual per capita clothing is $1,177 or $3.22/day.

[12] Shelter—Four adults sharing a two bedroom apartment for $774/mo would spend $6.45 per day. Average shelter expenditure (including household operation costs) for a Winnipeg household for 2009 was 35% of average household income ($68,642) or $24,025. Assuming average family size of 3.5 persons = $24,025 / 3.5 = $6,864 per person ($19.07/day).

$11.00 per day.[13] This is by no means to say that such a life would be enviable in any other aspect than its freedom from the need to generate a large income. This gives us occasion to point out that the sort of simplicity we are advocating is certainly a life with a higher level of consumption than that required barely to meet subsistence needs. But we should also note the perennial truth that the Greek philosopher Epicurus (d. c. 270 BC) pointed out: "The wealth demanded by nature is both limited and easily procured; that demanded by idle imaginings stretches on to infinity."

What is sufficient for mere physical survival is thus quite easy to identify as is knowing how much is "enough." We pretty much know when we've drunk enough and eaten enough and breathed enough. We know when we are warm and safe from the elements. The limits imposed by nature—the size of our stomachs and bodies, the measure of our physical appetites—are not easily exceeded to any significant degree. Moreover, unless human numbers are exceedingly large, meeting these needs is not even particularly problematic from a sustainability perspective.

Even though the survival needs listed above are non-negotiable in that they must be met somehow, from a sustainability perspective, it still matters a great deal just how we meet them. Our two liters per day of required fluids coming from tap water rather than wine flown in from France or Argentina would make an enormous difference in environmental impacts. Likewise, whether our 2,200 calories per day are coming from locally grown vegetables and grains, or instead, we insist that they must be sea foods caught in S. E. Asia, or beef pastured in Brazil, those calories would incur very different ecological footprints. But in these matters, we are already moving away from that which is minimally sufficient for physical survival and into a realm of desires that are learned from and shaped by our culture.

---

[13] Total dollar cost to sustain one human being meeting needs through a market system and not own production, foraging, hunting-gathering, etc.: $10.54 per day—$316.20 per month. At current minimum wage (2009 - $9.00/hr), this can be obtained for 1¼ hours of labour per day. The corresponding figure for the average Winnipeg household based on total consumption expenditures would be $65,074 / 3.5 persons per household / 365 = $50.93 or $1,527.00 per month.

The next category of needs for which we must make sufficient provision pertains to our psychological and social well-being. Clearly, even our physical survival can be threatened if certain social and psychological needs are not adequately met. Children in orphanages, for example, if not stroked and cuddled enough, and lacking the opportunity to bond with an older caregiver who authentically loves them, will fail to thrive and sometimes even die. Moreover, despite our popular habit of celebrating the rugged individualist, people don't do very well if left alone. Solitary confinement is our most severe punishment for wrong-doing. So interdependent are we that in aboriginal cultures, banishment from the community often meant death. Today the epidemic of depression afflicting elders in our society can often be traced to loneliness.

In Maslow's hierarchy of needs, the psychological and social needs I'm outlining are included in his "safety/security, love/belonging and esteem" needs categories. We need to feel both physically and emotionally safe. We need sexual gratification, the affection and esteem of others, experiences of beauty, education and intellectual stimulation, secure and meaningful work, meaning and purpose in life, and many of us need offspring. How much of these is enough is rather hard to specify, or whether they can even be measured at all. But the human capacity for contentment clearly suggests that we are capable of finding enough esteem, safety, sexual pleasure and love, at least for limited periods. Lacking these experiences (and they are *experiences*, not *things*), we may fail to develop our full humanity and emotional maturity, and sometimes we even fail to thrive physically. It is highly relevant to note that human beings were obviously capable of meeting all of these needs for hundreds of thousands of years before the invention of consumer culture. Meeting our psycho-social needs does not require Facebook, or McDonald's, or a Lexus. The genius of consumer culture is that it convinces us that such things are necessities.

Since we were capable of meeting our psycho-social needs before the invention of consumer culture, and even before the invention of market exchange economies or industrialization, it should be fair to say that the economic cost of meeting these essential needs is very low or zero. Since little or no material consumption is required, living a life that is psycho-socially rewarding for us is thus clearly sustainable as well. The mere fact that we did survive and thrive and manifest psychological well-being for several hundred centuries clearly proves, I think, that human well-being is only loosely related to material consumption. That there are many aboriginal cultures extant today whose members achieve a healthy adulthood without the benefits of living in a consumer culture, provides further evidence in support of our conclusion. Thus, it is clearly possible and there is ample precedent, both historical and contemporary, to claim that people can live at low levels of material consumption while experiencing high levels of personal development and psycho-social well-being.

So what is consumer culture then? What were we thinking when we invented it? And what can we do about it now, if anything?

As soon as we move into the realm of consumer culture, we are obviously talking about a human artifact. This is something we invented, or perhaps some of us invented, for their own purposes and then foisted on a naive humanity—although I find this conspiracy theory implausible for reasons I will explain below.[14] The power of consumer culture resides in the fact that some of us have struck notes that easily resonate in the rest of us such that we collude in our own oppression.

Any economy must meet our basic physical needs or the economy itself will disappear because its customers will perish. The demand for the goods that fill these needs is intrinsic to our human nature. But we use material goods to assist with meeting or expressing many of our psycho-social needs as well. This capacity human beings have to substitute need satisfiers is the key focus of consumer culture development. We need love and esteem. But we can learn to perceive a diamond ring as evidence that someone loves us, and we can use diamond rings to express

---

[14] The idea that most of us are unwitting victims of conspiracies of advertisers, capitalists, and even governments intent on using consumerism to narcotize the masses and cement their own power is not new. See: Durning (1992) in which he argues that it has been the commercialization of television, the advertising industry and the appropriation of public spaces to commerce that induces high levels of consumption. These enterprises are clearly under the control of a minority and secretive elite whose interests are conflated with market capitalism. See also: Adam Curtis *Century of the Self* (BBC, 2002), a documentary dealing with the conscious development of consumerism from the theories of Sigmund Freud and their application in the development of public relations by Edward Bernays and propaganda by the Nazis. The documentary concludes with the clear implication that hyper-consumption is a sort of political opiate that pacifies the masses in democratic societies and is used by political parties to maintain their hold on power.

our love. How a psychological experience as rich, warm, complex and essential to human nature as love can become associated with a colorless, hard, cold, bit of stone attests to the miraculous ability we have to teach ourselves to believe almost anything. So I recognize the realm of consumer culture to begin just over the border between where we meet our psycho-social needs directly through the intrinsic reward of relationships on the hither side, and the yonder side where we start substituting extrinsic material things for relationships through enculturation and social learning. Consumer culture teaches us to want what it wants us to want by offering us substitutes for what we really want. As others have pointed out, these substitutions can be significant for many people (Segal 1999). If we have not been fortunate enough to find real love in life, the services of a sex trade worker might be consoling on occasion, as might owning a pet, or collecting long lists of friends on Facebook. The pleasures and distractions that material things can offer are certainly significant.

Consumer culture's happy place, however, is the realm of learned needs and desires. In the early years of the twentieth century, when cheap mass communication teamed up with mass literacy, mass production and the science of persuasion through marketing and advertising, brought us the birth of consumer culture. Consumer culture goes far beyond the inherent human need for material things necessary to our survival or even to our comfort. Consumer culture makes a science of creating learned needs. Since humans are capable of learning almost anything, there are no practical limits on what people can be taught to want. We can learn to spend our hard earned money on pet rocks. We will spend it on a brand to signal our status or taste. We will spend it on ideas like *security*, or *choice*, or *options*. Because learned needs are psychological rather than material, we get no clear signals from our bodies that the need has been met. So it can be refocused through advertising, fads, regulations, and social comparison giving the captains of commerce a nearly limitless field in which to make a profit. On top of all this, we humans can want something and not know consciously that we want it. We can be learning something and yet not consciously be aware that we're learning it. All of these aspects of the relation between people and the stuff we consume is relentlessly exploited for profit. The whole range of activities associated with this way of being in the world is probably what distinguishes consumer culture from all other cultures of history. In consumer culture, we don't consume to live; we live to consume, and we strive to make each other consume all the more.

Our culture might be compared to the amniotic fluid in which we develop from conception onwards. Recent studies of fetal learning suggest that even in utero, we are influenced by the moods and experiences of our mothers. Certainly after we are born, we're immersed in an ocean of social messages arising from the larger culture that are teaching us what matters and what doesn't, what we should want and what we should dislike, what we must do to win and how detestable it is to lose. Much of this is taken in at a time in life when we cannot, for developmental reasons, reflect critically on what we are learning. We're busy making our arms and legs work, mastering our toilet training, and learning one or more new languages. We don't have the time or mental capacity to question or debate the rules of a game we're still learning to play. So it's during this period that we learn to look for contentment and happiness through the satiation of desires, without really distinguishing whether our desires are innate or learned. We discover that unsatisfied desires are unsettling and uncomfortable, and even when they are temporarily sated, we anticipate with fear losing the objects that answer our desires even temporarily. We learn to try to possess, control, defend, and compete for these need satisfiers. And whether in pursuit of objects that satiate desire, or in trying to conserve the temporary respites we enjoy, we are dragged into competitive struggles with others that rarely add to our contentment; instead, they just ignite new rounds of craving. And consumer culture is always standing in the wings, offering us everything we think we need in this fruitless exercise.

Not only does consumer culture provide the material things we actually need, and also the things we've been taught to want, it forces consumption. Perhaps the greatest current myth in "developed" countries with consumer cultures is the idea that we are, on account of our material affluence, freer than any previous generation. Somehow all this consumption is supposed to liberate us to realize our dream, a dream that too often turns out to be what author Salmon Rushdie has called an "empire of obesity and trivia." North Americans in the twentieth century work more hours every year than peasants in the Middle Ages who didn't have the benefit of all our time-saving technology (Schor 1992). Far from using science and technology to liberate ourselves from toil, in the hands of consumer culture, it is applied to design products that wear out faster than they must, a practice called "designed obsolescence." This forces us to replace goods that otherwise might have lasted, hence condemning us to work more, produce more, pollute more and waste more. We also write building codes, zoning regulations, and a myriad of professional codes of practice and occupational regulations in such a way as to require building larger homes than we want, farther from our workplaces than they need to be, and that force consumption of all sorts of special equipment, clothing, and training activities that have little or no relevance to working more effectively. Mass communication is used to shape fashions, spark fads, and set trends that continually move the goal posts of what is considered decent or basic to a healthy life. The same mass media also frighten people into buying security systems even as crime rates are dropping, and all manner of personal protection devices for home, work, and school. Large pharmaceutical companies are busy medicalizing and medicating all sorts of conditions which are normal to human aging, such as wrinkles, reduced erectile function, and skin tags even as they leave unattended the need for new antibiotics to treat serious diseases. There is even a medication to treat restless leg syndrome rather than simply getting up to take a walk. The complete enmeshment of North American urban planning with the automobile is legendary and forces nearly everyone, at great financial cost, to operate their own personal global warming machines just to get from place to place. And all of this is mostly under the control of undemocratic, publicly unaccountable, corporations guided by a single motive—maximization of profit— the prime directive of which is also written into law.

In the meantime, the captains of consumer culture are also busy neutralizing any alternatives to themselves. International trade agreements like NAFTA and the WTO place severe restrictions around any economic deviations from the rules they themselves mandate. Some of these commit signatories to the treaties to continue supplying exports at historic levels once these levels have been established, even if this means depriving their own populations from needed resources. Development of more sustainable alternatives to our current technologies, goods and services is also made more difficult by more liberal patent and intellectual property protections than in the past—the effect of which are to lock competitors and generic manufacturers out of markets as long as possible.[15] Corporations also routinely eliminate competition and alternatives to their own product lines both by acquisitions and mergers that absorb competing firms, and also simply by destroying the basis for future competition. A classic example of this was when a cabal of auto manufacturers, oil companies, and tire makers joined forces to buy up and then decommission metropolitan transit companies that competed with automobiles. General Motors is also notorious for recalling and crushing all of its EV-1 first generation electric cars in the late 1990s on the pretext that there was no market demand for them at the time. In fact, it was at least partly because such cars require almost no aftermarket service, a major profit centre for car companies (CBC NewsNetwork. *Who Killed the Electric Car?* 2010).

What can be the meaning of *sufficiency* in such a culture? Many of the forces of science, technology, innovation, and corporate power reinforced by government policies and the armed violence of the state collude, consciously or unconsciously, to make our individual lives as precarious, demanding, and insecure as possible. We sense this every day, even if we don't connect the dots as we've tried to do just now. All of this aims to keep us earning and buying, which is the motor of consumer culture. Is it any wonder then that most of us think of sufficiency as something quite precarious, frightening and joyless?

4. Bringing Mindfulness and Sufficiency Together

One response to the death spiral of consumer culture is mindfulness practice. Mindfulness practice can help us develop

---

[15] The effect of the NAFTA (North American Free Trade Agreement—a pact among Canada, Mexico, and the US to liberalize trade relationships) has been in some instances to undermine the regulatory and guardian functions of the sovereign nation-states by imposing a super-ordinate claims and resolution process which is unaccountable to the citizens of the signatory countries (DePalma 2001). There has also been a great deal of debate concerning "TRIPs" addenda to the free trade agreements (Trade-Related Intellectual Property agreements) which have the effect of subjecting signatories' intellectual property rights regimes to a lowest common denominator standard that works largely to the benefit of major economic players and which also has the effect of stifling innovation and technical development by corporatizing information (McLeod 2001; Shiva 2001; Chataway, et. al. 2000, 469–484; King and Stabinski 1999).

insight into how desires arise in us, how futile it can be to think that trying to satisfy desires will lead to permanent contentment, and how interdependent we are with the ecosphere and with other people. Mindfulness also helps us develop insight into our own mental activities, feelings, imagination, memories, and thoughts.

Bringing more mindfulness to our physical appetites can certainly contribute to better health as well as a greater exercise of environmental responsibility as we become sensitized to overconsumption—even of what is essential for us. But I think the greatest relevance of mindfulness practice to our sustainability dilemma is precisely in the realm of psychological needs, and especially learned needs—the desires most systematically preyed upon and exploited by consumer culture. Bringing to these experiences of distraction and desire a sense of calmness, penetrating insight, and consciousness of what we *really* need, physically, emotionally, socially, spiritually—this can help us connect with a natural, spontaneous, and wholesome wisdom within ourselves about what is good for us and good for the whole. Continually refreshing this awareness of what is good for us through on-going mindfulness practice will give us basis enough for deciding what to do (right action) and what to cease doing.

I have had many opportunities in the past to speak with individuals, groups, and the media about simple living. I'm often asked what people must do to have a calmer, more centered, less debt-ridden and consumptive life. Mostly what these people are used to hearing is a list of normative prescriptions—new commandments if you will—of what they need to do to be saved from the consequences of living in a consumer culture. They are often disappointed when I tell them I don't have any such thing. All I can suggest is a method by which they might discover their own answers. But it will take some time, persistence, and diligence on their part.

And this is also the best proposal I can make in the context of our present discussion. We need to establish the personal habit of cultivating mindfulness every day. We also need to connect with others who will help us learn how, help us sustain our practice, help us teach our children, help us celebrate and be loyal to what mindfulness reveals to us. And from this place of lucid stillness, we can discover insight into everything arising within us, including our desires to consume. We can interrogate them one by one: Where did they come from? What do they want? Is what they want something that will contribute to our well-being and that of the whole, or will it merely be a temporary pleasure or distraction from what is really well for us? How will pursuing this desire affect the great web of being in which we are members? Is this desire something we recognize spontaneously as a healthy one, or is it something that's being forced into us, something that feels emotionally harsh in any way, something we're being taught or cajoled into servicing? And who benefits most if we pursue this desire? Is it authentic, or is it merely something arising from the myriad of power, pleasure, and control fantasies of the ego? If we learn to take the time to parse the desires that arise in us, we will at least be conscious in our choice of life or of self-destruction.

Well meaning and intelligent people may disagree that we are so subject to learned needs or to their manipulation. Thomas Hobbes' view of human nature still carries considerable weight with many contemporary audiences, especially economists. Maybe mindfulness doesn't matter a whiffle because human nature is a seething cauldron of numberless desires which are inherently insatiable and no amount of insight will change it. But this still leaves us in the same place. We still have the same problem. Insatiable human appetites are driving us up against the immovable limits of the ecosphere and resource supplies. Whether we've been taught to want more and more, or it is wired into us, it comes to the same thing. Our survival and well-being requires that we moderate our consumption. It seems to me that our first task is recovering this value from our cultural memory (because it certainly isn't new), giving it priority of place, and maintaining it there. When it comes to reminding ourselves of the things we need to keep in mind every day, that's what cultures are for. We need a replacement for consumer culture, and I propose one based on *mindful sufficiency*. But I also hasten to add that I think this will be a joyful and loving culture as well, since a great deal of the violence, stress, and suffering we endure every day arises from consumer culture itself. These stresses could be transcended by adopting a different narrative of the good life.

5. Mindful Sufficiency in Practice

There are a great many ways that a culture of mindful sufficiency can be built up in practice. It naturally implies a changed perspective of education, technology, politics, economics, and community development. Imagine that at some point a great awakening occurs that human civilizations are in peril and something has to be done (or perhaps more accurately, there are a great many things we need to cease doing!). It's not hard to picture then, that all the means we know of would be recruited to meet the challenge of survival. We can visualize social marketing campaigns, education reform, regulation of design obsolescence, reclamation of the language of frugality and prudence, and a wide array of economic and social policies that are at least not prejudicial to simple living as is now the case. But for the balance of this essay, our focus will be on our lives as individuals and how mindfulness of sufficiency might find practical application.

5.1 *Mindfulness of waste*

We discovered above that the very meaning of the word "affluence" implies waste. Waste is the primary product of consumer culture. To produce more than is needed is to produce waste. To make things poorly and quickly so as to maximize profit also produces waste. To consume more than is needed is to compromise one's health and well-being as when we encourage addictions by consuming too much food or drink. What good does it do us to have lights on in unoccupied rooms? Or to have rooms with no use? Or to waste water during bathing or laundering our clothes? Thus the first focus of mindfulness practice in service of sufficiency is to become mindful of what we waste, how we waste it, and then to take steps to eliminate waste. Waste is consumption without utility. Waste is especially egregious when we plunge ourselves into debt to achieve it. It makes no sense at any level other than conspicuous display to impress others—we have so much wealth we can even waste it! No such attitude toward material things could be acceptable in a sustainable culture.

The focus of mindfulness practice in reducing waste is upon both the things we authentically need and also the comforts and luxuries we enjoy. Our intention everywhere is to reduce waste wherever we find it. Very skillful here is adopting technology that can increase the efficiency with which we use energy and resources. Efficiency measures reduce the energy and materials needed to deliver a specific benefit or perform a certain function. A shower head, for example, that uses 30% less water to get you just as clean is a more efficient device than the one using more water.

Another way of reducing waste is in the selection of the things we choose to consume. Many spend considerable time shopping around for the best price on an item they want. Probably less time is spent even considering whether the item is something the need for which is arising authentically from our daily round of living. We may fail to compare the operational features of the item to assure that they fit well with what we need. We may fail to investigate how the item was made, where it came from, and the effects it had on other beings as it made its way to us. Thus we can reduce waste by spending some time to select the most functional, best made, most environmentally friendly product we can find for the need we've discerned. Considering all these things will certainly slow down the shopping process, which itself can contribute greatly to sustainability and personal well-being.

Yet another way of reducing waste is the familiar advice to recycle. When things we own reach the end of their useful life and cannot be repaired or reused for some other purpose, then recycling as much of the materials as possible is another way of avoiding sending valuable resources to landfill that will have to be replaced with virgin materials.

5.2 Mindfulness of stored value

Even though we may become skillful at reducing waste, we can also bring mindfulness to what I call stored value. This refers to all the goods we have in storage in one form or another. It is estimated, for example, that 50% of food is wasted annually in processing, transport, supermarkets and kitchens worldwide, much of it having been lost because portion sizes are too large, people are overeating to begin with, or the food passes its best-before date while still in storage. The United States, a country that generally enjoys the best in food conservation technology and inventory control at wholesale and retail levels, still loses as much as 30% of its food, worth USD $48.3 billion annually (Stockholm International Water Institute, *et al.* 2008).

The average North American household also stores considerable quantities of all sorts of goods and materials in various cupboards, closets, sheds, garages, out-buildings, rented storage facilities and sometimes second or third residences such as cottages, seasonal homes, or time-shares. The first decade of the new millennium witnessed explosive growth of 81% in self-storage facilities in the US alone (Self-Storage Association 2007). We can also witness a steady increase in the number of garages included with new houses as a function of age. Single car garages were the norm from the invention of the car until the 1960s when double car garages became common. By 2000, triple or even quadruple car garages were being built, seldom to store cars per se, but rather all the other vehicles like boats, snowmobiles, personal watercraft, golf carts, trailers, campers, recreational vehicles, quads, and all their parts, accessories, and service add-ons that seemed so essential at the time. Closets are jammed with unused clothing, unworn shoes, the remnants of forgotten hobbies, and unfulfilled New Year's resolutions. Kitchen cupboards bulge with unused or seldom used dishes, seasonal or holiday dishes, and specialized single food appliances like waffle irons, wiener warmers, popcorn poppers, bagel toasters, and electric carving knives. Basements are jammed with the remains of hobby and craft endeavors, abandoned exercise machines, rusting bicycles, and every manner of sporting goods. Most of this sits precisely where it is because, while the denizens of consumer culture work harder than ever for the money to buy all this stuff, our most common complaint is a lack of time even for sleep or exercise or proper nutrition. So we are exhausted working for all the things we don't have time to use. Most important from a sustainability perspective, however, is the fact that all these goods represent resources that, because of the fiction of private property, the use of which we deny to others. This means that either they must forego the use of them hence impoverishing their lives, or else must find the means of obtaining their own copy of what we hide in storage, thus increasing demand for resources, energy, etc., with all the attendant ecological costs.

I'm not advocating that people part with things that bring real value into their lives merely to satisfy some abstract ideology of simple living. But it's a principle of natural justice that if someone is suffering from the lack of something that I have it in my power to provide, there is also a moral obligation upon me to provide it. Apart from the moral imperatives that surround the mere possession of wealth (not something we hear much about these days), there is the practical matter of the waste implied in remanufacturing and re-consuming goods that are already available in the world simply hiding in storage units, the contents of which their owners have probably mostly forgotten. As practitioners of simple living, this is a wonderful opportunity to start inspecting our hordes and meditating honestly on why we are keeping this thing from others? Just as in the matter of bringing mindfulness to all our consumption choices, we can equally do so respecting all of our decisions to possess something. Why do we own this? What purpose does it serve? Where did it come from? What use might it be to others? From what motives is our possession of it occurring? When all of these considerations are brought into our mindfulness practice focused on what we have in reserve, we will see right away how much room there is for change. We may also discover the truly liberating feeling of passing on to someone else something they genuinely need. In the same act we liberate ourselves from that particular impediment to the freedom of our inner being.

Possession is a privilege; also a burden; also a responsibility. St Benedict of Nursia (Chittister 1992, 104-106), the founder of Western monasticism advised his monks to: "regard all utensils and goods of the monastery as sacred vessels of the altar, aware that nothing is to be neglected. Cellarers should not be prone to greed, not be wasteful and extravagant with the goods of the monastery, but should do everything with moderation." If we consider our homes, indeed the Earth itself, as a monastery—a community most essentially defined as a school for spiritual development—then we can benefit by bringing this attitude of sacredness to all our possessions. In this light we can reflect, without self-blame, but simply to cultivate awareness, how are we treating the goods of our monasteries? Do they belong in our basements and garages or might they be more life-givingly deployed somewhere else? As the twentieth-century Tennessee philosopher and farmer Wendell Berry (Berry 1981, 281) observed: "We must daily break the body and shed the blood of creation. When we do this knowingly, lovingly, skillfully, reverently, it is a sacrament. When we do it ignorantly, greedily, clumsily, destructively, it is a desecration."

5.3 *Voluntary simplicity*

It is possible to aggressively reduce waste without making many significant shifts in our lifestyle. We make all the same consumption choices, we continue to seek the good life in terms of extrinsic material possessions, but we green-them-up (with green consumerism). It has long been known by product manufacturers that the existence of recycling programs actually increases the consumption of products whose containers can be recycled because it relieves consumers of the guilt they feel for generating waste. We can add to this the great cleansing that goes with passing along all the goods and resources we kept stored away for any number of reasons that we now no longer find compelling. When, however, we refocus consciousness toward voluntarily reducing our consumption of material things for reasons rooted in our mindfulness practice, then I say we are beginning to practice *voluntary simplicity*. Among other things, this involves switching our attention and effort from amassing extrinsic material possessions to cultivating intrinsic sources of well-being instead.

For centuries, people have gaped uncomprehendingly that a life guided by mindfulness and sufficiency might hold more reward than a life in pursuit of affluence. They firmly believe that if a little of something is good, more is better, and more without limit must be best of all, despite any experiential evidence of their own to the contrary. The craving for more and more is the voice of our evolutionary past still alive in us.

Voluntary simplicity has many definitions but what most share in common is the discovery that a good life is created by voluntarily limiting consumption of material things to that elegant sufficiency necessary for the maximum of well-being. From this point of view, it has always appeared highly irrational, and indeed self-destructive, to pursue material wealth for its own sake, or consumption without regard for its effects on oneself or others. Material things are means to sustaining our lives in service of the purposes that give them meaning, not ends in themselves. Simple living rests on discernment of sufficiency rather than the blind pursuit of affluence. The cultivation of mindfulness is essential to discerning sufficiency as well as directing consciousness in a way that truly provides for well-being. Paradoxical as it may sound, sufficiency assures enough for everyone, while affluence promises poverty and chaos—as we are now seeing every day. As the famed British economist E. F. Schumacher (Schumacher 1973, 42) remarked:

> For the modern economist this [principle of sufficiency] is very difficult to understand. [S/he] is used to measuring the 'standard of living' by the amount of annual consumption, assuming all the time

that a [person] who consumes more is 'better off' than a [person] who consumes less. A Buddhist economist would consider this approach excessively irrational: since consumption is merely a means to human well-being, the aim should be to obtain the maximum of well-being with the minimum of consumption.

To actually work, voluntary simplicity has to be voluntary. It has to begin with a personal and conscious choice to live differently, in spite of public opinion to the contrary, and every day, in spite of what our instinctive appetites prompt us to want. This is not to say that simple living is contrary to nature, but that it draws upon different natural capacities than those engaged in meeting basic survival needs or pursuing extrinsic sources of pleasure. We certainly have appetites for pleasure and material comfort, but we also have an appetite for reason, wholeness, and living in a way that is life-affirming.

Simple living has to be voluntary because there are no historical examples of imposed simplicity (such as that of the Puritan sumptuary laws) that have been sustained for very long (Shi 1985, 8ff). And it must be voluntary because the historical examples which have persisted for many centuries (e.g., Benedictine monastic life—1500 years; Quaker simplicity—400 years; Buddhist monastic simplicity—2,500 years) have all involved free consent based on reason, experience, and personal commitment. Finally, voluntary simplicity must be voluntary because any simplicity we live involuntarily is something from which we will always be trying to escape—such as the poverty and deprivation many people experience today as a result of the 2008 financial meltdown, war, environmental disasters, or personal tragedies.

For skeptics, the most irritating thing about voluntary simplicity is that there are lots of examples of people who have, and are, living it. It's not a theory or a utopian ideology. Many of these people were, or could have been, winners in the general scramble for more. Gandhi was a lawyer and could have been affluent, but vowed to own nothing that could not also be owned by the poorest of his compatriots and worked to build a nation instead. Siddhartha Gautama was already a king, but left it all to search for Nirvana. John Woolman was a successful business owner in eighteenth-century New England who had to keep scaling his business back to free time for prayer and preaching, which mattered more to him than success in business. Thomas

Treherne wandered the English countryside in ecstasy wearing leather and eating bread and water because he wanted to study happiness and how little might be necessary to attain it. Francis of Assisi left his father's lucrative rag trade and a lifestyle of wenching and singing to reshape Medieval European monasticism. Jesus of Nazareth and John the Baptist had no place to lay their heads, but tramped the Judean countryside teaching the joy of God's love and mercy. Seneca was richer and smarter than the emperors he served but chose to live the threadbare life of a Stoic philosopher. All these were real people.

In case you think that this is a way of life reserved for spiritual athletes or exceptional eccentrics, know that there have been, and are, tens of thousands of historically obscure Puritans, Quakers, Mennonites, Amish, monastics of every tradition, Cathars and philosophers, poets and social reformers, New Catholic Workers, Cynic philosophers, and Jesus Freaks, back-to-the-landers and Hara Krishnaites, Franciscan Tertiaries and Benedictine Oblates, wanderers and minstrels, soldiers and Samurai, and ordinary people—the multitude at the margin as it were—who have lived this way too and found it deeply pleasing. These are the people who most annoy the moguls of marketing. They are discovering through their own experience what is necessary for a free and happy life and what is not. This is not a matter of adopting an ideology. It is a matter of simply paying attention to our daily experience and taking it to heart.

5.4 *The question of luxury*

Before leaving the discussion of sufficiency, it's fitting to address the question of luxury. For most citizens of developed countries, consumption long ago ceased to be about basic needs, although Jerome Segal has argued convincingly that even in countries like the United States, there are still some basic needs which go unmet (Segal 1999, 45-72). But setting aside, for a minute, questions of policy, we find the technology, energy, and material resources have been available to solve the basic economic problem for much of humanity, at least since the last decades of the nineteenth century, with the broad implementation of electrification and adoption of fossil fuels as prime-mover energy sources. From that time onwards, a larger and larger fraction of household income has shifted toward discretionary purchases of luxuries rather than need-related purchase of necessities.

Detractors of simple living are eager to portray it as a joyless, comfortless exercise in asceticism, even though its most eloquent proponents consistently argue the opposite:

> It would be an error to suppose that the simplicity we seek has anything in common with that which misers impose upon themselves through cupidity, or narrow-minded people through false austerity. To the former the simple life is the one that costs least; to the latter it is a flat and colorless existence, whose merit lies in depriving one's self of everything bright, smiling, seductive. (Wagner 1903, 139)

Clearly, however, luxury consumption presents more of a problem both for maintaining a mindful approach to living and also a sustainable livelihood. Huge environmental impacts are currently incurred to procure luxury goods like gold, diamonds and other precious stones. The same goes for luxury foods like high-meat diets, coffee, tea, chocolate, and other luxury expenditures like over-powered, over-sized cars, houses, boats, and wardrobes. Most people do not go into debt for their next meal, although they almost certainly will for their car, house, vacations, and bling. There is no question that for many people these goods bring great pleasure and for nearly everyone, at least some of them do. I'm not a proponent of asceticism for its own sake and I enjoy a good meal, warm clothes, and a hot shower as much as the next person. I'm also completely confident that a sustainable livelihood can be established that includes enough of most of these things.

But among the many figures of history who point out that consumption entails responsibilities, few are as eloquent as John Ruskin (Ruskin 1996, 63):

> It is impossible to spend the smallest sum of money for any not absolutely necessary purpose, without a grave responsibility attaching to the manner of spending it. The object we ourselves covet may, indeed, be desirable and harmless, so far as we are concerned, but the providing us with it may, perhaps, be a very prejudicial occupation to someone else. And then it becomes instantly a moral question, whether we are to indulge ourselves or not. Whatever we wish to buy, we ought first to consider not only if the thing be fit for us, but if the manufacture of it be a wholesome and happy one; and if, on the whole, the sum we are going to spend will

do as much good spent in this way as it would if spent in any other way. It may be said that we have not time to consider all this before we make a purchase. But no time could be spent in a more important duty; and God never imposes a duty without giving the time to do it. Let us, however, only acknowledge the principle; once make up your mind to allow the consideration of the *effect* of your purchases to regulate the kind of your purchase, and you will soon easily find ground enough to decide upon.

If other examples of this general principle are needed we have only to look at diamond mining, made notorious because of blood diamonds coming from conflict regions of Africa and procured largely by forced labour or extortion. But even in North American diamond recovery operations, it is the economic return from only 1.5 carats of recovered diamond (300 mg.) that is needed to justify digging and processing a metric ton of rock and gravel, all of it using fossil fueled machinery and some of it occurring in ecologically sensitive regions (Campbell 2003).

Equally appalling is the energy and fresh water being squandered to retrieve oil from the bitumen tar sands in the Athabasca region of Alberta in Canada. When first extracted in the 1940s, light Saudi crude, some of the easiest oil in the world to reach, required no water and the investment of only one barrel of oil equivalent in energy to extract 130 barrels of oil for market. In the tar sands case, however, millions of liters of water are polluted in the recovery process which itself consumes one barrel of oil to produce only two barrels of crude. It is also 1.25 to 1.75 times more green house gas intensive to extract than conventional oil. The difference in these two ratios, 1:130 in Saudi Arabia compared to 1:2 in Canada represents one of history's most extravagant investments of energy which is consumed disproportionately in luxury motor vehicles (Alternative Energies 2011).

Thus, without being austere or negatively ascetical, we must suppose that a lifestyle of mindfulness and sufficiency will also interrogate luxury consumption as perhaps the most important class of discretionary choices that represent avoidable harms. In consumer culture, the only limit on our luxury consumption is our income, and easy credit often raises even that. The choice to consume luxuries is never represented by consumer culture within the context of all the other considerations we've cited that arise from mindfulness practice. These include our interdependence with others; the shift from extrinsic to intrinsic sources of well-being; a deepened appreciation for ordinary experience; a deeper sense of living in a moral universe; heightened awareness of the dynamics of desire, and so on. It seems reasonable therefore to recognize that some luxuries are more luxurious than others. Since what we are discussing is how to sustain a rich and rewarding life over the long term, not how to make ourselves worse off, we scarcely wish to exclude enjoyment of some comforts and luxuries along the way. But this cannot be determined solely by income. We need to situate such decisions within the context of interdependence, nonviolence, inter-generational, inter-species, and international equity, as well as environmental sustainability. If we are to live here for the long haul, we must be mindful both of the pleasures of luxury consumption and of its costs—which are considerable. Our willingness to pay these costs should not a badge of economic masculinity or privileged status, but rather a symptom of the depth of our addiction to pleasure. Our responsibility is to be informed, mindful, and deliberate in our choices, knowing all the time that we may not be the ones who pay the price for any given luxury indulgence—it may be other species or future generations.

MARK A. BURCH

4

COMMUNICATING SIMPLICITY

1. Introduction

It's reasonable to assume that any essay about simplicity and communication will have to do with the classic themes of Right Speech. To write (or speak) rightly, our words should be true, carefully chosen, compassionate, and ideally, few. They should issue from a sincere and honest heart, expressing goodwill and intended for the improvement of others, even when the subject is contentious, or our partners in conversation are malicious or uninformed. What we say should align with how we say it, how we hold our bodies, and the directness of our gaze. Above all what we say should be about something that matters. In all other cases, silence is preferable.

These themes continue to be highly relevant but they have been extensively explored by others in nearly every historical period and across many cultures. We have trouble managing our tongues (and pens) and there is no shortage of advice on this matter that I don't mean to repeat here. In what follows, I want to explore how we *communicate simplicity*, not how to communicate simply. For those who think that voluntary simplicity has something to offer the world in its present predicament, this must be a matter of considerable practical importance. Communicating simply is a matter of rhetoric and style. Communicating simplicity is an urgent task upon which the future of our species may depend. It is this second trail that I want to explore mostly because I think it is the one less traveled.

2. Have-You-Ever Metaphor?

An often used metaphor for humanity's sustainability predicament is the ill-fated Titanic, a luxury liner of massive bulk and inertia whose wealthy but clueless passengers are carried to their doom even as they sip champagne and listen to cheerful chamber music. Imagining this tragic event leaves us feeling as if we are being carried helplessly along in a huge vessel over which we have no control. We feel trapped aboard something which once set in motion, cannot be easily turned or stopped, even if we wished to do so. The image arises from the Industrial Age paradigm of great mechanical forces blindly following impersonal natural laws. It was the age of Newtonian physics and Victorian values that gave us an imperialist paradigm that aims to subject the world to human designs by sheer mechanical violence. Is it any wonder then that we too feel violated by these same relentless mechanical forces, along with the world we try to subjugate?

The image of the Titanic and all the associations it summons is an example of how the way we perceive and think can shape what we believe is possible for us. Discovering alternatives to being carried down with the ship implies creating new metaphors that help us see ourselves differently. Maybe we're not passengers on a cold iron ship fated to kill us because of its own design flaws. Maybe 19th century mechanistic images are less helpful in the circumstances than are more organic ones would be. Instead, maybe we're more like a flock of birds, or a school of fish. We're a shining multitude capable of launching, stopping and turning on a dime. We are not a mute, mechanical mass of metal, or even a pile of silicon chips that must be plugged in and programmed to do what they do. We are a self-energized, self-aware, self-replicating, self-repairing, self-organizing, self-actualizing, solar powered, completely organic, totally recyclable, omni-local, interdependent, and fully conscious *community*. What holds us together is not rivets and wires but *communication* among self-conscious beings. We are the makers not the victims of our technology.

With the possible exception of Facebook, we generally don't share anything and everything with anyone and everyone. *What we communicate is constructed from a nearly infinite array of possibilities depending on how consciousness is oriented and on the story metaphors we tell ourselves about life, the universe and everything. In the previous essay, I proposed that a synergy of mindfulness practice and a lifestyle ordered to sufficiency rather than the pursuit of affluence might be foundations for a more sustainable culture. Assuming for the time being that it is messages about mindful sufficiency that we wish to communicate more broadly (so as to keep our flock from hitting the "wall" of our unsustainable way of life), this essay will focus on what sorts of communication might be most helpful in building and transmitting this new culture. Communication is the glue that keeps the flock flying together and communication tells us where the flock is going. Communication is also an essential process for education.

3. The Company We Keep

Encouraging a culture of mindfulness and sufficiency can face challenges arising from the misfit between what mindful sufficiency is about and the media we might use to communicate it. As early as the 1960s, philosopher and media theorist Marshall MacLuhan helped us appreciate that both the content of a message and the medium carrying it have profound effects on the societies within which they circulate (MacLuhan 1967). In a consumer culture already saturated with the influence of mass media, we may think that promoting mindful sufficiency implies recruiting television and radio coverage, getting celebrity endorsements to attract public attention, and then crafting a one-size-fits-all message that we hope will be taken to heart by people in the millions. But this understandable first response already disconnects what mindful sufficiency is about from the media we might use to promote it.

Today, mass media are mostly commercially owned, serve commercial values, and are engaged in commercial ventures. Their prime directive is to attract or drive people to the marketplace. They do this by broadcasting product advertising, but also by creating and continually reinforcing a generally consumeristic cultural milieu. Because the media themselves are so often used to selling things, to presenting unattainable fantasies as entertainment, to confounding fact and fiction, and to manipulating public opinion, virtually anything else that appears in these media runs the risk of suffering because of the company it keeps. Incredibility by association is compounded by the fact that no one can realistically sell a non-consumptive way of life and stay in business. So pervasive is the association of electronic media (increasingly including the Internet) with commercial enterprise that even when they carry non-commercial content, they still implicitly endorse consumerism because the content itself is being consumed in the process of viewing or hearing it.

Commercial media make money from businesses that sponsor their programs. It is unlikely that they will carry content that is anti-consumerist in worldview, as has already been discovered by *culture jamming* organizations like Adbusters (*Adbusters* 2012). To do so would undermine the very basis for their profitability. Even organizations like the Simplicity Forum (c. 2000), established specifically to promote simple living in the United States, has faced strong headwinds in trying to raise money from foundations to promote simpler living. Foundations are endowed with money generated through commercial endeavors. The interest on their original endowments depends on continuing and profitable economic activity, all of it driven by a consumer culture narrative of the good life. Thus it's not likely that such institutions will support activities that call into question the very basis of their existence.

There remains, however, the practical question of how mindful sufficiency and simpler living, as cultural innovations, can be diffused in society as a whole. This is important, partly because a cultural course change is essential if we are to avoid the wall of ecological and social catastrophe. But even more important is the fact that as we grow in mindfulness, our deepening appreciation for what is being lost to consumer culture, and also our growing sense of interdependence with all life makes such action imperative. So what forms of communication might better align with the values and culture of mindful sufficiency than those offered by the world of commerce? Will engaging them require multi-million dollar budgets, deep technical expertise, and World Cup of Soccer scale events? To address these questions, I want to distinguish two different species of communication, and then illustrate the role that each might play in diffusing a culture of simple living.

4. Communication of the First Kind

Communication is as old as the human species; indeed, as old as life itself. If we situate communication for a moment within the living communities of the earth, we see a multi-channel world of great diversity. I want to use the term *Communication of the First Kind* to refer to our most biophysically rooted and earliest means of communication. Human beings are flooded, body and spirit, with a multitude of odors, hues, tones, and tastes; with intuitions and images and dreams and visions; with songs and poems and hungers and hankerings. Long before we invented artificial communication technologies such as print, telephones, television, etc., we were (and continue to be) capable of a wide range of communication activities that include chemical, nonverbal/behavioural, visual and auditory, tactile and aesthetic communication, much of which we also share with animals and plants. We know the world and our place in it through experiences involving many senses. These experiences ground us in the pre-conscious depths of our cellular origins four billion years ago at the same time as they propel human consciousness toward whatever it is capable of becoming. We communicate but also steep, breathe, and maneuver in an ocean of on-going exchanges and relationships of social and ecological inter-dependence. It is also our bridge into the world of organic reality and with all that is other than human. These are examples of Communication of the First Kind.

The ocean of messages from both internal, subjective, unconscious sources and external, social, and natural environments, provides our most immediate and real context for living. Mindfulness practice can heighten our awareness of these messages simply by providing a way of bringing attention back to them and valuing what they have to say to us. One example of what I would call Communication of the First Kind involves the image-making powers of the psyche. It consists of the spontaneously appearing images that have their source in the less conscious regions of the psyche and their communication to conscious awareness. Unlike words, images can represent situations as wholes. They empower people to transcend the constraints of *Communication of the Second Kind* (to be explained below). They also give access to ways of knowing wherein whole new patterns can arise together with the sensory, motivational, and emotional "auras" that will later nourish acts of culture creation.

A noteworthy example of this is community visioning exercises. I've facilitated groups of people on a number of occasions who tell their personal stories about what it feels like to be living in consumer culture at this time. Nearly all of these stories involve feelings of sadness, despair, stress, worry, regret and loss, especially when participants are asked to recall what has become of the natural places they enjoyed as children. As we process these memories in more detail, we discover a myriad of reasons why we respond emotionally to consumer culture in this way. But we also soon discover that taking up each particular problematic situation and trying to deal with them one by one just lands us in a tangled thicket of complications, connections, and unforeseen consequences. No one, it turns out, wants to be living in a society that leaves them feeling overwhelmed and despairing. The way out, however, is not found by fixing one problem at a time, but rather by imagining a healthier future society. These images appear as highly energized, quite detailed wholes. Moreover, they tend to be shared almost at an archetypal level, as if they are not the product of individual minds. Once a life-giving image is discovered, it's a much more energizing and hopeful prospect to work backwards, building from the image the better world we want, than it is to try to salvage consumer culture which is clearly undergoing its own extinction.

Communication of the First Kind represents our innate capacity for holistic connection with the world of our experience. It is common to all humanity, not the reserve of technical experts, moneyed elites, or even of literate cultures. It is inherently democratic and accessible to the youngest child. It is our most direct contact with living. It grows up from the earliest foundation of our biological and mental development. In my view, it is this sort of communication that most directly relates to mindfulness and which the practice of sustainable living is most concerned to conserve, deepen, and develop. It pertains to what Anthony Spina (1998) refers to as our *Life World*—the world of personal relationships, lived with immediacy and intensity, that infuses life with meaning. Communication of the First Kind is also the source of compelling messages about whether or not we are living sustainably. We know by walking down the street and listening and smelling and tasting the air and sensing the emotional and physical vibrations around us whether motor vehicles are a wholesome thing for us and for the planet. And we know this in a way that is never communicated by reviewing statistics and reports about automobile accident rates or air pollution levels.

Ecopsychologist Michael Cohen (1993) has suggested that in addition to the senses of vision and hearing, which today we rely on most for our communication experience, we have 51 other senses that mediate our experiences of each other and our environment. Our culturally driven tendency to communicate mostly on just two of our 53 available sensory channels renders us both stupid and blind in ways that even our recent ancestors would find truly mind-boggling. It is precisely four million years of human evolution within this constellation of sensory and communication experience, Cohen contends, that produced human intelligence in the first place. We impoverish our sensory experience by focusing most of our attention on only one or two senses, he argues, and in the process we impoverish human intellect, our emotional well-being, and even our contact with reality.

Communication of the First Kind occurs face-to-face. Historically, it has been by means of Communication of the First Kind (relationships, art, dance, experience in nature, introspective practices, ritual, gossip, storytelling, etc.) that cultural innovations have diffused within society. Since it often involves the more tactile, intimate senses, it is associated with the feminine. In light of its historical role, we might even conjecture that it provides the very ground that defines human sanity and our whole capacity for future development and evolution. There is hardly any reason to believe that nature is finished evolving the human species, even within the context of pre-industrial cultural forms.

Nevertheless, Communication of the First Kind presents some limitations. One is that all parties to the communication need to be in the same place at the same time. Communication of the First Kind cannot be pre-recorded or re-broadcast. Consequently, it is inherently personal and limited both in time and space. It is inherently local.

Second, every act of Communication of First Kind has about it a quality of uniqueness and unrepeatability because it is partly defined by the flow of experience in time and place, and by social context. A common example of this is a joke that isn't as funny on the second telling as on the first. We account for this difference by saying, "You had to be there." That is, you had to be present in the original physical and social situation to appreciate the humor. Since the flow of situations can never be duplicated, each act of Communication of the First Kind is unique in detail, if not in general outline. This lends to each occasion of Communication of the First Kind a special richness and unrepeatable preciousness. At the same time, however, it presents limitations when it's desirable or essential that a large number of people receive the same message, or that certain messages be preserved and transmitted over and over again.

Third, Communication of the First Kind is limited by the fact that, while it is "multi-modal" and therefore very rich, it moves at the speed of the human nervous system. Indeed, for both Communication of the First and Second Kinds, the speed of human neural processing sets the outer limits of any communication experience, not the speed that machines can transfer information from one place to another.

Which brings us to Communication of the Second Kind.

5. Communication of the Second Kind

Today, whenever we think of transmitting something from one person to another, we naturally think of mass media communications. Our society is dominated, indeed obsessed, with the technology that mediates what I call *Communication of the Second Kind*. The affluent North American adolescent is fully equipped with a smart phone, entertainment centre, laptop computer, iPod music player, and high-speed Internet access. Every credible business has a website, and every government is plagued by concerns about cyber-terrorism and information security. I call this Communication of the Second Kind because it is a historically recent, technically-mediated extension of human communication that rests upon the innate, and far older, layer of communication faculties that are the natural birth right of everyone—Communication of the First Kind.

The content of second-kind communication technologies is symbols and images. It is abstract, quantitative, mostly visual, and linear. The technologies that carry these interactions mostly use only two sensory channels—vision and hearing—and at least as often, they aren't mediating communication between people at all, but rather between people and machines, or even between machines themselves.

Communication of the Second Kind offers some unique advantages as well as displaying some limitations of its own. In thinking of communication as a means of diffusing mindful sufficiency in North American culture, it will be important to keep these in mind since they will inform virtually every decision we make going forward.

Among its advantages, second-kind communication does not require that everyone be physically present in the same place at the same time since messages can be recorded and rebroadcast at different times and across wide geographical areas. Since their content is symbolic rather than real, they are best suited to communicating news about something as a substitute to experiencing the thing itself.

Another strength is the general belief in popular culture that whatever appears on mass media is important—whether or not this is true. For better or worse, media coverage confers status and currency to any event or cause appearing in them. Since access to mass media like television is rather expensive and technically difficult to arrange, the net effect is that messages appearing in them tend to represent the views and values of the mostly corporate and government enterprises who can afford to produce them. While this size and wealth advantage has to a considerable extent been off-set by the Internet and inexpensive video and audio production equipment, this freedom of access has been counterbalanced by audience fragmentation.

Finally, the mass media create celebrities. In North American popular culture (rapidly becoming a global popular culture), causes, products, or events endorsed by celebrities acquire an aura of status, urgency, and importance. This is totally unrelated to the qualifications of the celebrity in question to confer such endorsements or even to know much about the product or cause they are endorsing. The relationship is purely commercial. While this is highly illogical, it is nevertheless a potent psychological truth that can't be ignored.

For all the glamour they confer and for all their pervasiveness, mass media also display many limitations. The fact that most mass media convey essentially the same message to everyone requires that messages be designed to appeal to a lowest common denominator of public interest and aptitude. This is not well-suited to dealing with inherently complex challenges like climate change, energy policy, or conservation of species diversity.

While mass media are necessary to heighten public awareness of a cultural innovation like mindful sufficiency, media awareness campaigns are not, on their own, sufficient to spark its adoption. Research on the effectiveness of advertising suggest that such approaches are both expensive and of limited value in actually changing behavior (McKenzie-Mohr 1999). Yet today, creating a media image, an online brand, and some name recognition for an issue, is seen as tantamount to actually doing something about it.

Third, for all the variety of technical gadgets available, Communication of the Second Kind still represents only a thin slice of the communication bandwidth available to us through

Communication of the First Kind. With the convergence of information technologies, the concentration of information and control of media infrastructure in fewer and fewer corporate hands, and the digitizing of everything, this range is getting narrower by the day. Conversely, however, there are legions of geeks who busy themselves with inventing new generations of technology capable of artificially replicating the full sensorium of experience that such communication systems cut us off from. This seems to me very much like inventing white bread and then reintroducing vitamin and mineral supplements that we could otherwise have ingested simply by eating whole grain bread to begin with.

Fourth, the very nature of technology-mediated comm-unication is elitist, centralized, and increasingly controlled by a razor-thin cadre of technical specialists and corporate interests. Despite the best efforts of media rights activists, mass media continue to serve the interests of undemocratic corporate and government elites. Especially ironic is the association between the use of Internet-mediated communications and a sort of anti-corporate and anti-establishment anarchism that sees Internet freedom as the most modern rallying point for resistance to corporate and government oppression. But these very same advocates of Internet freedom don't seem to hesitate in surrendering the most intimate details of their daily lives to corporations which are of historically unprecedented scale and few in number. Their cell phones allow their every movement to be tracked, their every purchase recorded, their every con-versation monitored. Their Internet use can also be monitored and parsed for every web search, every topic of interest, every social connection. This is scarcely what we would associate with freedom.

Fifth, because Communication of the Second Kind is inherently symbolic, it is always a message about something-at-a-distance, rather than immersion in the thing / event / experience itself. Most of us understand the difference between a television program about the Amazon rain forest and the actual experience of being in the Amazon rainforest, even though some people today probably think that they are doing important work for environmental conservation simply by making and watching television programs about it. While it's obviously better to be aware of rain forest conservation issues than to be unaware, it's a bit delusional to think that by watching a television program about rain forests, we actually know something about them in the same sense as would apply had we actually been there.

Sixth, and paradoxically, despite the remarkable trend toward corporate concentration of second-kind media outlets, at the same time there is a fragmentation of media audiences driven by the development of its own technologies. The number of televisions and radios per household in North America is now at saturation. There are only twenty-four hours a day in which to consume these media. Penetration of household computer technology and Internet use is rapidly reaching saturation as well. The total potential audience for any one program has always been finite but now it's declining. Satellite systems, cable distribution systems, and now, the introduction of digital technology, vastly increases the number of different programs available. Moreover, there has been a great expansion in programming for niche audiences. The ultimate fragmentation of audiences will result from Internet streaming of video and audio programming which in the long run will make possible individual tailoring of program content and delivery times. The result of all of these developments is essentially to eliminate one of the mass media's greatest advantages—the promise of reaching a mass audience.

Audience fragmentation is further intensified by a corr-esponding profusion of communicators. Viewed by some as a resurgent democratization of media, inexpensive video and audio production equipment, cell phones, readily available editing software, and cheap band width have all made it possible for virtually anyone to produce media content and distribute it themselves. But this may be as much a limitation as a liberation. Because of their scale, budgets, and technical capacities, the traditional corporate mass media could claim a certain credibility with the general public. But in the rapidly emerging world of "everyone as audience—everyone as producer," literally anything goes and it's *caveat emptor* in the marketplace of ideas.

The diminishing capacity of mass media to actually reach the mass audiences they used to deliver to must be weighed against the high fixed costs of producing programs for these media. If the same or larger costs are being incurred to reach ever-diminishing audiences, the financial—to say nothing of the strategic—realism of turning to mass media to promote cultural innovation is questionable.

In addition to all these considerations, there is a range of other issues concerning whether Communication of the Second

Kind media contradict the meaning of mindful sufficiency at another level altogether. Some eminent, well-intentioned advocates of simpler, more sustainable living, view mass media, and especially the Internet, as indispensable means of promoting global sustainability. I want to address each of the grounds on which these proposals are made, with deepest respect and affection for the thinkers making them, but from which I must differ because I don't think the proposals make sense. I fear that time and resources which could better be applied elsewhere may be wasted by pursuing these avenues.

First, a perennial concern is raised that television, and now video media, streamed on the Internet, fail to realize their potential because commercial and entertainment content dominate these media. They could and should be used instead to inform and engage the mass of society in solving sustainability problems (Elgin 2009, 130ff). Mass media should be used to educate and inform, not just sell stuff and entertain. Through such broad programs of information and engagement, citizens would be better equipped to think critically about pressing sustainability issues and participate more effectively in democratic decision-making.

As desirable as this sounds, it doesn't fit very well with the effects that television actually has on human brain activity and motivation. The medium of television itself evokes brain potentials associated with daydreaming and unfocused attention (Burke 1996). This happens at a pre-conscious level, before we are even aware that our brain activity is being changed. It tends to induce passivity and suggestibility (Hanson 1996). Television viewing promotes a sedentary lifestyle of community disengagement (Edsall 1995). It is also the breeder reactor for consumer culture itself, exposing viewers to a relentless stream of commercial messages. The medium itself is one that tends to render its viewers passive, uncritical, and compliant (McGrane 1998). Based on the research evidence, it would appear that television, and to a considerable degree the internet as well, is perfectly suited to the tasks it is already performing—serving as a conveyor belt for government and corporate propaganda fed to an increasingly narcotized and uncritical public. It seems an unlikely mechanism for fostering anything like a literate, engaged, and active citizenry.

A second reason offered in favour of using mass media to promote sustainability is the idea that television today provides the images and ideas that comprise our shared frames of reference for viewing the world (Elgin 2009, 156). Having a shared frame of reference is pre-requisite to cooperative, broad-based action. This insight was originally offered by MacLuhan as well in his *global village* concept and later his global theatre, but has been echoed many times since in the work of others (MacLuhan 1962). It's important to note, however, that simply because something is widely shared does not necessarily mean the results will be positive. Mass media can, and are, being used today to spread ignorance, misinformation, and prejudice with equal effectiveness to enlightenment, facts, and goodwill. For example, two separate studies have shown that viewing Fox News coverage of current events such as the Iraq War and the US Public Health Care debate actually leads to increased misinformation and confusion about the issues (World Public Opinion.org 2010; NBC/*Wall Street Journal* 2009). Given the diversity of values already present in society, there seems to be little basis for believing that in the case of the sustainability crisis, we would have any more luck recruiting people to a common point of view than on any other issue.

Next, there is considerable evidence that mass media can be addictive. A CBC documentary aired in 2010, "Are We Digital Dummies?", reported that perhaps as many as 10% of Internet users suffer corrosive effects on social interaction skills and the capacity to function effectively in ordinary reality. Enlightening is a quote from a reviewer of massive multi-player online games (Chatfield 2010) who digressed from his review of the soon to be released "Cataclysm" by Blizzard Games, to wax philosophical about the meaning of online gaming in the lives of gamers themselves: "We play games because their miniature worlds are places where everything makes sense, where effort brings rewards, where neither we nor the place ever grows old." That is to say, gamers seek immersion in a world of unreality. Peter Pan couldn't have said it better.

Immersion in the world of the Internet is so addictive that one young man in California actually had his legs amputated because they became gangrenous when he failed to move away from his computer console. Well-heeled Internet addicts are now being carted off to addiction treatment centres with prog-ramming specific to their needs. It is not clear, therefore, how such a medium could reliably heighten human consciousness, voluntary action, critical thought, improved information, or public involvement in the issues of the day. The very definition of addiction suggests that freedom is compromised; we become less able to make the free, *voluntary* choice for a simpler way of life, which is one of the key values of mindful sufficiency.

A final rationale for engaging mass media to address the sustainability challenge is that a consensus of global values must develop before effective action can be taken on issues of global scope such as climate change or over-appropriation of planetary productive capacity (Elgin 2009, 155). This might be construed as calling for the same sort of centralized media campaign in service of sustainability as it currently serves in the cause of commerce. This may or may not be a welcome development, depending on your point of view. While centralized control might have been possible when mass media consisted only of radio and television, in the age of the Internet this is technically impossible because of how the operational architecture of the Internet is designed. It's probably also socially impossible because of the libertarian / anarchistic views shared by many Internet activists. But the recommendation can also be questioned at the level of appropriateness to what the sustainability crisis may require.

It may be that the reason why so many centralized, big-picture, one-size-fits-all planetary rescue plans have failed to catch on (e.g., the World Conservation Strategy in 1980; Agenda21 in 1992; the Kyoto Protocol of 1997, etc.) is because the sustainability crisis, while global in scope, cannot be solved by a single globalized program of reforms. This is the case because the global problem of sustainability has arisen from a diversity of local contributions of which, in many cases, local people are fully aware. These might be more effectively addressed by bringing mindfulness to their local contexts, awareness of place, memory of local wisdom, capacity to generate local networks of know-ledge, practice and solidarity in meeting the local manifestations of misdirected desire, addictive consumer behavior, and erosion of community.

Given all these considerations concerning both Communication of the First and Second Kinds, what sort of approach might be more consistent with sharing the message of voluntary simplicity more widely?

6. What is Needed Now?

The notion that expensive mass media promotional campaigns might be sufficient means of propagating the values of mindful sufficiency in our culture may be mistaken. Such an approach at best runs the risk of casting the promotion of simple living back into the cultural mold from which we're trying to extricate it. At worst, it threatens to invalidate these efforts entirely by placing them in the company of fantasies, idealizations, and commercial interests devoid of reinforcing messages from Communication of the First Kind. The last thing we really need is more information *about* our problems. What we need instead is *transformation* of our culture, beginning with how we live our own lives. Transformational communication does not happen simply by repeating the same clichés used by our favourite pop culture celebrities. Transformational communication happens between people, really present to each other, using all the "channels" we have.

If we want to advance the practice of mindful sufficiency, we need to find means that are consistent with its central values and vision. This immediately commends forms of communication that are direct, democratic, holistic, deeply entrenched in authentic human experience, decentralized, low-tech, and the use of which we actively deepen mindfulness, communities of interdependence, and meaning. Clues to these forms of communication can be found by exploring how those without access to electronic technology propagate change. We need to understand how new learning diffuses through animal pop-ulations where access to money or technology plays no part at all. In short, we need to share the treasures of mindfulness practice through Communication of the First Kind as well as through Communication of the Second Kind, if we aim to promote transformation as well as awareness.

If we believe that the world is truly a system of relationships, then it is responses-as-messages on which we need to focus, and it is message *relevance* that matters at least as much as the size of audience we're reaching. What is required is insight and involvement, not necessarily large amounts of money. We need sufficient insight into the sustainability dilemma so that the messages we fashion are powerfully compelling for other people. They need to carry within them a communication dynamic, a quality of social contagion that is self-propagating. They need to be viral. I stress here transformational responses to the sustainability challenge, not only messages about it that are popular or widely viewed. We need creativity in how to frame and communicate these responses. And we need involvement sufficient to live these insights with integrity and accept some sacrifices in seeing them replicated. A negative example of this has been the success of radical Islam, which uses minimum technical and financial resources to achieve remarkably impressive effects relying instead on the intensity of the relevance of its message to its adherents and their seemingly limitless commitment to achieving their ends. There is nothing about money, or about centralized high-tech media that assures insight, creativity or commitment. Which brings us to communicating in a first-kind manner.

7. The Message Is What We Do

The fact that human beings are intensely preoccupied with social comparisons assures that any sensible (visible, audible, tactile) efforts we make to adopt the values and practices of mindful sufficiency will become messages sent by example and, unless we live as recluses, they will be immediately detected. Commercial media already exploit the power of social comparison by presenting advertising imagery that attempts to substitute for the face-to-face social comparison activities of daily life. Since the goal of advertising is to deliver us into the marketplace, it is not concerned to mediate forms of experience that deliver us into either community or into mindfulness. Nevertheless, the contrived and vicarious role models offered by mass media are not nearly as compelling as the real life examples of happier people we might meet in person. It is through these personal meetings that we communicate in a first-kind way.

Probably the most compelling way to communicate the value of mindful living is to live it deeply and authentically ourselves and just share our life with others. This doesn't require becoming evangelistic or aggressive. On the contrary, what is more consistent with the spirit of simplicity and mindfulness is a genuine, unpretentious cultivation of its values. It includes a neighbourly readiness to share this as and when appropriate, i.e., to cultivate community rather than privacy. It's more effective to be joyfully present and available to others through the good things we discover in simple living than to evangelize an ideology we hope others will adopt without ourselves having to demonstrate its practicability. In this way, we are not telling others about mindful sufficiency, but rather simply living it in visible ways. The deeper and more authentically we cultivate this way of life, and the more generously we invite others into experiencing its benefits, the more compelling it is as an act of communication and the more dynamic we become as engines of cultural transformation. We cannot convincingly share what we don't authentically live.

8. Immersion Learning

Immersion learning could also provide a means of diffusing mindful sufficiency (Bender 1989). We learn by imitation and direct instruction, of course, but in immersion learning, we enter a whole new environment where everything in our surroundings immerses us in what we aim to learn. Travel to unfamiliar cultures has this effect, as does immersion learning of languages. These are very much first-kind communication experiences and highlight the difference between these communication styles— the difference for example, between learning French from a computer screen as contrasted with living in France for a year. Creating opportunities for curious people to live various expressions of mindful sufficiency over short periods of time would allow them to experience what it is like rather than learn about it as a detached curiosity. It might be possible to create special learning centres for this purpose, at least at the outset. They would later be followed by intentional communities created with mindfulness and sufficiency as key articles of a Community Charter. Simply being in such places and joining in a daily round configured to other values than those of consumerism could provide a powerful first-kind medium for sharing the values and practices of more sustainable living.

A limitation of all immersion learning is transferring its lessons to the outside culture once people return from the demonstration setting and resume their former lives. Eventually, we must see the appearance of whole communities that practice more sustainable living and then the decision will simply be whether or not to join in. Examples of such places already exist in the growing number of eco-villages being established around the world (Global Ecovillage Network). But before then, any immersion learning process must be mindful of participants' needs to re-enter mainstream consumer culture and take steps to help visitors transfer their learning as much as possible back into the old context. This may be very difficult to do, however, as Thomas Kuhn (1962) pointed out: Whenever different paradigms are represented in the same cultural space, they appear to be incommensurable. They speak with different languages to different aspects of our experience. Transiting from one to the other can be very challenging, and maintaining two at once in consciousness is by definition, impossible.

An existing movement within voluntary simplicity to form voluntary simplicity study circles (Andrews 1997) offers some of the characteristics of both social comparison and immersion learning approaches. Study circle participants explore many new ideas and examples of simple living while also participating in a short immersion experience of being in a group attracted to the same values and practices as oneself. Extending and developing the study circle process may be an excellent entrée to important forms of Communication of the First Kind required for making the transition toward a more sustainable culture.

9. Going Artsy

Culture is an all-embracing idea that includes language, cuisine, beliefs, values, institutions, governance, technology, and the arts. The role of the arts in developing a more sustainable culture is, in my view, grossly underrepresented and perhaps even undervalued in most discussions of how we can meet our sustainability challenges. But if we think for even a moment about how we each came to absorb the ideas, images, stories, and feelings that define our way of life, both the fine arts and folk art play major roles. The songs we sing and listen to, the stories we tell ourselves, the selection of subjects that appear in our art, the screenplays and scripts that underpin our movies, television and drama productions, the stories we tell our children, the dances we perform and the occasions we perform them—all these and many others are examples of how the arts communicate culture. The most intimate expressions of these artistic creations are those that are expressed as Communications of the First Kind.

Of course, artists have to eat and fame happens to be part of the allure of art for some people. Therefore, an artist must be a commercial as well as an aesthetic success if she or he is to keep on eating and making art. Second-kind communication media represent the logical channels for exposing one's art to a large audience, becoming better known, and thus making more money. But even among the financially successful in the artistic community, there is continual preoccupation with retrieving intimacy, connection with their audience, authenticity of portrayal, personal scale, depth of insight, and ideally, a level of communication with others which is transformative of both artist and art appreciator. We engage with art when it touches us sufficiently to change our lives, or at least our outlook on our lives.

I think any transition to a more sustainable society and a culture of mindful sufficiency will involve deep engagement of the artistic community. We very much need visions of what a more sustainable society will look like in the future. We need songs that celebrate the revelations of mindfulness and the rewards of discovering our deep relationships of interdependence. We need stories to tell our children (and ourselves) that remind us of the things we so easily forget if we slip out of paying mindful attention to what is real. We need artistic works that once again engage the full human sensorium and don't settle for mere visual or aural bedazzlement. While I have no artistic talent of my own, I can see art all around me and I sense its absolute fundamental significance in transmitting and shaping culture. I have also felt its power to transform me at emotional and intuitive levels that are hard to articulate in words.

A great tragedy in consumer culture is that so many of our artists are either transfixed by the catastrophe unfolding around us, or else they have sold out to the commercialism and narcissism of mainstream culture. Their art expresses only their individual struggles with their various neuroses and fails to reveal anything to the rest of us about the realities of our own lives—something I think is an integral part of the vocation of an artist. What our time in history needs are visionary artists who can see past both themselves and the present darkness that surrounds humanity. This act of visioning is not to promote some ideology like a workers' paradise, nor to offer unattainably idealized images of the future. We need artists who can portray that within us which offers real testimony to our powers of transformation and evolution. We need an art of hope, rooted in mindfulness, but breathing us into a future wherein human life still means something and the human adventure is continuing.

To do this, of course, implies that artists themselves make this journey. We cannot spin convincing yarns about a world yet to be born unless we have ourselves already visited those terrible regions where these transforming energies are at work. I am not at all naive about what this process involves. But this is and always has been the meaning of real art and real artists navigate these waters. Who will come forward then and help us? Who will make this journey and come back with a vision to save the people?

10. Spreading Viruses

The most compelling argument for relying principally on mass media to broadly promote a more sustainable way of life is the notion that there is no other practical way of reaching large numbers of people in time to avert the ecological collapse in store for consumer culture. While it is true that electronic communication systems offer instantaneous broadcast of the sort of communication they can carry, for many reasons already mentioned, this may not be the way of reaching people that best aligns with what mindful sufficiency is about. Worse than not being effective, they threaten to undermine the very values sustainable livelihood requires. Admitting this requires that we come to terms with all our fears of being ineffective, or of not diffusing the sustainability message in time to avert ecological collapse, and to forego the popular delusion that whatever creates a "buzz" must be important and is having a deep effect. Moreover, sustainability advocates are just as vulnerable as anyone to the vanity that one is having a positive effect on things simply by being well known.

To supplement our deeply ingrained propensity to use mass media to promote ideas, I would offer the hopeful principle of *six degrees of separation* linking everyone on earth. This notion proposes that every person on earth is separated from every other by only six steps of contact. If a message is passed from one person to all the people they know and thence onward, the message would only have to be repeated six times to reach everyone on earth—seven billion people. Critical here is the fact that the message must be meaningful enough to be valued as relevant, and contagious (viral) enough in its urgency, attractiveness, or humor, to assure that it will be passed along.

To scale this down a bit, if each person practicing a strong form of voluntary simplicity chose to share this way of life enthusiastically and personally with just ten other people, and these ten felt benefitted enough to share it with ten others in turn, this circle of sharing would only have to pass through nine iterations to directly reach a billion people—the "consumer class" of planet Earth. Since the traditional North American nuclear family itself still consists of about four people, a substantial part of this work can be done in one's own household, and by a tiny extension, to one's immediate neighbours. Most of us could easily engage many more than ten other people.

The nine degrees of separation principle requires no technology at all, no money, and no mass organizing campaigns. It can achieve its purpose entirely by word-of-mouth, face-to-face relationships. It is amenable to infinite variation and spontaneous, creative innovation, unlike the standard canned messages of the mass media. It encourages the dialogue in relationships which even the most advanced forms of interactive media fail entirely to duplicate in subtlety, precision, and flexibility. Most important, since *relationships* mediate the diffusion of this cultural innovation not technology, our introduction to mindful sufficiency can be leisurely, prolonged, deep, and most important of all, personal. It is therefore infinitely adaptable to local circumstances, history, and culture. There is no need to learn a new language to engage machines, no matter how intuitive the interfaces.

Though the diffusion of a sustainable culture by this means would be agonizingly slow at first, like any geometric progression, its expansion at the end of the sequence is explosive and complete. What drops out of the picture is any access to celebrity or claim on expert status for those sharing the lifestyle of mindful sufficiency. Sustainable living would not be purely a "message" or a "program" that some people have that they then use mass media to transmit to others who don't have it—the old consumer model of communication. Rather, the practice of mindful sufficiency would be a communion among people spreading out from a common centre in a shared set of values and practices. Or even better, it might be something originating from a diversity of centres to find expression in a diversity of ways. It would be egalitarian and accessible to everyone. Best of all, it would require no expensive bureaucratic organizations to manage. It would be a self-stoking process unfolding entirely outside and 'round-about the money exchange economy and all of its coercive institutions.

What might be most necessary in sparking this sort of process is strengthening the idea among existing practitioners of mindful sufficiency that its practice is something that the crisis of sustainability calls us to "pay forward" through relationships. While many expressions of simple living are strongly communitarian, others are quite solitary. Yet the times call for generosity and trust. If we can see what we gain from simple living as a summons to pass it on, we will have tossed the pebble in the pond. Moreover, we will be stepping into a more egalitarian, creative, and grounded future than anything currently promised by high technology, globalized markets, and elitist power structures.

A common question that arises in connection with introducing mindful sufficiency into mainstream culture is how many people are already living this way? Or, how many people do we have to convince before this reaches a tipping point to become a cultural reality? Implicit in these questions is the assumption that the more people who adopt an idea or a way of life, the more likely it is to be *true* or *rewarding*. All those people can't be wrong! Well, history shows that "all those people can be wrong" and the mere popularity of an opinion or practice doesn't make it true or valuable on that account. It only makes it popular—something the current Internet generation who believes so naively in the *truth* being whatever opinion is widely shared, has yet to learn.

Some fear that large-scale sustainability problems involving the day-to-day activities of a large number of people require an equally large scale and populous response to resolve them. But those fears may also be groundless. This is the old Titanic metaphor come back to haunt us again. While the problems created by consumer culture are indeed very large scale, and vast numbers of people participate in the culture (probably because they see no choice or have no time or energy to create anything different), only a relatively small number create and direct consumer culture. It may be that the task of cultural transformation, the task of shifting consciousness, does not require a mass conversion to mindfulness and sufficiency. Rather it might involve merely engaging those who create and direct consumer culture, or those who will someday be culture creators themselves. In this connection, it is the opinion leaders and artists and educators and daycare workers—particularly daycare workers—who are the key role models or idols who might be most instrumental in diffusing a new consciousness in society. We have no difficulty these days appreciating the power of *asymmetric warfare* where lightly armed but determined fighters have repeatedly stopped the massive armies of super powers. Why should we doubt the potential efficacy of a nonviolent asymmetric social change process.

It is important to keep in mind that those who currently style themselves as society's leaders, people with formal power in government and business, are the custodians of the old paradigm. It is their worldview that is dying because it has failed so totally to bring human activities into harmony with the planet, and human beings into harmony with each other. It already is this traditional group of leaders who cannot decipher the lyrics of the new songs wafting on the breezes from the future, because we speak different languages grounded in different worldviews. Whoever will shape the future culture of sustainability may not be many in number. But whoever they are, they are, or soon will be, standing at those critical balance points where the tiniest push at the right time may birth a new world. We have only to hope that their mindfulness is deep when the time comes. As Thich Nhat Hahn is said to have remarked: "We need more buddhas. . . more buddhas!"

11. The Way Ahead

In considering a research/action agenda for mindful sufficiency, it is not my intention to set up a polarity between media-driven and personal approaches to promoting sustainable livelihood. What I do suggest, however, is that neither can be substituted for the other and we need both. People must become aware of more sustainable ways of living as options that are being lived and practiced by people like themselves, not just eccentrics, atavistic back-to-the-landers, or celebrities. For this purpose, Communication of the Second Kind is both useful and appropriate.

Complementing this awareness-building, however, we should consider activities that aim more precisely at understanding how to share and support others in the practices of sustainable living. Study circles may already offer an excellent test bed for this sort of activity and we might well apply ourselves to the task of understanding how to nurture "super study circles" that carry people through conversation into solidarity, innovation, and action/non-action (Burch 2009). To do this, it will be useful to deepen our understanding of how a good joke makes the rounds, what has made twelve-step groups so ubiquitous and successful, and how animals transmit knowledge from one generation to the next. When we better understand these sorts of happenings, we may at last have grown beyond our technology to a wider understanding of our humanity.

MARK A. BURCH

4

EDUCATING FOR SIMPLE LIVING

1. Introduction

In the following pages I aim to explore education within a culture of simple living and some methods that might serve the new educational project implied by such a culture. The historical and survival challenges we currently face as a species also requires that I approach this discussion from two distinct but intertwined perspectives:

First is the trans-historical role that education plays in our perennial efforts, both as individuals and as societies, to fashion a good life. The desire for a good life arises spontaneously within us as a fact of our inner experience. It is basic to our species. It draws us continually to transcend our historical situation through self-transformation and cultural evolution. This is education for a better life.

Second, is the specific role education can play in helping us front the survival challenges posed by the imminent demise of consumer culture. We face the historical confluence of challenges such as the Hubbert[16] peaks for many critical resources including oil, climate change, the end of economic growth, and grid-locked institutions of governance, to name only a few. This more or less

---

[16] The "Hubbert Peak" refers to a theory developed by American geophysicist M. King Hubbert in 1956 to the effect that the consumption of a limited non-renewable resource will generally follow a bell-shaped curve as the resource is consumed. Applied most directly to petroleum reserves, the theory predicts that when 50% of the resource is exhausted, steadily diminishing production on the downslope side of the bell curve will drive commodity prices upwards with significant economic impacts. The concept of the Hubbert peak has lately been generalized to other non-renewable resources which can be expected to show the same supply/cost relationship as they are depleted. https://en.wikipedia.org/wiki/Hubbert_peak_theory

assures the end of material affluence as either a desirable or attainable goal for personal and social development. Our historical situation is driving a "transition" toward some new culture and worldview we cannot yet fully articulate (Hopkins, 2008). The only certainties are that the consumer culture of the past cannot be maintained for long and that it arises from a delusional worldview. Education has a key role to play in helping us evolve our worldview, and hence our culture, in directions that are more consistent with human well-being and ecological sustainability. This is education for human survival.

Finally, I take an essentially psychological perspective of our search for well-being and how we meet our survival challenges. Peak oil is a problem today because human beings are over-consuming oil in pursuit of inordinate desires for power, comfort, and wealth. Climate change is threatening every ecosystem on Earth because human beings are releasing excessive green house gases in pursuit of limitless affluence. While peak oil and climate change certainly threaten our survival, they are not something Earth is doing to *us*. They are instead the outer-world consequences of how we think (how we orient consciousness) and what we desire. While improved technology, better policies, and more humane social relations are undoubtedly necessary conditions for a better life, they are not sufficient. Such practices fail to address the essential motivational, attitudinal, and cognitive causes of the challenges we face. Since, as individuals, we are all prone to falling into unwholesome psychological states, it only seems sensible to engage every available cultural mechanism we have to compensate for this tendency. Education can make a major contribution to this end.

2. Educating for a Better Life

Education for simple living is based on a different perspective of human nature and what makes for well-being than the perspective promoted by consumer culture. It begins with telling ourselves a different story about what sort of creatures we are, why we are here, and how we can flourish into the deep future. This story partly determines what we believe is possible for us.

A starting point on the question of what education for simple living might imply can be found in something written by Thomas Moore (1994, 59) in one of his lesser known books, *Meditations*:

> We [now] study to get diplomas and degrees and certifications, but imagine a life devoted to study for no other purpose than to be educated. Being educated is not the same as being informed or trained. Education is an 'education,' a drawing out of one's own genius, nature, and heart. The manifestation of one's essence, the unfolding of one's capacities, the revelation of one's heretofore hidden possibilities—these are the goals of study from the point of view of the person. From another side, study amplifies the speech and song of the world so that it's more palpably present.
>
> Education in soul leads to the enchantment of the world and the attunement of self.

Education draws forth the human capacities we associate with *soul*, but also does this so that ". . . the speech and song of the world is more palpably present." Put differently, education develops within us the capacity to be attuned to enchantment. This is accomplished in a process which is both personal and relational, both subjective and objective. We do this not in order to achieve something else like a high income or celebrity, but because attunement to the speech and song of the world contributes intrinsically to our well-being. Education aims to shape and in-form how we are in the world. This is different from learning merely how to add to what we have. In Moore's words, the goal is to be educated—to have that which is potential within us drawn forth so that it can appear in the world and become a fact of human history.

Education of this sort begins within person-to-person relationships. This may seem obvious, but in consumer culture it is by no means obvious. Today both learners and educators spend more and more time interacting with machines in order to transfer information than they spend with each other drawing forth soul and experiencing enchantment. A recent rather extreme example of this approach to education is the MOOC—Massive Open Online Course, an education delivery system which is entirely computer mediated. One of its strengths is that the same course can be delivered to thousands of students at the same (Communication of the Second Kind), but it discards almost entirely the experience of education as a meeting of souls such that both are touched and transformed (Communication of the First Kind).

I remember spending considerable time as a child doing dishes with my mother. Working side by side was a time when we could talk about our days, how we were feeling, what we dreamed for the future. There was no formal instruction going on during these conversations but there was considerable soul sharing which helped me discover what my own soul was about. But this apprentice-style learning, the learning we absorb by working with others older and more experienced than we are, is something that has largely disappeared from modern life. It requires a different perspective of work than is common in consumer culture which sees youth not as a preparation for adulthood but as a protected, prolonged recess from any connection with the real world. This is an educational challenge as well as a social one. It represents an attitude toward education that would have no place in a culture of simple living which aims to strengthen and intensify our immersion in real world experience.

Our perennial search for a better life is a vibrant developmental dynamism intrinsic to our species. This energy is always present and active, but it can sometimes be directed in ways that are unskillful and unwholesome. A culture that encourages manifesting this energy exclusively as competitive material acquisitiveness is both a historical aberration and an ethical error. Maybe competitive acquisitiveness is imprinted right in our DNA as consumer culture claims. But perhaps it is a learned attitude that we absorb from an education system designed to serve consumerism and its familiars, capitalism and state fascism. The answer is often determined by what we emphasize.

I propose that our developmental energies can find more appropriate (ecologically and socially benign) expression if we think of education as the process of progressively drawing forth and realising the human potentials that contribute to well-being. At the same time, we aim to do this while incurring an ever-decreasing impact on the ecosphere. Moreover, education provides the tools and relationships that help us harmoniously integrate the qualitative development of our personal well-being in synergy with the requirements of the ecosphere and of just and equitable human relationships.

One aim here is to liberate education from the chokehold of consumer culture and economics. Even momentary reflection on personal experience demonstrates that increasing our income secures an increase in well-being, but only up to a point. There is no simple or direct relationship between affluence and quality of life, or development of *soul* for that matter. Not all values are economic values. Indeed, economic values are decidedly limited in their power to determine well-being and personal development (See: Alexander, Samuel 2012, for an extensive review of research).

Achieving the goal of drawing forth (educing) the intrinsic human capacity for joy, growth, and well-being in synergy with the ecosphere and with other people also calls for a re-orientation of technical and economic development.

A society that educated for lives of voluntary simplicity hopefully would not orient technical development to create products and services simply because this was potentially profitable. Instead, economic and technical innovation would be directed to developing soul in symbiosis with the ecosphere. This would certainly imply doing more with less, but not in order simply to maximize profit. We would strive to do more with less so that the development of human potential could be a more equitably distributed opportunity for human beings. We would employ technology so that the life processes of the ecosphere could be protected and enhanced. Our aim would be to achieve the maximum increment in the development of human potential at an ever-diminishing real cost to society and the ecosphere. The measure of our success would be a planet growing wilder and wilder inhabited by a race of healthy, happy, peaceable, and soulful human beings. This is a fundamentally different vision for technical development than that it should simply be the hired brains of economic avarice.

Given this general perspective of education, what might be some more specific aspects of education for simple living and a better life?

3. Educating for Mindfulness

Simple living has been perennially identified with conscious living, with deliberate acts of mindfulness, and with deep rootedness in our human capacities and limitations. The mindfulness we seek to cultivate through simplicity of living is rooted in the powers of consciousness and the immediate experience of life-in-this-body. What Stephanie Mills (2002) has called "Epicurean simplicity" is deeply situated in our primordial physical powers to encounter life as warm animals, creatures capable of ease and pleasure, and through the capacities of our bodies, to become architects of friendships, communities, and intimacy. It also implies a heightened appreciation for the full range of our human experiences, without undue judgment or censorship.

In the first essay above, I discuss at some length the meaning and cultivation of mindfulness as well as the changes its regular practice brings to conscious awareness. Recent research has shown that the consistent practice of something like mindfulness meditation (Vipassana) is often accompanied by a growing preference for simple living (Elgin 2010; Kasser & Brown 2009). Mindfulness practice gradually produces a number of motivational, perceptual, and cognitive changes that help practitioners experience greater richness in everyday living, perceive greater connectedness between themselves and other beings with whom they share the Earth, and an increasing preference for compassionate and nonviolent ways of interacting with others. I believe these changes are necessary conditions for assuring human well-being over the long term and are absolutely essential prerequisites to a lasting and fulfilling practice of simple living.

Mindfulness rarely develops spontaneously. It generally requires instruction and practice. It's also helpful if practice is supported and reinforced with the same insistent intensity that today we see devoted to promoting competition, entrepreneurism, greed, and individualism. It takes daily, conscious effort to awaken, and more effort and social support to stay awake. Despite the fact that some Eastern cultures have been exploring mindful states of awareness for perhaps as long as five millennia, there is no reason to assume that everything there is to know about consciousness has already been discovered. This implies both an educational and a research project in as much as mindful states of awareness may well have life-giving applications of many different kinds (e.g., Kabat-Zinn 1994).

If the cultivation of consciousness becomes a central cultural project for a sustainable way of life, then we might imagine educating for mindfulness evolving along at least two continua. The first of these would be *inward* and *downward*, that is, in terms of consciousness seeking to extend itself along its *depth dimension* toward its own subjective interiority. This is the world of what Carl Jung termed the personal and collective unconscious (Fuller 1994, 74), and what Ira Progoff (1969, 153), a later figure in the field of depth psychology, called the *organic psyche*. It is that inner domain of experience where we notice *psyche* (what we think of as mental phenomena) emerging from the domain of bodily processes (or what we think of as physical, or somatic awareness). This is the world of interior imagery, of dreams, of intuition and deep inspiration, of the immanent sacred, and of the ancient personal continuities between ourselves and our psychological emergence, both as individuals, and as a species.

The other dimension along which mindfulness might develop is represented by an outer-directed, expansive movement. It includes all our efforts and activities aimed at expanding the perimeter of awareness through learning, exploration, communication, discovery, technical augmentation of our senses, and coming to know the *Other*. Of course that Other may be another person, nature, the cosmos, or the transcendent aspect of the sacred. To this realm belongs science and communication, but not primarily as a means of manipulating and controlling the *Other-as-Object* (nature, other people), but rather as means of coming to know, appreciate, and relate to the *Other-as-Being*. The purpose of this sort of learning is to expand the perimeter of what we recognize as *inter-being*. Inter-being is the web of relationships that provides the enabling context that sustains our personal subjectivity—in descending scale, the cosmos, the ecosphere, and society (interpersonal relationships) (McMurtry 2002; Macy 1983, 24ff). It is through cultivating these two varieties of mindfulness that we find the balance that is a central value in simple living. Consciousness is the organ we use to gracefully balance and integrate the realities of our *inner* and *outer* experiences, the realities of our subjectivity as individuals who also flourish within a web of defining and indispensable relationships. The growth of consciousness is thus synonymous with the development of mature appreciation for these various realities and what they bring to our lives. It is also prerequisite to making responsible choices.

Education for voluntary simplicity in some sense must imply recovering a sense of self as positioned within our powers of consciousness, and not as is the case in consumer culture, of a self-increasingly alienated or projected into the material artifacts we use consciousness to create. Humanity's greatest achievement is not our technology, not economic affluence, not luxury comfort, but rather the fact that we are self-aware. The chilling modern preoccupation with developing silicon-based intelligence that will supersede and surpass the organic intelligence that spawned it is a particularly alienated example of our powers of self-awareness held in projection on our artifacts.

For many who practice voluntary simplicity, the physical side of life is not something from which to escape through fantasies of constructing alienated mechanical replicas of ourselves. Rather, it's an aspect of existence with which we hope to cultivate a deeper and more vibrant appreciation. It's precisely our ability to become conscious of these inherent potentials that brings us a sense of richness in living. These abilities pre-exist anything we might make or own. They are not enhanced by material affluence which may paradoxically numb us to the richness of life itself. We discover that it is through focusing consciousness mindfully that consciousness itself can grow, and a world of experiential richness opens up that is the inherent birthright of every human being, regardless of how much or how little we own. Learning mindfulness doesn't require owning anything tangible. Rather, it involves learning to attend closely to our sensory and emotional experiences, our immediate consciousness of self and other, and activities that foster in us a *beginner's mind*—freshly awake, non-judgmentally aware, compassionately open to the moment. In this way we discover for ourselves what is essential to our well-being and how easily that can be provisioned.

So education for mindful simplicity includes all those activities that help people reconnect with, develop and appreciate their inherent physical, psychological, and interpersonal capacities. It is rooted in sensory and perceptual learning, cultivating appreciation, but also extends inward into dream work, intuitive awareness, and also outward to discovery learning of nature both human and infra-human, and the full range of knowledge and abilities needed to deepen our dialogue with the immanent and transcendent sacred.

4. Educating for Collective Remembering

A perennial role for education is transmitting the deposit of human culture and knowledge from one generation to the next. This includes acquiring the skills and knowledge necessary to a fruitful and cooperative co-existence with other people and with nature. This sort of education is a chance for future generations to learn from the mistakes and build on the achievements of their ancestors. Education in a culture of simple living would also perforce imply remembering our mistakes, celebrating our achievements, and outfitting ourselves to participate fully and constructively in the human adventure.

Making progress toward achieving this value will require considerable recovery and reconstruction activity in its own right. The industrial and commercial mentality that so pervades consumer culture has not failed to diffuse into education as well. Many education administrators and school trustees firmly believe that education is a business and that educational institutions should be run like businesses. This has produced a strong bias in favour of programs and curricula that are oriented toward the goals and activities of business in particular and consumer culture in general. It is common today to think of education as merely a training process for future employment or an investment that we expect to pay handsome financial dividends.

While education must certainly prepare everyone for productive roles in the economy, it cannot be only that or we lose a great deal that is very precious. To neglect history, music, the arts, physical education, pure science, the study of other societies, times, and cultures, is to condemn learners of all ages to a generalized amnesia that narrows life, drains it of many rich sources of pleasure, handicaps people in their capacity to enjoy a rewarding leisure, and most pernicious, renders a population vulnerable to tyranny by propagating ignorance and apathy.

If the simple life is the examined life, richly lived, then its indispensable foundation is education that is both broad and deep, especially in values other than those of the market. If life is about more than getting and having, then learners need to discover what riches lay beyond the frenzy of getting and having. Equally important is the need to weld strong connections with both our history and our visions for the future. Without being slaves to irrational traditions or inherited hatreds, we still need a sense of rootedness in history as well as a sense of responsibility toward future generations. Lacking this, we are limited to the narrow cell of our own personal concerns. We have little sense of where we come from, where we might belong, or where we might be going. Lacking historical and cultural perspective, we fall prey to lacking all perspective, unable to place events in context, or to value and protect what is worth valuing and protecting (See Alexander, Bruce K. 2000).

Thus, education for simple living implies education in cultural memory. Personally, I think it would be extremely valuable if we heard less about war heroes, captains of commerce, and megalomaniacal empire builders, and more about those happy souls who discovered how to fashion lives of fruitful simplicity. In consumer culture, we don't hesitate to give detailed attention to the lives of tyrants, torturers, and frauds. Why not also study the lives of people who are happy?

5. Educating for a Life Economy

Any economy serving a culture of mindful sufficiency and voluntary simplicity would be an economy that aims to promote life, and more life, and not an economy that chronically conflates life with growth and profit as consumer culture does. What may be profitable is not always life-giving. When important costs of production are being externalized in myriad ways, an economy can be death-dealing instead. The very concept of sustainability calls for a life-serving economy. Such an economy regenerates resources, conserves genetic and species diversity, preserves habitat, actively removes toxins from the environment, recycles its materials, and aims continually to improve the quality of life for people independent of the quantity of their material property. Education in such a society would prepare people to participate in a life economy.

One vision of such an economy is offered by Maria Mies and Veronika Bennholdt-Thomsen (1999) in their book, *The Subsistence Perspective*. The key feature that distinguishes sustainable societies from consumer societies, according to these authors, is that the former represent life-economies whereas the later exemplify death-economies. In life economies, productive activities aim to enhance and sustain the conditions necessary for life, and more life. It is the social consensus about protecting the conditions that provide for a diversity and fecundity of life that guides how human beings will relate to each other and how they will use nature.

From this perspective, organic permaculture and cooperative enterprises constitute life-sustaining technologies since the focus of organic food production regimes is the creation and maintenance of healthy, diverse, food-producing ecosystems, not just high agro-industry profits. Similarly, co-operatively organized enterprises constitute life-serving ways of collectively organizing production since the benefits of economic activity are equitably shared. Such arrangements promote and sustain more life, rather than being organized toward profit accumulation in the hands of a few.

By contrast, consumer societies require death-economies—economies that extract resources beyond sustainable levels, employ toxic materials, systematically inflate their benefits by externalizing their costs and impacts, and that can exist only by parasitizing earlier, more foundational subsistence production activities. John McMurtry (2002) has argued that the globalization of consumer culture is occurring—just as was the case with the original enclosures that occurred in sixteenth-century Europe—at the expense of the civil commons, i.e., all the non-profit productive and social assets we have collectively fashioned to sustain our communities, families, and bioregions—public libraries, concert halls, public schools, pension plans, health benefit plans, daycare facilities, voluntary organizations, etc. Consumer culture can survive only by enclosing and exploiting the civil commons just as it does the ecological commons. Moreover, according to recent research published by Mathis Wackernagel (et al.) (2002), the aggregate effect of this death economy has been to expand the ecological footprint of humanity to 1.20 times the sustainable global carrying capacity for our species. This value does not represent what would be required if everyone on Earth lived like North Americans. It represents the current condition of ecological overshoot caused by the global consumer class (about 20% of the population) consuming and wasting well beyond what the planet can provide over the long term. As more and more people aspire to consumer culture lifestyles, this condition of overshoot can only worsen.

By contrast, education for voluntary simplicity implies developing an understanding of our place within Earth's life system, and providing us with the knowledge and skills to live a life of qualitative abundance within the quantitative limits offered by that system. It implies the cultivation of a discriminating intelligence that can distinguish what activities serve life, and what activities propagate death, even if the later gains for us a measure of temporary prosperity or comfort. This sort of education also entails developing the capacity to take delight in the diversity and vibrancy of life and to discover pleasure there. It calls for integrating the feminine principle in a more dialectical relationship with the masculine. Education for life can never tolerate the subordination of women or the reproductive economy to the extractive economy that feeds consumer culture.

Equally important, the transition to simple living implies dethroning the myths that have proliferated around money, the assumed power of money to confer security, and the man-ipulation of money as a means of livelihood rather than simply a medium of exchange and measure of comparative value. Education for sustainable living must re-establish respect for all activities that contribute directly to the production and sustenance of livelihoods especially when these activities occur outside the market system. It calls for renewed respect for the people who perform such work—foresters, fishers, farm workers, homemakers, artisans and trades people, artists, and creative thinkers. Educators need to help learners to discriminate activities that are truly productive and restorative from activities that are essentially derivative and parasitic. This learning needs to occur in an experiential way so that we internalize its lessons as personal experience, and not simply as a factoid on a test on the way to a real job that earns money.

Education for mindful sufficiency would then imply drawing forth and developing all those skills and attitudes that equip us to participate cooperatively in life-producing and life-sustaining activities. It also implies transmitting from one generation to the next the full inventory of practical knowledge about how to live wisely and sustainably in relation to each other, to this particular place on the Earth, and to all that is larger-than-personal (Hopkins 2011, 152ff). Recognition of this fact is partly represented within the Transition Culture movement with its emphasis on re-skilling, i.e., education activities that help us recover our traditional knowledge (pre-fossil fuel age) of how to sustain life over the long term in our specific place on Earth. It presupposes gender equality and a knowledgeable respect for the work of reproducing life. It places the generative powers of the living world at centre stage, and all those conditions that sustain and support the generative powers of life.

In addition to all this, education for a sustainable livelihood requires cultivating the sort of awareness and active involvement necessary to a defense of the civil and ecological commons. It is easy today to assign responsibility for the despoliation of the commons to a misguided and rapacious class of capitalist entrepreneurs (the "1%") or to benighted consumption addicts. Of course, it is essential that we come to recognize the vital importance of the defense of the commons to the sustenance of life and human civilization. We also need to actively take up that defense when the appearance of particular individuals, policies, or enterprises threatens it. But at a deeper level, we can focus attention within ourselves on every movement of greed, fear, exaggerated self-interest, or alienated individualism since these provide fuel for the aggressive pursuit of gain through the exploitation of the common good. Such impulses are the common heritage of humanity not only the failings of particular individuals. Our best defense against them is mindfulness of their presence and influence, insight into their dynamics, and a collective resolve not to let them undermine the general human welfare.

Finally, education in a culture of simple living includes mindfulness of scale. This is clearly implied in the very meaning of sufficiency, which is a fundamental value of voluntary simplicity. As Herman Daly (1995, 180-194) has so cogently argued, any sustainable economy must establish limits on its overall scale such that the total scale of the economy can be carried within the ecosphere. Economics provides no means of establishing these limits because the discipline of economics suffers from severe theoretical and practical shortcomings that render it blind to energy and material flows in the ecosphere. Hence, the limits on the scale of the overall economy can only be set based on collective commitments to values and moral principles such as those we have been discussing. An economy can be efficient and still be ecologically unsustainable and socially unjust. Therefore, economics must be situated within a context of scientifically determined biophysical limits on resource and energy flows, and ethically determined limits on how much social and material inequality we will tolerate in society. This implies an ethic of mindfulness, sufficiency, and social equity as the bedrock of any sustainable society.

6. Educating for Self-reliance

Some of the most colorful figures in the simple living literature advocate and practice strong forms of self-reliance. Sometimes these practices border on aspirations to self-sufficiency, *living off grid*, going *back to the land*, or even pursuing ways of life that lean toward ascetical extremes (Segal 1999, 180-200).

More common, however, has been the recognition that cultivating self-reliance in the ordinary affairs of daily life, meeting at least some needs directly through our own productive activity, contributes considerably to well-being. Self-reliance is the alternative to dependency. Self-reliance is often the guarantor of a measure of personal freedom and latitude to make one's own choices in life. Moreover, the practices that contribute to self-reliance also help build self-esteem since we come to know ourselves and develop our capabilities as constructive, productive, and capable individuals skilled in what is required to provide for ourselves and our families. These lessons are a powerful antidote to the toxic dependency psychology of consumer culture—a psychology that directly or indirectly emphasizes our helplessness, incompetence, and radical dependence on the market to provide for our needs. Today, this dependency takes its most familiar form in staggering personal debt loads and relative ignorance concerning how to perform basic life sustaining tasks such as growing food, making clothes, maintaining shelter, etc.

So I suggest that education for simple living also includes training for self-reliance, and this in very practical terms. Those who lose touch with the realities of growing and preparing food, building shelter, making clothing, creating entertainment, making art, etc., are also losing touch with some of their essential human creative powers. We can also lose the sense of direct personal immersion in the biophysical world that sustains us on a daily basis. Lacking such contact, we cease to know where we really live. We cannot love what we do not know. What we do not love, we often fail to appreciate and protect. Thus education for simplicity and self-reliance is also a form of education for the defense and conservation of the civic and ecological commons. As Wendell Berry has noted, it is awareness of ourselves as participating members of a community of life that is in a specific place—i.e., really here, really now, and with these neighbours whom we personally know—that we have any sense of continuity with our past, any appreciation of the values of our present life, or any hope of protecting these values from the corrosive effects of a globalized market system that can only see them as "profit centres" (Berry 1987).

Self-reliance can also be interpreted in a larger-than-personal sense. It may be even more important in the long run that we re-diversify our local economies through building stronger systems of regional self-reliance. Free market globalizers aim to de-skill the entire world into a mere aggregation of global regions specialized on the basis of their comparative advantages. This tends to destroy the traditional diversity of skills found in local communities. While such a strategy may be economically efficient as long as global trade can feed on cheap fossil fuels, this program cannot be sustained for more than another decade or so (see Rubin 2009). In the process, the world's societies are seeing their indigenous diversity of labour specializations atrophying or disappearing entirely as their leaders chase after the doubtful promises of the global marketplace.

A humane future requires re-constructing dense networks of local and regional self-reliance through production from local resources using local labour to meet local needs. Only local people are knowledgeable enough in the ways of regional ecosystems to understand how to use them sustainably. And only when production for local use is carried on locally, do we have a clear view of all the externalities of this productive activity and its effects on people and the environment. When we clearly know that our future well-being depends on caring for what is at hand, we are far less likely to fall prey to the psychological disconnection, disinformation, and apathy that plagues global consumer culture. Most know nothing about how the products and services they use affect ecosystems and societies that are safely out of sight (see Esteva & Prakash 1996, 277-289).

Thus education for simplicity and self-reliance has a collective aspect as well as a personal one. It implies learning, practicing, and sharing all those skills and values, attitudes and cooperative abilities needed for a truly regional, organic, and sustainable way of life. Naturally, the values of mindfulness and sufficiency will provide the guiding vision for this project, but it must go beyond simply looking out for one's own self-interest. Also essential is re-constructing the bonds of social and economic cooperation, a sense of mutual responsibility, and a sense of shared fate. In a world as inherently interconnected as ours, consumer culture's adulation of radical individualism is both deluded and suicidal. We flourish together or we perish together, and not abstractly, but in concrete relation to this place, with these people who are our neighbours. So, while each of us blossoms by learning to take care of ourselves, we surpass ourselves when we learn to take care of each other. When we pass this threshold, we move into the world of collective self-reliance, itself a proper focus of education for simple living.

7. Educating for Transition

In discussing education for a culture of simple living, there are some relevant situational factors to consider. First of all, living simply by choice as a pathway to the good life has always been a more or less marginal undertaking. The historical record suggests that most people, most of the time have wanted, and continue to want, just a little more, and often a lot more. We are prone to believe that more is better until invited to a more penetrating awareness of the sources and consequences of this belief, or until for other reasons we are impelled to search for alternatives. Because those who have discovered alternative approaches to the good life are a minority, this necessarily positions education for simple living from the outset in a transformative context vis-à-vis the majority of the population.

Equally important is the fact that in many societies around the world, the penetration of consumerist values is deep and pervasive. It has been at least two generations since very many people in North America or Europe have had any direct personal experience of the values represented by the more self-reliant, community-centered, and non-monetized ways of life characteristic of rural and farm communities of the first few decades of the twentieth century. Thus for North Americans who dwell in urban centres, perhaps 85% of us, living simply elicits no personal memories from which to reconstitute its values and practices, except for occasional brief holiday excursions on camping trips or the like. In these circumstances, then, to propose a life of voluntary simplicity woven up from threads of material moderation, cultivation of enhanced consciousness, personal and collective self-reliance, and deep cultural remembering—all of this represents new territory—a task of exploration and transformation rather than recollection and re-affirmation.

Another pressing fact of our current situation is the urgency of humanity's sustainability predicament. Learning to live in greater harmony with the ecosphere and more peaceably with each other is no longer an undertaking we can comfortably assign to future generations we hope will be more enlightened and willing to change than ourselves. Everywhere, the wild facts of life are revealing this attitude for what it is—denial and delusion. The fossil fuels that have allowed us arrogantly to believe that the sky is the limit are themselves limited, and within a decade or two will be astronomically expensive (Campbell & Laherrere 1998). Under the pressure of consumer culture's relentless hunger for material resources and energy, every major ecosystem on Earth is in decline, being harvested at or beyond their sustainable yields (World Resources Institute 2001). As we have already noted, the aggregate effect of this process has been to expand the ecological footprint of the human economy well beyond the carrying capacity of the planet (Wackernagel 2002, 9266). To these observations we could add growing population, increasing inequality of incomes, growing risk of pandemic diseases, pervasive cynicism regarding institutions of governance, and many other factors. At the end of the day we can recognize the urgency of a transformative agenda for education, not merely an informative program that takes a hands-off position with regard to issues of value and destiny. We simply don't have another generation in which to learn how to live sustainably. I can scarcely imagine that such assertions could be received by current educational leaders without controversy or resistance. Yet it remains perhaps the greatest challenge of educating for mindful sufficiency to "...become a means of preserving the world against death" (Eastabrooks 2002, 10).

To this end, while education of the young remains a priority as always, education for simple living must also focus on the current generation of adults and young adults—precisely those of us whose consciousness is most thoroughly colonized by consumer culture. In these circumstances, an approach to education that merely seeks to conform us more closely to our existing predicament is catastrophically misguided. Education for the current generation of adults must have a transformative focus to undo the trauma and psychological colonization propagated by consumer culture. Later, we may hope, education can become truly evocative and developmental—aimed not at transformation of consciousness to avert catastrophe, but to deepen, extend, and develop consciousness so that it then becomes the instrument for realizing all that we are capable of being. Presently, however, any educational program that serves life must at least partly devote itself to helping people make the transition from our self-destructive way of life to creating something more viable over the long term. This leads us directly to the second role of education—education to meet our survival challenges.

8. Educating for Survival

8.1 *In delusion is destruction: Correcting unskillful beliefs about the nature of things*

I have already mentioned that humanity currently faces a confluence of challenges which threaten our future. The now broadly international Transition Towns movement identifies peak oil, climate change, economic contraction (driven jointly by resource depletion and the contradictions of a debt-based monetary system) and grid-locked institutions of governance as four particularly pressing issues of global scale. (Hopkins 2011, 28-39). If we don't meet these challenges with resourcefulness and creativity they have the potential of ending civilized human societies as we know them. But to these challenges we could also add a lengthy list of others such as depletion of top soils, water shortages, extinction of species, pervasive toxic chemical pollution, carrying capacity over-shoot, ocean acidification, shortages of strategic materials, and many more which, even if peak oil and climate change didn't exist, would still have the potential to end consumer culture and perhaps the human species as well. These realities have led Senior Fellow of the Post-Carbon Institute Richard Heinberg to characterize the world of the near future as gripped by "peak everything" (Heinberg 2011).

Education has a role to play both in helping us fashion a good life and also in meeting our pressing survival challenges. But I don't think these are separate endeavours. In what follows, I want to bring the perspective of education proposed above to bear on a complex of delusions that I think pervade consumer culture. In the process, I hope we can glimpse an educational agenda (a detailed curriculum is beyond the scope of this writing, but a start in this direction has already been made; see Burch 2012) which compensates the delusional thinking that is driving the demise of consumer culture—and not to sustain consumer culture—but to replace it.

If I have a false idea about some detail of reality, we call it a "mistake." When a false idea plays a central role in my worldview or identity, however, such ideas are called delusions. If I believe that invisible back-rays originating from the constellation Pleiades cause me to be unlucky in love, my friends might gently suggest that I see a psychiatrist. But if I believe that an invisible hand guides the economy ensuring efficiency and general well-being far surpassing any individual's ability to comprehend or control—I could be an economist. I might become a prime minister or privy counsel to presidents. When such ideas are shared by large numbers of people, they are collective delusions. They become non-negotiable dogmas of popular culture in proportion to the number of people who share them. People who create these ideas become famous and get Nobel Prizes—such as the celebrated gentlemen who brought us derivative trading regimes and credit default swaps. The prizes are especially generous if what they are telling us is something we want to hear anyway. We like it when experts tell us we really know what is going on in the world and that we can control events. We can know with particular certainty that we are dealing with a delusional belief when loyalty to the belief is utterly unaffected by its repeated failure to predict the future correctly or to adapt us successfully to life in the real world of ecological and social relationships. (A recent Canadian Broadcasting Corporation documentary directed by Josh Freed (2011) compared the accuracy of assessments made by "experts" in judging the authenticity of art, wine, political trends, and most tellingly, economic performance, and found that their judgments are no better than chance, or the predictions that might be made by lay people. Nevertheless, the cult of expertise brings us considerable consolation.)

Oddly, we think that harboring delusional beliefs is a good thing. Why else would we comfort each other in moments of disillusionment? Why else do we think that deluded children are cute, and chastise anyone who might undermine their beliefs in Santa Claus, the Easter Bunny, and the Tooth Fairy for spoiling their childhoods? Why do we spend so much time and energy helping each other reconstruct delusional thinking in the face of experiences that test or destroy these false notions such as divorce which shatters the delusion of everlasting love, and death which challenges the delusion of personal immortality? We do so because we fear being overwhelmed by anxiety. So, it seems we prefer being emotionally comfortable to being sane. This preference has many consequences.

I think that at the heart of consumer culture is a pervasive set of delusions which are so basic to how we see the world, life, and everything, that we accept them as cultural givens. This complex of delusions is the psychological source of many of the outer-world developments which now threaten the future of humanity and which necessitate a major cultural transition. One role of education in service of survival is to help us become conscious of these delusions and replace them with more adaptive beliefs. By "more adaptive" I mean beliefs which better fit human activities within ecological systems and limits. More adaptive beliefs also help human beings live more peaceably with each other so that conflicts between people do not themselves cause further ecological harm.

In the following section, I describe what I think are eight widely accepted but false ideas underpinning consumer culture. I also describe eight corresponding *psychological transitions* and the educational project they imply that I think could compensate each delusion.

8.2 *From growth to life*

The customary apology for economic over-development is that an economy must grow or die. The ideology of growth utterly pervades both consumer culture and political discourse as the highest goal of all human activity. Because the global economy rests entirely on a debt-based monetary system, growth is a fundamental economic requirement or the system will collapse. But the halo that surrounds the idea of growth is applied in a host of other cultural narratives as well. In short, in consumer culture, we must be growing in every way, every day, or else we are dying. In this way, the dogma of the desirability of growth comes to be augmented psychologically by the fear of death.

But the opposition of growth to death is a false one. To recognize growth as one characteristic of life is altogether different from thinking that the absence of growth is death. Living things indeed grow, but they also come to maintain themselves in dynamic equilibriums—what in biology is called *homeostasis*. To live is to grow, surely, but unlimited growth is pathological. Thus sustaining life over the long term involves at least as much knowledge of how to stop as how to go. While localized dis-equilibriums and chaos can certainly be found in living systems, these conditions are usually transients on the way to some new steady-state. Life displays both moments of growth, change, and chaos as well as periods of stability, order, and homeostasis. Also relevant are the intentions behind our actions: Obsession with growth is driven by self-centered greed, whereas concern for life is motivated by Other-centered love. What is delusional about consumer culture's ideology of growth is ignoring this more holistic perspective of life founded on love. To think that the purpose of the economy and our institutions of governance is to promote growth rather than to serve life is deeply delusional thinking that leads to catastrophic results.

Correcting this delusion might begin by recognizing that life is a more comprehensive category than growth. Growth and life are not synonyms. Life includes and transcends both growth and death. Maturity, equilibrium, and death are as integral to the life system as are birth, youth, and growth. Any culture that doesn't recognize these facts and equip its people to live them with grace, inner peace, and conscious awareness is deluding itself and multiplies suffering.

The critical psycho-spiritual mistake of consumer culture is that it fails to confront the emotional reality of death honestly and skillfully. We wish death was not a reality. So we try to escape it partly through focusing attention on growth. By extension, perhaps, we aim to grow our incomes, our possessions, our reputations, our "marks" in the world, as a way of transcending or escaping death. But because the means (pursuing growth at all costs) is not appropriate to the goal (resolving our anxiety about death) we remain fearful and insecure—a perfect potential market for whatever gadget or bauble is next in the queue promising false transcendence through consumption.

Consumer culture worships youth in denial of aging. It worships growth in denial of limits. It worships change in denial of homeostasis. All of these forms of denial underpin the delusions that youth can be made perpetual and aging is a curse, that people and economies must grow continually or else they are dying, and that everything must be changing continually or we are not making progress. To better fit our lives within the larger and more comprehensive ecosystem that supports all life, we need a more comprehensive and inclusive vision of life itself, and especially of a good life. If a good life is merely having more and more things that help reinforce and maintain denial of aging, mortality, and death, then it can lead nowhere except to its own contradiction. Cancer is growth contradicting itself. Mummification and the Peter Pan Syndrome are youth contradicting itself. Psycho-social dislocation, addictions, social chaos, and anomie are change contradicting itself (Alexander, Bruce K. 2001).

Thus, in moving toward a more life-affirming culture, we need stories, music, drama, art, and activities and rituals that ground our culture in a narrative about life and not just growth. In this task, the cultivation of mindfulness, deep cultural remembering, framing human life within the larger life economy of the planet, and a recovery of community are highly skillful means to help us honestly face our ego-centered fear of loss, separation, change, and death. It is the ego's fearful clinging to what it thinks will make for its own immortality that distracts us from the span of life which it is rightfully ours to experience and enjoy. Only by counteracting this fear by being reliably present to each other can we lessen the suffering it brings. No technology can do this for us. It is a form of human companionship which our culture can either well or poorly prepare us to offer each other.

8.3. *From technical "progress" to development of consciousness*

In his book entitled *Graceful Simplicity*, Jerome Segal (1999, 119-158) traces a debate that occurred among the eighteenth-century intelligentsia about the nature of progress. Some parties to this debate argued that on the historical evidence, there was no basis to think that human character was any more virtuous in modern times than in the ancient civilizations of Greece, Rome, or Egypt. The most notable domain in which cumulative progress could be discerned, they observed, was in science and technology. At the time this discussion was going on, European inventors and entrepreneurs were soaring on the hubris of Newtonian mechanics and enjoying the first real fruits of scientific knowledge applied to enriching and comforting human beings. The sky seemed to be the only limit and we would eventually surpass that as well.

Since then, we generally equate *progress* with technical innovation rather than development of human well-being. Societies with more advanced technology are perceived as more advanced in every way—morally, intellectually, aesthetically, and perhaps even spiritually. The teachers of character improvement and spiritual development have seldom had anything as flashy to show as the wonders summoned by the magicians of technology. Despite the daily proof of what can happen when improved technology falls into the hands of people of unimproved character, popular culture is deeply pervaded by the delusion that technical advancement is the same as general cultural advancement. So enmeshed are we in this delusion that today we even look to technical gadgets as solutions for essentially non-technical problems. I've already mentioned green consumerism (based on the development of more environmentally friendly materials and technologies) as a pseudo-solution for the impact that the insatiable human desire for luxury can have on the ecosphere.

Because technology is a blunt instrument which includes no intrinsic basis for moral judgment or answering questions of value, it is, taken by itself, a bad metric for progress. I propose instead that if we are to mark progress—that is, qualitative improvement in the human condition—the appropriate frame of reference is inner, not outer, and with reference to consciousness itself, not the artifacts it produces. I make this suggestion because our state of consciousness literally is our experience of well-being. It is the values that structure consciousness, the habits that guide it, the aperture of inclusiveness or exclusiveness that focuses it, and it is the capacity of consciousness to register truth as we discover it in the universe and in subjective experience that are most determinative of human well-being. It is for this reason that people living at very different levels of technical development can experience comparable levels of well-being. Therefore, I propose that consciousness itself—its development, deepening, extension, and right orientation—should become the principal focus of concern and the primary measure of human progress. The technology needed to support the development of human consciousness, and through this work, the qualitative improvement of character and increase in well-being, is very different from that needed to produce more material goods and dominate one's neighbours militarily. It seems intuitively obvious that there is little point in becoming richer or more powerful people unless we also become better people. In this task, educating for mindfulness as well as deep remembering of the past are extremely skillful means. Continuously improving technology without also continuously improving human character merely guarantees improved tools for multiplying suffering. This is *prima facie* absurd. Asserting the priority of developing consciousness as the guiding principle for all development decisions might help assure that we pursue the right goals, even though progress is slow, rather than pursuing the wrong goals with increasing speed and efficiency.

8.4 *From affluence to sufficiency*

Also central to consumer culture's worldview, and related to the delusions of both the growth imperative and mere technical innovation as progress, is the pursuit of limitless affluence. Note that the dictionary definition of *affluence* is "profusion, abundance of worldly possessions, wealth" (Shorter Oxford

English Dictionary 2007). Implied in the idea of affluence is provision in excess of need, superfluity, and therefore waste. In its farther reaches, this is the realm of the *Cornucopians*—the group that adheres to the bizarre doctrine that Earth has a limitless capacity to produce the limitless number of things people can be taught to want. But since affluence means "more than enough," what is more than enough can have no limit nor can it be anything other than waste (consumption without utility). A culture that defines the good life as ever increasing affluence delivered through endless growth and technical development is therefore orienting its entire economy and innovative capacity to the production of waste. While people clearly use material consumption for other reasons than meeting only essential physical needs, constructing a whole way of life around the production of waste is clearly delusional. This has happened because consumer culture includes no analysis of what material consumption is for, what contribution material consumption makes to well-being, how over-consumption can diminish well-being, and therefore has no concept of sufficiency.

Compensating the delusion that material affluence is the preferred pathway to overall well-being requires an educational process that engages mindfulness practice, deep cultural memory, and knowledge of what makes for a life-oriented economy. Within mindfulness practice in particular, we need to learn just how, and to what limit, material things are needed and which needs they are appropriate to fulfill. Consumer culture tries to conflate material consumption with meeting nearly every human need, material or non-material. Mindfulness practice, on the other hand, is a skillful means of awakening to our actual material needs and the appropriate material means of fulfilling them. It also enables us to distinguish non-material needs and discern non-material ways of meeting them. Most important for the future of the Earth and of humanity, however, is the fact that mindfulness practice makes it possible to interrogate desire itself, to what degree pursuing desires, in fact, makes for well-being, and if not, what is a more skillful path to attaining well-being.

On this basis, we can imagine a much more life-affirming worldview with cultural practices to match. It would include a clear awareness of *sufficient provision* as the guiding principle for a sustainable livelihood rather than maximization of waste in pursuit of profit. Since we all harbour innate tendencies to always desire more of everything (Miller 1995), both a cultural ethos of sufficiency and daily mindfulness practice supported by encouraging communities are essential to compensate the delusional desire for affluence.

Lacking mindfulness, any suggestion that living more simply can lead to a qualitatively richer life just sounds incredible. From within the consumer culture delusion system, simplicity appears to be the opposite of richness, complexity, abundance, and choice—all values we prize for a variety of legitimate reasons. But once we take time to develop mindfulness of consumer culture itself, we become conscious of how consumerism is actually impoverishing people and the planet; how spurious complexity is now outrunning both our capacity to comprehend our situation and manage it effectively; how any prospect of future abundance is actually undermined by excessive current consumption; and how consumerism is actually reducing choice by destroying the social and ecological structures that make choice possible. Mindfulness reveals that consumerism is in fact leading us into a future of poverty, hideously complex problems, material scarcity because of resource depletion, and a future of *involuntary* simplicity in which all prospect of choice is only a distant memory.

8.5. *From markets to ecosystems*

The current hegemony of economic thinking, both in popular culture and in public policy, subordinates ecosystems to markets. Life serves profit. This inversion is carried to such an extreme that some think economic models can be used to manage ecosystems like businesses. This represents another instance of delusional thinking because it assumes that the laws of thermodynamics and of energy and material flows within ecosystems can somehow be reversed at the whim of human beings. It also places the proper object of management, i.e., our own behaviour, in projection on nature, i.e., that it's ecosystems that need management when for eons they have managed themselves quite well, thank you. Economic thinking needs to be subordinated to, and nested within, eco-systemic thinking because that is the way nature works. The human economy subsists within the ecosphere or it doesn't subsist at all. Economic activities must conform to natural systems and processes.

There is fairly universal agreement these days that markets allocate labour, capital, and resources more efficiently than do centrally managed economies. But to recognize that markets allocate resources efficiently doesn't address the question of whether such allocations are just, or whether they are environmentally or socially benign. Instead, consumer culture uses markets to build an unsustainable and inequitable society, hurtling toward collapse with optimum efficiency.

Remember that "free" market capitalism emerged triumphant from the Cold War due more to its opponents' failings than to its own virtues. There are few today who will openly question capitalist market economies perhaps because capitalism, democracy, freedom, human rights, and technical progress are fused in a single overarching narrative of modernity. In fact, they are merely historically contemporaneous, and only in some places. They do not necessarily require each other at all. We can find examples of socialist democracies (Sweden), capitalist regimes that violate human rights (Chile), totalitarian regimes with free markets (China), states where citizens enjoy considerable freedom and respect for their rights but which are technologically undeveloped (Bhutan, Kerala, etc.), and technologically and economically developed countries which routinely violate human and democratic rights in pursuit of their own interests (the United States). Today, it is not hard to understand the popularity of market capitalism operating in a liberal secular democracy when the only alternative on offer seems to be neo-Medieval Islamic fundamentalism.

Because consumer culture strongly enforces a taboo against questioning "free" markets, any discussion of alternatives sounds like advocating one or another form of oppression—not a popular position to advocate. But we need to disentangle the demonstrated efficiency of markets from consideration of other values which are not necessarily efficient, but which still matter to us, such as economic equity, local self-reliance, and ecosystem integrity.

Alternatives to the hegemony of economic thinking can be found on a number of fronts. Bennholdt-Thomsen and Mies (1999) propose that it should be the Earth's capacity to provide conditions congenial to life, which is the real economic bottom line, and that any culture that encourages its people to expend life in exchange for monetary profit is deeply deluded and violent. A subsistence oriented economy existed in the past and could exist again in the future—changed in form and using improved technology, to be sure—but an economy which is more concerned with the health and productivity of ecosystems and more inclined to power itself on current sunlight than any imaginable consumer culture.

The Permaculture Movement is another example—an ecological design discipline that aims to create designed ecosystems based on an intimate knowledge of, and respect for, the possibilities of a specific place and culture (Mollison 1991). Permaculture substitutes the short-term pursuit of profit from agricultural production of monocultures with the long-term process of developing intact, viable, and productive ecosystems capable of feeding human beings as a side benefit. By seeking to optimize the system for ecological resilience, permaculture mimics nature more faithfully than extractive approaches to food production aimed at maximizing profits.

Yet another cultural innovation, albeit leaning toward the technological side of the conversation, is restorative architecture (Riu 2012). Key here is viewing the buildings required for a good life not as gadgets that stand between people and the environment, or against the environment in the interests of people, but rather working with the environment to meet human needs. Restorative architecture aims to design buildings that generate their own energy, produce and recycle their own water, process their own waste, perhaps even grow and repair themselves rather as a body heals itself following injury. Such buildings would rely heavily on local materials, current sunlight, and the dynamics of local climate and terrain to subtly transform these elements into spaces congenial to human activities. They resemble organisms more than human artifacts, yet they provide for legitimate human needs.

The work of transition required here is breaking the hegemony of economic thinking on the worldviews and decision-making practices now current. This is not to say that con-siderations of cost and benefit be thrown to the wind, but rather that conscious efforts be made to re-think economics from the bottom up as is being done by the advocates of "steady-state" economics, appropriate development, and others (Daly 1995; Schumacher 1973). Any economic theory that takes the market as its point of departure effectively establishes a bias that promotes economic exchange ahead of every other consideration. Economic exchange needs to be situated within ecological and social relationships, not superordinate to them, before human societies can fit well within the ecosystems upon which they depend.

8.6. *From individualism to community*

Apparently as part of its natural evolution, the human psyche developed what Sigmund Freud called an ego to provide a focal centre for consciousness and help mediate interactions with the environment of objects and other people. The very nature of the ego is that it is bounded. It perceives and feels itself as set apart from its environment. This "distance" is a useful fiction for getting certain needs met and laying the foundation for later psychological development. Even today, many psychologists consider *ego strength* to be a sign of a healthy personality rather than what it is, a delusion.

The Renaissance Period in Western culture celebrated the ego through its cult of individualism which in turn has been monstrously amplified by consumer culture. Strong, indeed impregnable, belief in one's individuality, one's individual rights, and the supremacy of one's individual desires and needs is immensely useful to consumer culture. It motivates individual efforts to earn income as well as maximizes consumption in the disposal of that income. A society of radical individualists anxious to advertise their uniqueness and aggrandize their egos is vastly more profitable for business than would be a society of humbler people more intent on living simply, finding common ground, and sharing their material possessions.

As mentioned before, *ego consciousness* has its uses in helping us adapt to our surroundings and interact with each other. When much social interaction is focused on strengthening this "useful fiction," however, we become delusional because we overlook a more essential fact of life—our connectedness to everything and everyone—and in fact, the radical dependency of the ego on these relationships for its very existence.

It is through a relationship that each of us is conceived. It is through a succession of molecular and cellular relationships that we grow and develop physically. It is through a multitude of social, informational, emotional, and intellectual transactions that we develop as persons. It is interdependence and cooperation that sustain us in existence at every moment. "No [person] is an island..," John Donne once observed. This observation is more than a mere poetic metaphor.

When advertising presents us with amplified and distorted images of the sovereign ego while obscuring, minimizing, or derogating our relationships with others, it can have disastrous consequences for sustainability. It promotes strong tendencies to aggressive self-assertion and narcissism which in turn encourages choices that can be destructively individualistic. We lose the ability to perceive or care when our individual choices and behaviors are having adverse effects on others. Such behaviour blinds us to our interdependence with human and non-human others. Ecosystems are all about relationships, and not so much about individuals. Losing sight of the reciprocal relation between individuality and collective connection is suicidal.

The taboo in consumer culture against portraying individuals as constituted by their relationships is propagated mainly in two ways. The collective or larger-than-personal perspective of our existence is defamed by labeling it "communist" and therefore linking it with past statist abuses of human rights. Alternatively it is considered "mystical" or "idealistic" and therefore beyond the compass of the "hard-headed" realism we so admire in the "self-made man." This willful unwillingness to recognize our connectedness, whether by rendering it scary by branding it "communist" or otherworldly by calling it "utopian"—in either case condemns us to a form of delusion, which is having grave consequences for our own and future generations.

Just as the forces which, in the past, suppressed and violated the dignity of individual rights have been shown to be contrary to human well-being, so too it can be shown that pathological narcissism joined at the hip to self-indulgent consumerism can be equally corrosive of well-being. Every person is, to borrow a metaphor from Arthur Koestler (1967), Janus-faced—after the Greek god Janus who was depicted as having two faces. There is an aspect (face) of our existence that is individualistic and that is served fairly well by notions of a separate ego and individual rights. But the very same being can also be represented in terms of connections, relationships, and interdependencies, which are just as compelling and determinative of well-being as are references to individuality. The fallacy underpinning many conflicts of the twentieth century was the idea that these two aspects of our humanity are necessarily at odds with each other in the public sphere.

If we are to escape the cul-de-sac of environmental catastrophe on the one hand, and perpetual interpersonal and inter-social conflict on the other, we must construct an understanding of ourselves and others that conceives of our individuality in terms of our relationships, and which also nuances our social obligations with respect for our individuality. Unless both these perspectives are present in how we think of ourselves, the result is violence of one sort or another. Either society oppresses the individual, or individuals become so self-absorbed that their inner lives are pervaded by isolation, depression, and paranoia. Then our collective life suffers for lack of individual energy and engagement.

Surprisingly, perhaps, some useful metaphors for this relationship have been made available to us from quantum physics and its concept of *entanglement* (Arntz & Chase 2004). The concept of entanglement applies strictly only at the quantum (subatomic) level of matter and energy relationships. It denotes an observed tendency of the physical state of one subatomic particle (or wave) to be directly affected by the state of another particle or wave, even though these two phenomena are widely separated in space. Thus two particles are conceived as entangled or connected in a sense, when the physical state of one is determinative of the other, even though they are not in observable physical proximity. Since according to the Big Bang theory of cosmic evolution, at the moment of the Big Bang, all matter was co-terminus and co-existed before space-time unfolded, all matter is entangled with all other matter. The conclusion implied by this theory is that at the quantum level at least, everything really is connected to everything else.

Extending what is a quantum physical theory as a metaphor to discussion of other issues can be hazardous. But this has not stopped many speculative thinkers from doing so. Mindful of how such transfers can lead to more confusion than clarity, the notion of entanglement is however, still quite descriptive, as a metaphor, of other species of relationship relevant to our discussion.

For example, there is abundant evidence of what might be called ecological entanglement observable in how meteorological, hydrological, and nutrient cycles, energy exchanges, genetic diffusion and food webs link physically distant organisms and populations in relationships of mutual interdependence. Not only are nutrients and energy cycled through these relationships, but also pollution, toxins, and mutations. Everything each of us does from breathing, eating, excreting and reproducing has consequences for other species and physical and biological systems elsewhere on Earth. These effects are often proportional to the physical quantities of matter and energy appropriated by human beings, as well as their toxicity. A consumer culture that maximizes consumption of matter and energy in the deluded belief that this will also maximize well-being, is a culture that creates maximum impacts on the ecosphere through these relationships of interdependence.

We can also identify examples of psycho-social entanglement. From the very beginning, we are fundamentally social beings. We are conceived in relationships. We are socialized and educated through interactions with other people and life forms. Power is essentially relational and exercised through social connections. The whole construction of the ego and our cognitive universe of learned knowledge and skills is built up and maintained through interactions with others. This reality of connection also makes us vulnerable as individuals to cultural determination of our values, attitudes, and behavior, and vulnerable to mass social hysterias, delusions, and mob thinking. Some thinkers have even proposed that the human species as a whole is psychologically entangled at the archetypal level—the level of inherited psychic structures that define characteristically human ways of behaving (Jung 1981; Progoff 1969).

Finally, many spiritual traditions assert that we are spiritually entangled. This claim arises from the intuition that we live in a moral universe with larger than personal connections and responsibilities. It's expressed in such metaphors as everyone being "children" of the same God (Judeo-Christian), or of a people who receives its identity from a common source or heritage (Judaic, Islamic), or of diverse peoples who nevertheless comprise a single ontological whole by virtue of their connection within the sacred dimension of the universe (Medicine Wheel). Evidence of spiritual entanglement is difficult to verify publicly but it is often authoritative for individuals who experience it subjectively. For many spiritual teachers, the essence of spiritual experience is liberation from the sense of a separate self (ego consciousness) and experiencing oneself instead as at home or belonging to the cosmos, i.e., connected to the universe rather than a stranger in it (James 1958; Progoff 1973; Walters 2001). Thus our deepest spiritual experiences may not be theistic at all, but simply awakening to, or perhaps remembering, our fundamental identity with everything.

An appreciation for our own fallibility is a corollary of the various scales at which entanglement can be discerned and the very complex linkages and interactions which are possible in a connected universe. The meaning of individuality is therefore relative. Since it is the ego and its rational functions that constitute individuality, the compass of what the ego can grasp is limited compared to the vastness of a connected universe. We are only apparently individuals and our egos exist, relatively speaking, for only a very short time. Because our individuality is both limited and transient, we can never, as individuals, grasp the whole. Therefore our perceptions, thoughts, decisions and actions relative to the whole will always be more or less fallible. Therefore, the way to happiness and harmony if that's what we want is: (a) compensating the ego delusion by cultivating consciousness and remembrance of our connectedness to everything else; (b) cultivation of humility in recognition of our limitations and fallibility and, (c) living simply so that the negative consequences to others of our relative ignorance and fallibility are minimized. This, too, is an inherently educational and transformational project that exceeds the abilities of most individuals acting alone. We need support from each other in community, assistance from the lessons of the past, and specific training that helps us escape the delusion of ego-centered existence, and live instead as who we truly are.

8.7 From mine to ours: The transition to a commonwealth of goods

Today many people believe that possessing wealth automatically confers entitlement to use it any way they like, short of breaking the law. This claim on the freedom to dispose of our material property as we please is another attitude deeply rooted in individualism and powerfully amplified by consumerism. Much advertising today is not about products or services at all. It's about freedom. It aims to intensify the individual sense of entitlement to break all constraints, defy all boundaries, ignore all limits, because we can afford to do so. Hence, the financially successful person can drive an SUV that appropriates three times the fuel and produces three times the pollution of a more modest car, proportionally depriving future generations of these resources and exposing everyone to increased air pollution here and now. Very few people would question the SUV owner's entitlement to do so, if he or she can afford it. He might even be envied. This very same logic applies to anyone who drives any sort of car at all when compared to people who so far have not been able to afford one.

Only a few centuries ago, some people thought that the possession of wealth conferred obligations in addition to entitlements. The doctrine was noblesse oblige. Wealth was a divine trust or at least partly the result of unmerited good fortune. People then recognized that success or position can be as much a matter of good luck as of hard work. A case in point is the accidental matter of the family, society, racial group, or historical period into which one is born. Possession of wealth entailed responsibilities to the community and to God, the creator of all wealth. The wealthy person was a steward on behalf of God and the less privileged members of society. How wealth was deployed was a weighty decision surrounded by clear moral imperatives. It was not merely a matter of deciding which of one's own competing appetites should be indulged at the moment. Compare this to the prevalent attitude today that if I am born into a wealthy family and experience good fortune in my business, it is not a gift of Providence, but proof that I must deserve it.

Whether or not one believes that wealth entails spiritual and moral obligations, there is no doubt that wealth in our society is a claim on material consumption. Matter and energy are degraded or transformed whenever money is spent. These facts of life have consequences for current and future generations. Conscious beings survive who recognize their connectedness with others and respect the obligations those connections imply. Those who don't, perish. It's nothing personal. It's just the way the universe works. The entitlement we think accompanies the mere possession of wealth needs rethinking in our society. We are not free to do what we like with what is "ours" without regard for others because such an attitude is arbitrary, groundless, false and ultimately self-destructive.

The idea of "private property" strongly reinforces that of individual identity and underpins claims of entitlement to exclusive use of resources and space. We can even find analogues of these ideas in the behavior of infra-human species to establish "territories" from which they try to exclude others. But is it appropriate to take as the moral compass for human choices the behaviors of infra-human species? Or is nature just nature, doing what nature does, and can human beings aspire to something more? Or might human beings even be nature aspiring to something more? While we trace our origins to natural evolution, is evolution, in the human case, repeating itself, or is it surpassing itself?

Regardless of how we answer these questions, it seems promoting the "privacy" of private property can lead to as many abuses as contrary efforts to disentitle people from the property they can rightfully claim to provide for themselves.

I would suggest that a more holistic and truer understanding of property must include many qualifiers: That the mere physical possession of something does not automatically confer an entitlement to it against the claims of all comers. Many things we possess come to us by luck or happenstance and might likewise have come to others just as well. Therefore, the ferocity of our defense of our claims to what we have might be softened by imagining how we ourselves would hope to be treated by more fortunate others should our circumstances be reversed. We ourselves, as well as the things we think we own, in fact belonged, still belong, and will in the end continue to belong to the Earth. They are more truly on loan to us for the duration of our stay, but not eternally. The idea of private property should never be extended to the point where it deprives others of resources essential to their lives, whether or not we personally enjoy an abundance of the resource in question. What we might well do in service of sustainability and social harmony is nuance the hegemony of private property, personal ownership, and individual advantage in favour of a commonwealth of goods rooted in a multi-generational and multi-species perspective of "rights."

In terms of simple living, these reflections imply that we hold our possessions lightly and that we order our lives so that there are fewer of them. From the perspective of sustainability, overcoming the delusion of private property opens up the possibility of owning in common and sharing with others things that before we thought we must own individually and protect from others. Fostering such a reorientation of attitudes is inherently an educational and a long-term project.

8.8 *From competitive balance to cooperative synergy*

By far the dominant conception of how to sustain consumer culture, or more generally, civilized human existence, is to seek balance. It is finding a balance among economic, environmental and social values—often represented as three intersecting circles with their common intercept being the holy grail of sustainability—that provides to nearly everyone the common sense paradigm for sustainable development. Talk about balance always sounds so respectful, inclusive and open to compromise. There are very few advocates for imbalance who don't also run the risk of being taken as threats to civil order. The concept of balance also appeals to our desire for equality because achieving balance between competing interests implies a sort of teeter-totter arrangement where both sides can get at least part of what they want. Finally, balance resonates with our pre-existing delusion of ego isolation, i.e., I stand here opposed to you over there. This implies tension, separation, and opposition that can only be resolved through balance. So people who seek balance between opposing interests are considered realistic, and those who consistently help us find balance—however temporary—we think are wise.

The problem is that the universe doesn't work this way. Nature is not organized as a flat aggregation of equally legitimate interests that are in tension, or that can be traded off in negotiations moving toward balanced compromises. Neither is nature organized simplistically in opposing pairs which would make balances between such opposites easy to achieve. Instead, nature is organized as complex, nested systems of holarchies (Koestler 1967). Some elements of these systems are subordinate to others and some are super-ordinate. Relations between elements in the system are not democratic. Subordinate elements are foundational to the existence of their super-ordinate counterparts. They cannot be traded away in the spirit of compromise. More concretely for this discussion, the economy, human social life and ecosystems are not spheres of interest that occupy the same level of practical significance the claims of which can be balanced or traded off against each other.

Instead, the ecosphere and its well-being are foundational to the imbedded complex systems—human societies and economies—which are built up within it. The claims that the ecosphere might make—if it had a voice—the claim to maintain its own physical and reproductive integrity, to carry out its life functions free of toxic agents introduced by humans, to evolve along the vectors of its inherent dynamics without artificial manipulation of its store of genetic memory, etc.—these claims are absolutely fundamental to sustaining the living system upon which all human activities depend. There can be no question of balance here if what is meant by this is some calculus of value that trades a bit of death to the ecosphere in exchange for a bit more human prosperity. Until people recognize the holarchical structure of nature, comprehend and limit the danger inherent in ego-assertiveness that expresses itself as a will to dominate nature, we will never be able to find a sustainable way of life, much less the serenity we long for in pursuing balance. Whatever economic benefit we want to achieve must be secured within what is required for a healthy ecosphere and an equitable society. Social conflict will always undo economic progress. Ecological collapse will undo both. The direction of these relationships is non-negotiable.

Any future culture of simple living must evolve beyond the delusion of "balance" as the main goal of real politik. As discussed above, the search for balance presupposes separate interests that are in competition for the same scarce resource. What I'm proposing instead is the principle that every conflict originates in perception which is too superficial or individualistic. When a society encourages development that inflames individualism, enshrines the "privateness" of private property, and intensifies every competitive instinct of individuals, it multiplies and intensifies conflict because it is multiplying and intensifying delusion. When a society en- courages mindfulness of interdependence, relationship, shared fate, and collective self-interest, it multiplies and intensifies the potential for cooperation and synergy. Moving beyond seeking balance among interests competing for power and scarce resources might help us move toward cooperative collaborations seeking symbiotic relationships of mutual benefit.

Cultivating mindfulness of these relationships needs to become a matter of daily psychic hygiene. We need to slow down our pace of life. We need to teach these practices to our children with as much dedication and self-sacrifice as we give today to hockey practice, soccer, or extreme fighting. Then we will begin to tip the balance toward a different sort of future. When we notice any sort of conflict arising, and when this becomes a universally recognized signal that we are mis-perceiving our situation—that we are overlooking some aspect of our interdependence—we will rediscover the ancient basis for cooperation and social harmony.

8.9 *Reproduction is a right*

In its fevered efforts to appear environmentally enlightened, CBC television recently aired a story about a single mother in Toronto who was diligently teaching her seven children to replace incandescent light bulbs with compact fluorescents. Upon a moment's reflection, however, it's clear that the sustainability challenge in this particular household is not the light bulbs. To say as much is politically incorrect. It brings into view decisions, or the lack of them, concerning one of the most intimate and personal of human acts—reproduction. Yet our future is threatened at least as much by sheer human numbers as it is by our consumption habits. Earth might be able to support a billion or so humans living simply. It almost certainly cannot support nine billion of us in hot pursuit of affluence. Some sort of conversation is required about whether reproduction can remain an entirely private, individual, and inviolate human right when the consequences of over-population are not borne solely by the individuals making the decision to procreate. Just as there is a fundamental point of natural justice which turns upon entitlements to property, there is an equally compelling point which turns upon the act of reproduction. At the moment, this right is effectively quarantined in the realm of individual rights.

Thinking of reproduction as an entirely private matter is delusional because procreation has both social and ecological consequences, depending on the consumption expectations accompanying each addition to the family. Past efforts by states to limit procreation as in the case of China, are odious to us because they seem to be an excessive exercise of state authority. A more palatable alternative to such draconian measures might be an educational program that places the act of procreation in a broader perspective by including alongside its individual and private aspects consideration of its social and ecological consequences. Should this be part of the broader educational program presented above, individuals would probably find grounds enough upon which to base their personal decisions.

9. Education as Therapy

To summarize so far, I've proposed that education for simple living, just like education for life in a consumer culture, calls for a particular program of learning and enculturation. I've proposed educating for:

- mindfulness
- collective remembering
- participation in a life economy
- personal and community self-reliance
- preparation for psycho-social transition

While certainly not exhaustive, I see these as central guiding principles for any curriculum for simple living. I hope it goes without saying that a curriculum for simple living would also include all the nitty-gritty practical skills proper to each of these principles, not simply an intellectual assent to their importance.

I've also suggested that the perspective that informs these principles can also be brought to bear on the critical survival challenges facing humanity at this time in our history. The causes of our survival challenges originate from a cluster of widely shared and mutually supportive delusions that pervade consumer culture's narrative of the good life. A critical task of education is to support psycho-social transitions from delusional ways of thinking and acting to a alternate worldview that better aligns our thinking and behavior with what is required for ecological fit and social well-being—education as therapy, if you will. These include transitions:

- from growth obsession to concern for the well-being of life
- from developing superfluous technology to developing consciousness
- from policies that serve markets to those modeled on ecosystems
- from valuing affluence to prizing sufficiency
- from pathological individualism to persons-in-community
- from private property to a commonwealth of goods
- from seeking a balance among competing interests to seeking cooperative synergies within nested holarchies of social and ecological relationships
- from viewing reproduction as an individual right to a social and ecological act

Keeping these considerations in mind, I would now like to take up a brief discussion of education methods that might fit well with the perspective of education just outlined.

10. *Transformational Learning*

Traditional education can be described as informational learning. Much modern pedagogy assumes that it is transfer of content (information) from one person who has it to someone else who doesn't have it that forms the core of educational activities. Despite calls over many generations to broaden the meaning of education, mainstream practice still consists mainly of thoughts transferred from one brain to another. Emotional, physical, intuitive, aesthetic, or spiritual learning occurs mostly by happenstance or in special niche programmes, if at all.

Transformational learning subordinates acquiring facts (although it certainly includes that) to changing the orientation of consciousness. By "orientation of consciousness" I mean new thoughts about the world and our place in it, but also a new felt sense of this relationship; access to, and a deeper appreciation for, a wider range of our personal experience including emotion and intuition; awakening to our physical and psychological interdependence with other people and species; recognizing that consciousness is socially constructed, not a property of individual brains, and that consciousness develops and changes through interactions in relationships (community). The tools appropriate to this sort of learning involve a greater role for activities like storytelling and visioning in education for simple living than mere transmission of facts.

My understanding of transformational learning has grown from a synthesis of ideas and approaches developed by several other scholars and educators as well as my personal experience as a practicing educator.

For me, transformational learning in service of simple living starts from the assumption that people are curious about voluntary simplicity because at some level they desire a change in how they live. So educating about voluntary simplicity is not in the first instance a matter of transferring information from one person to another, but rather drawing forth (educing) what is already present in learners. It's about making conscious our already existing predisposition to change. We aim to provide a safe setting and relationships within which we can explore the origins, meaning, and implications of our desire to change. We hope to offer support and validation for personal change. And hopefully we seed the development of a community where change can continue to flourish. When I meet people for the first time who are interested in voluntary simplicity, I believe they are looking for a different sort of life than the one they have or else they wouldn't be showing up. I don't assume that everyone is looking for the same thing because it sometimes turns out that we are not. While no activity can be all things to all people who participate in it, I've found it helpful, nevertheless, to hold this work as lightly as possible so that it can be whatever it needs to be for the people who show up for it.

A second principle that informs my understanding of transformational learning is a particular perspective on how people change. Today, the dominance of information technology in consumer culture begs the argument that information is what sparks change in our lives. This is a bias shared by many educators as well. Give people enough information, or the "right" information, and they will automatically arrive at the "right" conclusions and will be motivated by sweet reason to act in "appropriate" ways. Especially in a consumer culture which preaches that "more is better in every way," more and more information delivered faster and faster is supposed to somehow substitute for both the knowledge of how to structure the information in useful ways and the wisdom necessary to discern which information matters and which doesn't. I don't ascribe to the view that personal change arises from acquiring more information. For many sorts of change, information is essential in the later stages of the process when a decision to change has already been made, but it is not necessarily sufficient to spark change on its own.

In many cases, it is transrational factors like dreams, visions, fantasies, and sometimes pre-conscious or wholly unconscious emotional processes that drive change at the personal and even societal levels (Curtis 2002; Progoff 1985). We humans are certainly capable of reason. We often use reason to rationalize not changing our lives. But we can also use reason for creating the changes we have already decided we want based on transrational inspirations and experiences. It appears to me, however, that it is very seldom the case that we make deep change in our way of life solely to conform them to the dictates of reason. Rather, making deep change seems to require subjective encounters with powerfully numinous imagery and emotions that exert a strong attractive influence. Related to this is the experience of meeting numinous people whose lived example is literally a guiding beacon for us—an experience that "in-spirits" us with energy and hope. Once these inner energies are mobilized, we use reason to figure out how to make our inspirations manifest as facts of history. Learning about simple living in a way that actually leads to life change thus requires making conscious the deeply inspiring and powerfully attractive visions we already harbor for such a life. The curiosity and desire for change is itself evidence that these motivations are already present to one degree or another and are seeking to manifest themselves in consciousness and in action.

Immanently useful in this connection is the important tool of journaling (Progoff 1975). Journaling is a literary form of what the twentieth-century analytical psychologist C.G. Jung called *active imagination.* Jung thought that by giving some concrete form to the images and inspirations arising within us, we could "befriend the unconscious," advance the project of our own growth, and access a deep wisdom in our relationships with others. He encouraged people to write, paint, sculpt, or sing whatever was arising from their dream life and waking fantasies, with appropriate limits in place, of course, to acting these out in real life. New media are making us a more visual/aural culture but in the process we are trading away one of the great strengths of literary culture: The act of writing or drawing can take something which is transient and ephemeral and solidify it long enough for us to meditate on it, suck out all it has to say, and in the process, develop a relationship with it. Journaling can be a starting place for recollecting our own awareness, or integrating our awareness after some new experience, or as a way of honouring and remembering some new insight. Journaling can also refer very broadly to any process that helps externalize an internal process so that we can relate to it differently. This need not be limited to writing per se.

Another principle that informs transformational learning is the work of the Brazilian philosopher, social activist and popular educator Paulo Freire (Freire 1995). For Freire, education is a process of social evolution rooted in the development of consciousness. Social change is the aim of real education. Social change is sourced in personal change, which in turn is sourced in the transformation of our conscious awareness. It's by interacting with others that we develop consciousness of our current life situation, name that life situation, and then imagine how to engage it as active architects of our own history rather than spectators (victims) of a history shaped by oppressive social forces or institutions. For Freire, consciousness is socially constructed. We grow conscious through our interactions with others. Relationships are essential to this process because no single individual has a complete grasp of the historical situation we live in. Each of us has a partial grasp of what is going on, even in our own lives. When we tell our stories to each other, naming as best we can the realities impacting our lives, and when we listen respectfully to each other's stories, we come to a more complete awareness of our situation and the opportunities it presents for change, if change is required.

Freire's work has had a profound influence on me personally and on how I invite people to explore change in their lives. Eschewing traditional didactic approaches to learning, we can invite each other into conversations, simulation games, and reflective activities in which the main content is the story of our lives—what it is like to live in consumer culture right now; what this culture has done to the people and places of our memories; what we hope for ourselves and our children in the future; how we feel about what we experience every day. The aim is not to implant an ideology. Rather, we aim simply to create a social space where everyone has permission and encouragement to pause, reflect, name what is happening to us, and imagine other possibilities whenever that is called for. There is also opportunity on many occasions to take this sometimes newly emerging awareness toward practical steps that implement both minor and major life changes. But my touchstone is always to help people cultivate changes in consciousness before undertaking changes in their way of life. Without doing this, we have no idea why we're doing what we're doing.

I think this approach is an important alternative to the pep talks we might offer about the virtues and benefits of simple living. In my experience, most people are already well aware of the difficulty consumerism has landed us in, and they know quite a bit about why—at least as this impacts their own lives. Sometimes this knowledge contains factual errors, but the facts of our situation are less relevant in the short run than whether or not we have a general awareness of the challenges we face and a felt sense of the urgency of change. People need time to tell their stories and hear the stories of others so that, first of all, we create a broad community of concern. Once this emotional bond is in place, and a sense of community is emerging, there is time enough to deliver up-to-date information about all the challenges and threats posed by consumer culture to the future of humanity.

Another strand in transformational learning is derived from the theory of complex living systems as described by Margaret Wheatley and Myron Kellner-Rogers (1996). What inspires me from the work of these thinkers is their vision of human beings, both as individuals and as societies, as creative, receptive, actively self-organizing entities. We are self-organizing systems congealing around identities which, once established, create a kind of psychological equilibrium that the system then functions to sustain and develop along the lines already defining each identity. We thus selectively perceive new information from the world so that we maintain some minimum level of historical consistency with how we already see ourselves. At the same time, however, we are continually admitting new information which feeds an on-going process of self-re-creation. Considered as complex living systems then, we are at the same time continually maintaining and re-creating ourselves. We are strongly motivated to maintain our identities, even if that requires changing. Similarly, we must be able to see our already established values reflected in some form in the new way of life we are being invited to enter or we won't enter upon it.

What has influenced me most directly from systems thinking has been the vision of human beings as complex, creative, self-maintaining, and self-guiding beings. We simultaneously conserve and create the identity that constitutes who we are. We simultaneously maintain some psychological consistency with our history, but we are also open to new experiences. The lesson for me as an educator is the need to take a humble and respectful approach to working with others. As educators, we cannot transform the lives of others. Only others can transform their own lives. This is probably a good thing. But as educators, we can frame questions and arrange experiences that provoke change in learners precisely because they are also open to such new experiences. Using good provocative questions (pro = "promoting", vocative = "conversation"), we can "disturb" some of the "certainties" which dominate our worldviews and behaviour. In this process, good questions and invitations to relationship are stronger catalysts than any lecture loaded with statistics or any appeals to pure logic. What happens to the questions and invitations we offer once they enter the labyrinth of a learner's consciousness is something over which we have very little control. Therefore, we can always expect surprises during any process as creative as this one. Much depends on trust and faith in ourselves and the goodness of others. At bottom this implies a deep trust in life itself and the healing intentions of our good angels.

Somewhat reiterative of the Freire and complex systems strands of the transformational learning model is the importance of first hand, personal experience in learning about simple living. It is far more stimulating and inspiring to hear first-person accounts, or to tell our own stories, than it is to hear presentations, no matter how skillfully constructed, "about" simple living. I emphasize getting this personal involvement even when it begins with incomplete or inaccurate information. People have a way of rounding out what they need to know about a subject after they start caring about it. My primary aim is always to spark further and future engagement with simple living. It's for this reason that I stress the importance of face-to-face, real life activities for which setting up websites, creating PowerPoint® presentations, or even publishing books or articles is no substitute. The chemistry, complexity and immediacy of real world relationships simply cannot be duplicated at the present time by any virtual proxies no matter how useful they may be in disseminating information.

Finally, and perhaps most important, is taking a positive, creative approach to everything we do. Those working for positive change in society can get mired down in criticizing the deficiencies of consumer culture. This is an especially honoured pastime in academia where it is believed that criticizing something is tantamount to actually doing something about it. But the exercise can be incredibly exhausting. It feeds cynicism and despair, and at the end of the day is both sterile and profoundly conservative. It's very easy to find fault with consumer culture. But why would you waste your breath pursuing such a conversation unless you believed that consumer culture is worth saving, if only it can be reformed in the ways argued by your critique?

A more radical and positive approach involves ceasing critique, or at most, confining it to its role in "conscientization" (Freire's term for growing consciousness), and fixing most attention on the good life we want to create through the process of exploration, discovery, visioning, and change on which we are embarking. I believe consumer culture is already dead and beyond resuscitation. The dead can be left to bury the dead. Those interested in living will take up the task of creating a life-giving culture and will do so immediately.

So these are the key principles that guide what I'm calling a transformational approach to education: (a) people interested in voluntary simplicity already desire change at some level in their lives; (b) deep personal change is motivated by transrational (not necessarily irrational) emotional, imaginative, aesthetic, intuitive, and spiritual energies which must be respectfully evoked before change can happen; (c) journaling can be a powerful aid in working with transrational content; (d) we change our lives by first changing our consciousness, and consciousness is socially constructed in symbiosis with others and evolves through communicating with others; (e) people are complex, self-regulating, conservative/creative systems who actively create and re-create themselves along lines of their already established identities and values; (f) first-hand personal experience is the foundation for growing consciousness in face-to-face symbiosis with others; (g) all learning activities should arise from, or lead back to a creative, life-affirming and positive place; mere critique is vain and ultimately sterile.

11. *Re-Visioning: An Exercise in Transformational Learning*

One example of transformational learning is workshops I have facilitated on Re-Visioning—essentially inviting participants to use imagination to address our sustainability challenges.

I begin the workshop with a memory and journaling exercise where participants are invited to recall one or more past experiences in nature—especially experiences from childhood—and they write detailed accounts of them in a workshop journal. I offer stimulus questions to help participants develop rich journal entries with lots of memory detail. Everyone then tells one or more of their stories to the group. As the stories unfold, many accounts are very emotional as people recall the wonder, sensory richness, and spirit of discovery and adventure that marked many of their experiences. Often participants want to tell more than one story. All are emboldened by the sharing of others to tell even more of their own history. I allow ample time for these stories because a great deal of community-building, shared trust, and respectful communication occurs as an unconscious parallel process to the storytelling.

I then invite participants to consider what has happened to these natural places since their childhood? We journal these accounts as well, followed by another round of storytelling. Not surprisingly, many of the landscapes and natural places of our youth have been degraded or destroyed by development of various kinds. As people share one story after another, the magnitude of this destruction becomes evident as something that touches everyone's life. I ask participants to focus especially on how they feel about these losses and how the landscapes now look and smell and sound compared to the days of their youth. Needless to say, these questions can sometimes evoke dark emotions. But we have already fashioned a learning community and together we can face and accept emotional content that as individuals we would be strongly tempted to deny or avoid. Fear, sadness, revulsion, anger, and a sense of loss are all framed as feelings that inform us about what we need in life to be well. In most cases, these experiences inform participants that development as we have always known it is no longer well for us—and we now know this at a visceral, personal level. Even when the landscapes of our youth remain untouched by capitalist exploitation, the very sense of relief and delight we feel in knowing that they have been preserved also informs us of what is well for us.

At this point, the group arrives at what Joanna Macy calls "the turning" in the workshop process (Macy 1998, 17). It's here that I introduce the idea that we humans are creative, imaginative creatures. The good news in the bad news of traditional development activities is that we chose to do these things, and we can choose something different if we wish. The question is, what do we wish? I then introduce a visioning process to visualize a future state of affairs where the shape of our lives, of our communities, and of our daily round of activities more closely matches what we intuitively know is well for us. Participants journal these visions in detail and then again share them as stories of hope, aspiration, and common purpose. In longer workshops, I have combined this visioning process with Delphi process, using successive rounds of visioning to bring the group into stronger and stronger alignment around the collective vision that emerges amidst all the individual vision-sharing.

After a vision has emerged that engages everyone in some way at a transrational level of their awareness, the time is right to share information about how we can set priorities and make our visions for simpler living realities. This is a sort of "back-casting" process that begins from a vision of possibilities that are "future distant" and then identifies the steps needed to reach the vision working backwards from the vision to our present situation and time in history.

Needless to say, this Re-visioning process can evoke strong feelings as well as other insights and responses. But it is precisely avoiding these feelings that blinds us to what is well for us, and keeps in place social and economic arrangements that are perverse to well-being. When a fuller range of our human experience is admitted to the conversation, we foster in each other an expansion of consciousness which reveals that we are not alone, that much that we tried to push out of consciousness is actually working on our behalf, and that we are creative, active, free beings who can shape our own history. In short, when these transrational forms of awareness take their proper and respected places in the conversation, we become capable of what Miriam Greenspan has called "the alchemy of the dark emotions" (Greenspan 2003). It is what Paulo Freire called "con-scientization" and the choices we make in the "limit situations" which conscientization reveals to us. It is what Joanna Macy means by "despair and empowerment work" (Macy 1998).

Finally, it is because we have not done this work of psycho-spiritual alchemy in our society, that we see epidemic levels of addictions and other unskillful responses to our crisis. Consumer culture devalues this work. The military industrial system of capitalism generates a continual state of crisis which is both dangerous and distracting from the real concerns that should occupy our attention and the fundamental work of education we need to pursue to meet our common challenges. Our time in history is calling on us to create a true pedagogy of simple living.

6

SIMPLICITY AND ECONOMY

1. Introduction

Above all, we shall then see that the economic problem is a convergent problem which has been solved already: we know how to provide enough and do not require any violent, inhuman, aggressive technologies to do so. There is no economic problem and, in a sense, there never has been. But there is a moral problem, and moral problems are not convergent, capable of being solved so that future generations can live without effort. No, they are divergent problems, which have to be understood and transcended. (Schumacher 1977, 140)

Vision

"The economy" is no longer our obsessive concern. People are interested in other things than making more money or accumulating more material possessions because now it is more broadly appreciated that these things provide only marginal assists to well-being. There is less frenzy, less viciousness and competition. Material provision must be made; all acknowledge this. But the pace of all our work has slowed, come down in scale to something we can really comprehend, hold, love. Everywhere there is a renaissance of craft and artisan production; local crafters meeting local needs, often making one-of-a-kind objects. More materials are harvested locally, more necessities are made locally, and more local people are employed in a diversity of activities. More pride is taken in our buildings which we now design to last a thousand years. Even now, our communities are beginning to breath an atmosphere of heritage and connection to place. But most of all, people have reclaimed their time from the tyrant of commerce. No longer

are the best hours of the day or its best energies claimed by wage labour and the dregs left for family, nature, and spirit. The equation has been reversed. Leisure rules, art matters, we take time to serve and enjoy being served, and around these important commitments we find time to provide what is needed for a graceful life. There are fewer millionaires to be sure, but also far fewer people who think that contentment comes from being a millionaire. Those who still strive, and grasp, and claw past others in pursuit of more are recognized for who they are— deeply troubled people, slaves to their desires—but no longer a threat to the rest of us. We've learned what an economy is for: An economy is for sustaining human life within planetary life. Those who think the economy is merely their personal highway to riches and power are now appreciated as relics of a less conscious and less civilized past.

"It's all well and good if a few people adopt a lower consumption lifestyle at the margins of the social mainstream—as long as there aren't many of them. But if simpler living becomes the norm in our society, wouldn't the economy collapse? Wouldn't the widespread adoption of mindfulness and a desire for sufficiency rather than affluence trigger another Great Depression, unemployment, and worsened development prospects for other countries who sell their products into our markets in a globalized economy? Who would pay taxes to support social services if everybody quit their jobs to live the Life of Riley? Isn't *mindfulness* just another word for navel gazing, and sufficiency something only a slacker would want? Isn't voluntary simplicity really a recipe for economic disaster?"

Various versions of these questions often come up in discussions about simple living and the prospects of its ever becoming a widely adopted way of life. They warrant close attention because at our current moment in history. Economic ways of thinking have super-saturated the modern mind—the result of several generations of consumer culture indoctrination. They are in fact a *totalitarian ideology* in the sense that practically every other value or perspective of what it means to have a good life, to solve social problems, to mark progress, or to achieve something noteworthy tend sooner or later to be subordinated to the language of money. One evidence of this is the number of people who think that a conversation is getting serious or getting realistic when it comes down to dollars and cents. Money, and the methods we have for understanding what people do with money—economics—literally defines both reality and adulthood for many people. By contrast, everything else is considered more or less unreal or extraneous to the more serious business of keeping track of money. Whether or not such values are sustainable, and whether or not such anxieties have a factual basis, are both secondary when compared to the sheer psychological force and prevalence of economic thinking. It is a daunting task to suggest that there is no basis in reality for fear of juju spirits when a whole society has been utterly convinced for several generations that such fears are justified.

It is definitely worthwhile to try to imagine what life might be like if the majority of people valued mindfulness and sufficiency of material consumption rather than compulsive over-consumption. To do so, however, requires quite a bit of context-setting. By this, I mean asking some fundamental questions about ideas which are currently taken for granted and which create an intellectual bias that can prejudice discussions and pre-ordain certain conclusions. Before we can imagine how an economy of simple living might operate, it is necessary first to deconstruct some of the popular beliefs that so strongly bias this conversation to the prejudice of simple living.

I must disclose from the outset that I am not a professional economist. In many quarters this might disqualify me from even offering an opinion on economic questions. But many have written on economic issues who weren't economists. Moreover, the influence wielded by economic thinking touches so many aspects of our lives that steering entirely clear of such questions would entail silence on a great many important matters. In my own defense, I'm tempted to point out that even those who are super stars in the field failed to predict the Tech Bubble of the late '90s, the decade-long recession in Japan, the collapse of Asian commercial real estate markets, the poverty of ethics in global financial markets, the 9/11 crisis and the impact it would have on markets, the deflation of real estate values in North America, and in 2008, the worst economic recession since the Great Depression. Economists can't predict much of anything really, unless the future resembles the past, which in today's world it certainly won't. Thus, in thinking about what the future might be like, I suppose my opinion is as good as an economist's, given the discipline's track record.

2. You are Micro, Everything Else is Macro

To begin, it's necessary to distinguish between what has been called micro- and macro-economics. The "micro" level is the level of economic activity where each of us actually lives. It's concerned with matters that are closer to the meaning of the old Greek word *oikonomia*, which is the root of the English word for economics, and means "care of the household." Microeconomics is of intimate, personal interest because it pertains to things like household incomes, debt levels, individual employment, family consumption patterns, savings rates, etc. The GDP (a macro-economic indicator) can go up or down, but it's not of much direct relevance to the individual until it results in personal job loss or incurring additional expense because the interest rate on mortgages has increased.

A great deal of the literature about simple living abounds with sage advice about how individuals can reduce debt, economize on household expenditures, and practice forms of frugality that are truly liberating if your aim in life is freedom and leisure rather than overwork and affluence. I don't intend to repeat this advice here. Suffice it that prudent stewardship of our money is an important part of sustaining the well-being of ourselves and our families. It's also clear that a large fraction of the population is in dire need of such information and skills as how we manage money has been deeply distorted by consumer culture advertising, easy credit, and unrealistic expectations.

When people raise concerns about what the widespread adoption of a lower consumption way of life might imply, however, they seem to be standing at the boundary between the micro world of household money management, and the macro world of national economies, trade surpluses, public debt, and so on. They fret about what would happen if the habits of those they judge to be economically under-productive individuals suddenly got scaled up to the macro-economic level. As an already confessed non-economist, this boundary is profoundly mysterious to me because advice being offered even by economists themselves to one side of the boundary doesn't seem to carry over to the other side.

One example of this boundary situation is the saving/spending dilemma. Individuals hard-hit by the economic recession and carrying too much personal debt are urged to reduce spending, pay down high interest debt, such as credit cards, and save more as a shock absorber against future market turmoil and to provide more for themselves in retirement. But reducing personal spending is bad for the macro-economy which aims for ever-increasing sales of everything, especially big things like houses, cars, major appliances, and expensive holidays. If people reduce their debt loads, this also reduces the interest and service charges they pay to lenders like banks, hence reducing bank profits. If they save more for retirement, they are foregoing current consumption—essential to driving short-term economic growth in the macro-economy, hence reducing employment—in favour of deferring that consumption perhaps for decades until retirement. From my layperson's perspective, this appears to be a completely schizophrenic situation.

Another issue that must matter to us all is the gross injustice of a certain asymmetry that applies at the boundary between personal finances and the macro world of what has been colourfully termed "swinging dick capitalism." Individuals may exercise admirable self-discipline and prudence in paying their bills, saving diligently, investing ethically, earning honest money doing honest work. But as soon as we put money in the bank, it enters the world of macro-economics, not the least bizarre part of which is the machinations of all manner of financial speculators, traders, and parasites. These are people—mostly men, mostly young, and mostly testosterone-ridden and adrenaline addicted—who don't really work for a living. Instead, they speculate on financial markets using money belonging to others, making bets on essentially unforeseeable eventualities, partly because of the immense sums that can be made in the process, and at least partly because of the buzz this gives them in the place where other people have hearts. They also specialize in cooking up complicated investment instruments that have nothing at all to do with the actual work of creating value in the world. When these instruments go haywire as they did in 2007-2009, they can have real, tragic, and utterly unjust consequences for us ordinary mortals living on the hither side of the boundary region between our households and the high rollers. The power that the swinging-dick capitalists exercise over us is, of course, our own greed in wanting to make money without working. So no one is entirely a victim in the system. Still, in my view, this is a social policy issue which cannot be resolved by individuals, but requires instead a new social consensus of values respecting what we allow our money to be used for in macro-economic markets, and by whom.

In any case, I mean to point out that the boundary between the worlds of personal finance and macro-economics is a blurry one with what appear to be some rather mysterious changes happening as we cross from one side to the other. Many uncertainties can thus grow up when we try to foresee what might happen if particular patterns of individual behavior became the general norm. The macro-economy appears to be, in fact, a "holon," where a greatly increased level of complexity can produce emergent properties and behaviors in the macro-economy that could not have been predicted strictly by extrapolating from the properties of its individual parts (households). This all amounts to a somewhat complicated way of saying that it is hard to tell what might be the consequences at the macro-economic level of the widespread adoption of simpler living at the personal level. Accordingly, there is as much reason to expect positive outcomes as negative ones, and probably a mixture of both. So I would like to move along now and take up more specifically some of the questions raised about how adoption of voluntary simplicity might affect the economy in general.

2.1 *Simple living would cause an economic depression*

To begin, let's consider the fear that simple living, widely adopted, would bring about an economic disaster—a depression (prolonged and severe contraction of GDP growth per capita)—or worse.

We should note, first of all, that depressions and recessions are already accepted by economists as part of the normal course of market cycles in capitalist economies. Since systematic records of economic performance started to be compiled about 200 years ago (c. 1800), there have been 18 major recessions or depressions that have stricken the North American economy lasting aggregately over 80 years, or 40% of the time. These are not rare occurrences and are in fact endemic to consumer culture. We therefore consider it normal that large numbers of people periodically fall into poverty, and governments acting on behalf of the wealthy, use the taxation and borrowing powers of government to bail out secured lenders (preferred shareholders and bond holders) while leaving the rest of us and our children holding the financial bag for decades to come. An economic recession is thus both a period of flagging growth and employment, but more importantly, it is a conveyor belt that transfers money from the poor to the rich, all propaganda to the contrary. It is a ratchet that moves wealth inexorably into fewer and fewer hands while leaving the majority less and less well off.

The most recent example is the credit crisis in North America of 2008 arising from sub-prime lending practices caused jointly by greed (considered rational in consumer culture) and unethical business practices. It was also being aggravated by rampant speculation in commodities markets for both food and petroleum—also an accepted activity within capitalist systems. To imply that adopting a simpler way of life would somehow expose us to risks we are not already running is therefore neither fair nor historically accurate. It might be fairer to ask whether simple living would *add* some new risk factor for economic depression to those we already accept with business as usual.

Second, anxiety about the possibility that simpler living will collapse the economy presumes that the economy will *not* collapse if it continues as it is. This is an instance of a fallacy shared by much conservative thinking—that the future will resemble the past if only we don't tamper with what has worked in the past. But there is mounting evidence that the past practice of externalizing the environmental and social costs of consumer culture cannot be sustained over the long term. Historically, when the human population was much smaller, and our technology much less powerful, it was possible to move on to new frontiers when the resources in a given area were exhausted. Today, with large populations aiming to live high-consumption lifestyles, traditional approaches to production and consumption can no longer guarantee that the future will resemble the past. It is the mainstream economy which will likely collapse under the weight of its unaccounted externalities and the dedicated practice of voluntary simplicity may be one of the best ways of preventing such a collapse.

Third, our past experiences with market cycles and economic recessions/depressions have usually been sparked by relatively discrete events like the stock market panics of 1929 and 1987, or the OPEC oil embargoes of the 1970s, the terrorist attacks on the World Trade Centre on September 11, 2001, or the current credit debacle arising from sub-prime lending practices. With these precedents providing the background of recent memory for any conversation about radical changes to our thinking about the economy, it is natural, though fallacious, to suppose that widespread adoption of simple living would be similar. But it seems extremely unlikely that the popular imagination would abruptly swing away from consumerism and toward voluntary simplicity, or that interest in simple living would suddenly spark a market panic like the announcements of valuation write-downs did in the sub-prime lending fiasco. A person's desire and capacity to live a strong form of simplicity generally develops gradually. The life stories of people who do this display considerable effort, application, and trial and error around exactly how to fashion a high quality of life on a low level of consumption. Moreover, there are a number of factors such as long-term debt obligations, the responsibilities of rearing children, and a variety of sources of social and financial inertia that make precipitous change unlikely.

Fourth, many discussions of economics assume that consumer culture with its extremely high rates of capital formation, competition, consumption, and spending are historically normal—simply because they are what the current generation has always known. But the consumer culture we are so worried to protect has only existed since the early decades of the twentieth century. Following the scientific and technical advances of the 19th century, industrial production was becoming so efficient that all of humanity's material needs could be satisfied on a much lower input of time and labour. This posed a crisis for capitalism which requires continuous growth to survive. So an alliance was formed among new mass media like newspapers and radio, an infant advertising industry, innovations in production technology including assembly lines and standardized interchangeable parts, and newly emerging specialties in applied psychology and marketing that made it possible not only to efficiently manufacture the goods and services everyone needed, but also to manufacture needs for products and luxuries that no one knew they desired until after seeing them advertised, mostly attributable to the pioneering work of Edward Bernays. The result has been consumer culture—in fact, a historical anomaly made possible only by cheap fossil fuels and a conscious program of developing a culture of hyper-consumption as a life insurance policy for capitalist profit (Curtis 2002). But to conclude from this that the only conceivable alternative to consumer culture is economic catastrophe seems questionable. One alternative to consumer culture is an economy which more resembles that of the late nineteenth century—not in the sense of a literal return to antique goods and technologies, but rather a return to more local and regionally-based, need-focused production using what have now become highly efficient production technologies, rather than fantasy-based hyper-consumption that is wrecking the ecosphere in the process. One of the effects of shifting to a needs-based production regime is likely to be a large increase in leisure, but not necessarily an economic collapse. As the philosopher and farmer Wendell Berry has observed:

> It [the economy] apparently can see no alternative to itself except chaos, and perhaps that is its chief weakness. For, of course, chaos is not the only alternative to it. A better alternative is a better economy. But we will not conceive the possibility of a better economy, and therefore will not begin to change, until we quit deifying the present one.
>
> The change I am talking about appeals to me precisely because it need not wait upon 'other people.' Anybody who wants to can begin it in himself and in his household as soon as he is ready—by becoming answerable to at least some of his own needs, by acquiring skills and tools, by learning what his real needs are, by refusing the merely glamorous and frivolous. When a person learns to *act* on his best hopes he enfranchises and validates them as no government or public policy ever will. (Berry 1970, 287)

Fifth, concern that simpler living might cause economic collapse takes an overly negative view of the capacity of the economy to innovate and adapt. One of the often cited virtues of "free market" economies as compared to centrally-planned economies is that consumer demand for goods and services supposedly drives production rather than state policies or political agendas. A shift toward a simpler way of living would undoubtedly include a shift in some of the goods and services people want. Why should this be of such grave concern to those most anxious for us to know what bold innovators they are, how much they thrive on change, and how prescient they are of the future? How could it be that the economy would collapse when it is managed by such obviously superior beings?

Finally, an economy oriented more coherently for mindful sufficiency might incorporate some key principles suggested some time ago by Herman Daly (1995, 180-194). The overall scale of economic activity, essentially the sandbox within which society allows entrepreneurs and speculators to play around, would be subordinated to certain physical and ecological limits established by science on the one hand, and by certain socio-ethical limits required for equity and peaceable relationships on the other. In consumer culture, ethical concerns are often forcibly separated from discussion of what benefits business—as if business interests operate in an ethical vacuum from the rest of society. But the events of 2008 have revealed what a short-sighted and destructive perspective this can be. While there has been an encouraging growth in businesses that aim to conduct their affairs in an ethical and environmentally responsible manner, the fair trade, ethical investing, and sustainable fractions of overall economic activity remains small. At this writing, US President Barach Obama is meeting with Chinese President Hu Jintao during which it has been reported that Obama sternly raised the issue of the Chinese record on human rights, but by the end of the day, both parties agreed warmly that this wouldn't impact their business relationship (Buckley and Spetalnick 2011).

2.2 *Simple living would threaten globalization*

Wouldn't reducing consumption in the developed countries have negative consequences for a globalized economy, and especially for the citizens of developing countries?

This is, of course, a complex question. Globalization is economically efficient because it distributes production to the areas of greatest comparative advantage around the globe. For some countries, globalization has brought economic improvements. For others, it has had negative consequences, or is a mixed blessing. Rather than conferring a generalized benefit, the record of globalization so far has been mostly to change the distribution of benefits within and between societies, creating new elites and under classes as it goes, but not necessarily creating overall benefits. Moreover, the economic benefits it can show have often been achieved with environmental and social costs paid elsewhere (McGrew 2000, 345-364).

If our primary measuring stick of the good life is economic efficiency, then globalization is a no-brainer. If, however, we prize other values instead of, or in addition to, economic efficiency, then the benefits of globalization are not as clear. The whole rationale for globalization is that through improvements in economic efficiency and production oriented around one's comparative advantages, everyone will be better off. But better off in what way? The usual answer is that we will all be monetarily richer—and therefore better off. But is a country better off if it surrenders its food sovereignty to a global market it can't control? Is a country better off if its diversely skilled citizens allow themselves to be de-skilled as they narrowly focus on activities or products in which they have a comparative advantage rather than maintaining an economically less efficient but more generalized capacity for self-reliance? Is a country better off if it trades economic efficiency for control over its own monetary policy, or for unrestricted access to resources that will be needed by its own future generations, or for its wilderness endowment, or for its remaining intact and healthy ecosystems? Should economic efficiency be traded for social harmony and cooperation? And do the citizens of developing countries really want the security of their children to depend on the whims of consumers or market speculators half a world away?

In addition to these questions, we must ask whether it is prudent to wager our future on a globalized economic system that may not even be sustainable for another generation? Globalization of the economy requires inexpensive trans-portation. Currently, this system depends utterly on fossil fuels. As oil and gas become more costly, both because of increasing demand and diminishing reserves, is it prudent for any country to trade its capacity to take care of itself for a profitable comparative advantage that can be enjoyed only as long as cheap fuel is available? And should we be investing so heavily in economic arrangements that virtually assure additional increments in climate changing green house gas emissions?

From the perspective of economic efficiency, an economy organized to deliver material sufficiency rather than monetary growth would probably represent a step backwards. Less money would be made in such an economy and it would probably be less efficient in its capacity to exploit comparative advantages, or less willing to do so. Conversely, however, a more nationally self-reliant, locally-based global community of local economies might display higher levels of social and ecological efficiency than consumer culture can. It might produce less money, but more social harmony, a higher level of skill diversity among its workers, an economy better integrated with the local environ-ment, and one less vulnerable to disruption by whatever fanatical madness grips a few humans this week in some godforsaken corner of the world. It may be that such an economy produces less monetary gain, and perhaps even less opportunity for monetary gain, but its citizens might be less interested in pursuing monetary gain once they had come to appreciate more fully the tenuous link between income and well-being (Alexander, Samuel 2012).

Economic and international development policy for the last fifty years has assumed that the citizens of developing countries will be better off to the extent that they integrate themselves into a global consumer economy. We've urged them to focus on making toys or growing tea for us rather than using local resources and locally adapted technologies to meet the basic needs of themselves and their families—needs that don't depend on psychological manipulation through advertising to manifest. In many cases, Northern importing countries do not need what they import as much as the Southern exporting countries need to export it. A recent example of this was the collapse in 2009 of Kenya's export market in Europe for cut flowers. When the economic recession hit Europe, eliminating cut flowers from daily shopping lists was merely the prudent elimination of a luxury expense. For Kenya, however, it was the loss of a major export market. This is not a happy recipe for national security or social harmony.

2.3 Simple living would threaten social services by reducing tax revenues

It has been argued, with some validity, that if people embraced lower consumption living in large numbers that tax revenues would decline thus threatening government funded social services that we all depend on, including those who live simply. Some social services like tax-supported socialized medicine in Canada actually make it easier to live simply since one needn't hold a full-time job to secure essential health coverage. Therefore, this concern must be taken very seriously.

If widespread adoption of simple living remains purely an individual choice and never sparks a larger conversation about a politics of simple living, i.e., development of a menu of political, economic, and social reforms that would flow from the changing social ethos, then hand wringing about lost tax revenues might be justified. It seems highly unlikely, however, that this would happen. Some of this anxiety might be due to a popular tendency to construe the meaning of simple living too narrowly. Again, our history of media exposure, our tendency often to think in terms of extreme opposites, and the custom in some quarters to think of simple living strictly as the practice of frugality, or else a way of life that celebrates laziness and indolence, could understandably lead to such a conclusion.

But consider the following: If voluntary simplicity is defined as including a reduction in the time we spend working, or a decision to live on a reduced income, then tax revenues would fall if we continue to derive them from the same sources, e.g., taxes on income. Pertinent to this topic, however, are two other considerations: (a) the question of what we need all this tax revenue for, and (b) an already long-standing discussion about whether taxing income is the best way of raising revenue for public services.

To embrace simple living involves much more than just working less, or spending less. It generally entails a gradual but pervasive lifestyle shift which involves diet, activity level, housing arrangements, how leisure time is used, etc. Governments currently spend large amounts of tax revenue on health care programs, social welfare programs, prisons, armies, police forces, national security measures, and huge incentives and subsidies to individuals and corporations to keep consumption and production expanding, i.e., to promote economic growth. If we imagined instead a society in which most people lived more simply, where there was greater income equity if not strict equality, more leisure time was available and that time was more focused on re-building community and environmental restoration, where people lived more active and self-reliant lives that engaged them more physically and directly in the getting of their living—if some of these things happened, it is also easy to imagine that there would be less *need* for tax supported social services and business subsidies. Moreover, the transition from what we have now to what we may have then could be a gradual evolution toward something different. As tax revenues declined, the need for them might also decline.

There is also the question of how we raise revenue for collective undertakings. Currently, a large fraction of taxes are derived from taxes on consumption, and corporate and personal income. There have been numerous proposals to shift this structure toward one that taxes social and economic "bads" like carbon emissions, pollution, and waste rather than "goods" like personal income. There is also a long-standing debate about many things that are done by governments to manipulate the economy or support specific corporate players in the economy through the use of subsidies, grants, incentives, licenses, etc. In short, there are things upon which governments currently spend tax monies that they might cease doing to good effect. It is certainly possible to realign the sources of government revenues so that they are less perversely stacked against those who would choose to live at lower income/consumption levels.

It may also be helpful to have a conversation about how society offers incentives for certain essential services that are perverse to achieving their intended goals. For example, why do we pay physicians regardless of whether their patients get well and stay well or not? Why do we pay the police to fight crime rather than prevent it? Why do we extend lengthy patent protection to pharmaceutical companies that fail to bring effective drugs to market which treat real illnesses rather than designer drugs for invented "conditions" that a generation ago were simply part of aging, or nothing that an honest day's work wouldn't cure? Why have we allowed taxation systems and legal codes to become so complex that they support an entire cohort of accountants and lawyers who add no value to society or the economy other than helping us navigate a labyrinth of their own making? Why do we allow the patenting of life forms and seed varieties by corporations when there was utterly no demand for this product in the first place, and which has merely become a thinly veiled program of subjecting the entire human food supply to corporate control? And why do we permit outright economic parasitism when banks and other financial institutions charge usurious interest rates for credit and service fees incurred merely to spend one's own money? Why do we tolerate governments (i.e., us) being left on the hook to bail out foundering financial institutions that write bad loans or corporations that despoil the environment and leave the mess to be cleaned up at public expense?

Such questions are not purely rhetorical. If our aims were promoting human well-being and ecological sustainability, none of these perversities would be tolerated. Since our aim has been to make money seemingly by making our lives as complex and burdensome as possible, any perversity makes sense if it's profitable. When doctors get paid for keeping people well, when police develop communities rather than oppress them, when drug companies produce compounds for real diseases that actually work without inventing illnesses in the process, when taxation and legal systems are made more transparent and equitable, when the cost of financial services is linked in some rational way to the price of actually delivering them, and when we cease rescuing at public expense the greedy, the adrenaline-addicted, and the criminal, then we may find that we need far less tax revenue than in the past.

Finally, so enchanted are we with the mantras of economic growth that we seldom appreciate that growth itself incurs costs, most of which are paid from public funds. A corporation or developer comes to town with attractive drawings of a new factory, promising hundreds of jobs and a boost to regional growth from the stimulus that capital investment often creates. Seldom part of these presentations is any assessment of the short- and long-term costs to the community—costs for social services, infrastructure, education, health-care, utilities, etc.—costs which often involve high fixed overheads whether or not the corporation succeeds in its business. Entrepreneurs sound dynamic and adventurous and forward thinking, but they live in a world of risks and benefits. They are accustomed to winning some and losing some and then moving on to the next game in the next town. The towns they play in, however, are often left with streets going nowhere, housing that no one can afford, excess capacity in public utilities, and unemployed workers applying for welfare if the company folds up. All of these costs take tax revenues which in a society more oriented toward simpler living might be reduced or entirely avoided (Meadows 2004).

2.4 If we don't buy stuff the poor will starve

The final objection to simple living that I will address is the recurring pseudo-concern respecting what would happen to people working in developing country sweatshops and brutally managed plantations if North American consumers stopped buying their products. I call this a pseudo-concern first because I fundamentally question its sincerity, and second because such an objection can only be raised in ignorance of the history of colonialism and economic exploitation standing just behind business-as-usual in North America.

Justifying one's own over-consumption on the grounds that continuing to do so is an altruistic gesture that provides employment to the less affluent around the world simply stretches credulity beyond toleration. While it may be true that in some cases, developing country workers in assembly plants, garment mills, and toy factories may be receiving higher monetary incomes than they would living in agrarian villages, it is also true that they are paid a criminally small fraction of the total price of most goods and services sourced from such companies and sold in the North. Our hyper-consumption mostly supports corporate profits and shareholder dividends in developed countries. In fact, it is a widely acknowledged fundamental of capitalism that it requires access to large pools of impoverished workers to keep labour costs low. As we see every day, in a globalized economy, capital will flow wherever labour is cheapest. As labour becomes more expensive, powerful incentives are created to invest in automated labour-replacing technology. So while we may try to salve our consciences with the delusion that shopping is essential to lifting the poor out of their poverty, the reality is that this is a particularly self-serving myth.

Second, while it is true in some cases that developing country workers may be better off in the factories and plantations of global corporations than they were a decade or two ago, this opinion is historically myopic. Today, much of the grinding poverty that people are trying to escape is itself the direct or indirect result of previous rounds of colonization, exploitation, evangelization, and modernization imposed on indigenous cultures by outside colonizers (Bernstein 2000, 241-270). In the sixteenth century, Europeans aimed to bring the blessings of Christianity to the ends of the Earth, along with a healthy dollop of greed for the gold, silks, spices, and the natural resources of distant peoples whom they scarcely considered fully human. In the seventeenth century, we were spreading the benefits of mercantilism. In the eighteenth century, we were shamelessly stripping the world of labour through the slave trade, and of resources for the first round of capitalist industrial expansion. In the nineteenth century, we aimed to share with the world the blessings of European "civilization," science and technology—no small fraction of it, our military technology—and to continue the flow of raw materials into a rapidly industrializing Europe and North America. In the twentieth century, our aim was to introduce "modernity" which would free the world from the shackles of superstition, ignorance, and the worst sin of all—underdevelopment—i.e., not being like us. These "civilizing" efforts on our part brought two world wars and a host of regional proxy wars during the Cold War period, most of them fought on lands belonging to "developing" countries. By the late twentieth century and the dawn of the twenty-first century, we are once again re-colonizing the world to "share" the benefits of globalization, structural adjustment, biotechnology, information technology and offering the chance of a lifetime to become full partners in the "crusade" against global terrorism. What we have been singularly incapable of doing is leaving other people peaceably to themselves to develop their societies, or not, along the lines they themselves choose. The truly stunning miracle of the last five hundred years is that any indigenous populations survive at all, given all the "love" and "concern" we have so selflessly lavished on them.

To suggest, then, that a continuation of this process of economic exploitation through further rounds of consumer culture expansionism is a moral obligation on our part seems an attitude deliriously out of touch with the lessons of history.

While considerably more might be said in defense of a lower consumption way of life that falls into the "ain't necessarily so" category, there will be value in focusing instead on just what the economic arrangements might be of a society that chose simple living, not as a requirement—for this has never worked historically—but as a widely and voluntarily adopted preference.

3. An Economy for Simple Living

Since the humbler meaning of economics as "care of the household" is tied up with well-being, no treatment of economics can be divorced from some underlying set of beliefs, whether explicit or implicit, about what makes for well-being (the good life). I understand an economy to be *the set of all human activities* (for not everything people do is economic), *together with the technology necessary to transform energy and materials provided by the Earth in service of a certain concept of the good life.* If we believe that a good life will be achieved by building bigger and bigger statues, then we get the economy of Easter Island and technology to achieve those goals. If the good life is ultimately found in an afterlife our conveyance to which requires the construction of massive burial monuments, then we get the technology and economy of ancient Egypt. If the good life consists in simply having more of everything we can imagine faster and bigger than ever before, then we get the blistering cancer of North American consumer culture with an economy and technology to match. My point is that there isn't just one set of economic laws that somehow exist independently from what we value. Just as historically we have wanted different things at different times and places, so we have seen different economies appear to serve them. This is both good news and bad news. The bad news is that our economic experiments have generally been pretty disastrous, and paradoxically, especially when, as pointed out by Ronald Wright in *A Short History of Progress* (2004), they were most successful.

The good news is that, on the historical evidence, it appears that human beings are capable of conceiving a diversity of "good lives," including ones that are far lower on the material consumption scale and far more sustainable than the consumer culture in which we now live. For most of human pre-history and ancient history, our economies were not concerned with money at all—money itself being a fairly recent invention.[17] Thus we find grounds for hope that we may not be genetically programmed to breed and consume ourselves to extinction.

It is this set of beliefs about what is a good life that is the hinge between present day consumer culture and how some proponents of mindful sufficiency imagine themselves living. In germ, I propose that an economy of sustainable living would be organized to achieve different goals and in different ways than our present economy. It would offer a different measure of success, engage different technology, and go about meeting human needs in a different way. These differences would not be so radical as to be unrecognizable to us, but they would definitely imply creating new institutions, dismantling others, developing a new menu of policies and development priorities from the ones current, and organizing everything to achieve substantially different goals. Some of these changes may require the recollection of historically older ways of doing things; other changes may require sheer invention. These goals are in no way foreign to our humanity—in fact, they would be authentically reflective of it. But they would be different from how we organize

---

[17] Metal objects which represented value which previously had been exchanged as commodities were first used as money about 5,000 BCE, and the first coins were minted by the Lydians around 700 BCE. Paper money was invented by the Chinese in the 3rd century BCE, but its use didn't become widespread for another two millennia. Today, money has taken the form of electronic and credit transactions, which involve no material objects at all, and whose value is established by both government fiat and currency market exchange values, neither of which are under the control of individuals. See: Mary Bellis, *The History of Money*, www.About.com Guide.

our economic affairs today, and achieving them would require a thorough-going and probably fairly lengthy process of social evolution—certainly a generation and perhaps more.

A very intriguing contribution in this direction is offered by Veronika Bennholdt-Thomsen and Maria Mies in their book *The Subsistence Perspective* (1999). These authors bring a feminist and Earth-centered perspective to a discussion of economics, in contrast to the male-dominated money-centered perspective of traditional economists. Their proposals spring from the idea that a subsistence economy, far from being concerned with mere survival, is instead an economy whose first concern is life and enhancing the conditions that make for more life, ecological productivity, health, and vitality. This is achieved through ecologically sustainable production regimes within ethically defined limits intended to protect the interests and well-being of life-oriented cultures. Such a system can thus be contrasted with "death-oriented" economies aiming for resource extraction and consumption with the goal of expanding commodity and luxury production so as to promote the interests of capital (profits) rather than promoting the interest of life.

Before moving forward, I think it is a mistake to treat the economic aspect of simple living apart from the other changes to society and politics that would likely coincide with the economic changes implied by a lifestyle of sufficiency rather than hyper-consumption. It's hard to imagine significant change coming to the economy without a parallel politics of simple living and changes arising, which are not about simple living per se, but which stem from other values shared by people who make a commitment to simple living. Surveys have shown that people who self-identify as living simply also display a preference for holistic approaches to health care, tend to choose locally produced organic foods, tend to opt for human-powered or pedestrian transportation, tend to be involved as volunteers in community-focused projects and activities, and so on (Elgin 1981; Johnston & Burton 2002; Pierce 2000; Young *et al.* 2004). While these are not direct results of simple living, they are attitudes and values correlated with it. It's reasonable to expect that in addition to opting for a less consumptive lifestyle, people with such values would also be working for changes to public policies, social welfare systems and services, settlement designs, transportation systems, and a host of other things that would have economic implications. Thus a shift to mindful sufficiency would involve a major social transformation, reflected in the economy to be sure, but elsewhere as well.

A first approach to an economics of simple living might consider the major economic sectors and how a shift to simpler living might be manifested in each. And let us remember that we are moving here from the realm of micro- to that of macro-economics:

3.1 *Primary production*

"Primary production" refers to activities which in fact represent *primary extraction*, or perhaps even primary *degradation*, of ecosystems by human beings. Such activities include mining, fishing, forestry, and agriculture/aquaculture. In Canada in 2007, about 2% of the workforce was engaged in extractive industries (*Wikipedia* 2008). The comparable statistic for the United States is 4.5% (Federal Reserve Bank of Boston - Bureau of Labor Statistics 2007).

Basic to mindful sufficiency are the axioms that simple living involves less consumption overall, and changes in consumption choices of material things which are necessary. We would expect then that people living in smaller homes or perhaps multi-family residences like co-housing or ecovillages would be consuming less metals, forestry products, heating fuels, furnishings and so forth, and that less of these goods would be allocated to mere social display than is current in consumer culture. Correspondingly, the scale of mining and forest harvesting activities would be markedly reduced, hence reducing employment in these sectors and corporate earnings from them. Partly compensating these losses would be improved con-servation of forest ecosystems, habitats, watersheds, species, and reduced environmental damage and health impacts from mining and forestry product industry wastes and pollution.

Conversely, however, it is reasonable to assume that a society that broadly adopted the ethos of simple, environmentally sustainable living, would be replacing a significant proportion of extractive primary production with recycling of primary materials. Jobs lost in the primary extraction industries might be more than replaced by jobs created in recycling and remanufacturing. It may even be the case that more jobs would be created than lost under such a regime as mining and forestry have become highly capital intensive and automated businesses, whereas recovering materials from manufactured products for recycling is more labour intensive and therefore more productive of employment. We might hope to see then, a contraction of mining and forestry activities compensated by increased employment in recycling/materials recovery industries and a reduction in the environmental externalities associated with present day extractive industries.

The question of fishing, aquaculture and agriculture deserves separate treatment because people who live simply need to eat just as much as those living consumptively. Differences here would likely arise from changes in food choices sourced in other motives than the desire to live simply, but which are often found together with such a desire. For two generations now, there has been a lively debate concerning whether a corporate agri-food system designed to maximize profit is the most environmentally sustainable, aesthetically desirable, or most health-promoting system that can be imagined. Abundant evidence now exists showing that perhaps 90% of food fish species have already been extracted from the world's oceans with a total economic collapse of the global food fishery anticipated within only a couple of decades (*Winnipeg Free Press* 1998). Global agriculture is depleting topsoil at many times its natural replenishment rate and agriculturally productive areas continue to be threatened by salinization, desertification, urbanization, fresh water scarcity, and climate change (Pimental *et al.* 1973). The global food system has also largely come under corporate control within regimes of globalized production from comparative advantages which has in effect recently subordinated commodity production for human nutrition to production of biofuels for transportation, or as a purely speculative financial investment (*Globe and Mail* 2008). While aquaculture may hold promise to alleviate some of the more destructive consequences of the industrial open sea fisheries, it is a developing industry with environmental and human health challenges of its own (David Suzuki Foundation 2012). Moreover, all food system production, processing, marketing, and distribution activities are highly fossil fuel dependent. It is increasingly clear that the current organization of the agri-food sector is neither environmentally nor economically sustainable in the long term.

Simpler living has generally been associated with a preference for a more localized and self-reliant lifestyle. People adopting simpler living tend to prefer organic, locally produced foods. They bring a somewhat more mindful approach to their food purchasing choices which includes consideration of the social and environmental aspects of the food system—considered as a system—rather than merely assessing the appearance and price of the foods they buy. An economy of simple living that included a sustainable and socially just food system would therefore likely see a downsizing of the global food production and distribution system with a corresponding increase in local organic production of food for local consumption. A less fossil fuel dependent food system would also likely see an increase in the demand for agricultural labourers as food production became less mechanized, or perhaps differently mechanized than today. A predictable loss of jobs and depreciation in the value of capital assets now employed by the global food production and transportation industries might nevertheless be replaced with smaller scale, more locally focused production for local markets. In a classic essay entitled "Does Community Have Value," the philosopher-farmer Wendell Barry convincingly illustrates that small scale production on family-owned farms tends to be associated with higher rural population densities and more profitable operations per hectare than are large-scale corporate farming regimes (Berry 1987, 179-192).

Given these considerations, it would seem that a general shift toward simpler living would have significant effects on the primary production sector of the economy and would imply substantial shrinkage of some major industries. These changes, however, could be accompanied by potential increases in employment and economic activity in materials recovery/ recycling and organic local production of foods as well as a transition to a more sustainable fishery.

3.2 Construction

A major sector of the economy is construction, employing in Canada in 2007 nearly 6% of the workforce (*Wikipedia* 2008). In the United States, the construction industry employs approximately 5.6% of the workforce (Federal Reserve Bank of Boston - Bureau of Labor Statistics 2007). The impact that simpler living might have on construction depends partly on how our future society envisions more sustainable approaches to meeting our shelter and transportation needs.

Since mindful sufficiency implies a general downsizing of one's material footprint in the world, it is reasonable to assume that this might also imply a downscaling of residential buildings, though the need for public buildings and commercial and industrial construction is more dependent on the scale of overall civic and economic activities. Barring a population collapse occurring for other reasons, a more sustainable and simpler approach to living would almost certainly imply fewer people living in fully detached single family houses and more living in multi-family dwellings. A generally lower level of material consumption might also imply a reduction in the scale of industrial and commercial buildings—particularly as recycling, remanufacturing, repair and maintenance businesses come to replace enterprises based on the processing of virgin resources. As people transferred their attention and energy away from increasing their incomes and placed it more on rebuilding family and community relationships, however, there might be increased interest in constructing larger and more attractive public buildings, libraries, museums, parks, and plazas.

Decisive to the implications these changes would have for the construction sector of the economy depends on how society answers the sustainability question going forward. There are at least four general approaches that might be considered to meeting the legitimate human need for built environments.

Our current approach views architecture as a semi-durable but ultimately disposable "product," the characteristics of which are determined by the profitability to be derived from building, selling, or renting whatever is constructed. Market capitalism is characterized by high rates of change that includes high rates of demolition and construction of buildings since both urban and rural landscapes are under more or less continual renovation. The result is a continually changing built environment that generates enormous quantities of waste and huge environmental impacts as everything is transported and built with fossil fuel intensive technologies and materials. In North America at present, with the exception of a handful of heritage buildings which must be doggedly protected at every turn from the predations of developers, the entire stock of public and private buildings is replaced on a cycle of less than 100 years. Everyone who now recognizes that such practices are entirely unsustainable in the long term has three alternatives to consider.

One approach might be to imagine simple living as implying even less durable buildings than we currently erect today. From this perspective, buildings could be designed to biodegrade more efficiently than they do today, and disappear completely shortly after the lifetime of their owners. One of the problems with much contemporary construction is that semi-durable buildings use some very durable components made of plastics, which will never degrade and thereby represent a continuing, if not eternal, pollution problem. If buildings could be made more completely biodegradable and/or recyclable, these environmental impacts might be minimized or avoided.

Among the benefits of this approach would be a rapidly degrading stock of buildings which would require continual reconstruction creating many jobs for builders and manufacturers of building products. It would also assure the relatively rapid disappearance of all sorts of buildings thus reducing the physical impediments to introducing new technologies or approaches to urban planning. It might also reduce environmental impacts because all materials would be designed for greater biodegradability or recyclability.

Among the disadvantages of this approach would be a very high "through-put" of materials and energy needed to meet human shelter needs—itself likely a challenge to sustainability even when renewable materials are used. Energy resources would still be needed in abundance to process and erect degradable buildings, which would have its own environmental impacts. Heritage buildings and with them a sense of history-in-place would be impossible. There would also be the matter of how well such buildings would protect people from the elements or continue to be healthy places to live as they degraded beneath us. In many respects, such construction might share many characteristics with the shelters built by pre-industrial cultures—biodegradable to be sure, but drafty, dirty, dingy and dangerous to one's health.

A second approach consists of construction designed to be much *more* durable than present practice. Here we would aim to develop human settlements consisting of buildings designed to last a very long time—centuries to be sure—rather like the best of the old cities of Europe and Asia. The logic of this approach rests on the assumption that it does not require ten times the materials and energy to construct a building that lasts ten times longer. As long-lived buildings came to comprise a larger fraction of the total building stock, assuming a relatively stable population, we might expect to see a reduction in the need for new construction with a corresponding saving in energy and materials. More durable buildings would therefore be more sustainable in the long run—especially if they were designed with sufficient flexibility to accommodate new technologies and new uses in the future.

Within this second scenario, we would expect a general contraction of the construction industry and building supply enterprises as the rate of construction of new buildings gradually declined. Counterbalancing this trend, however, would be a likely increase in building renovation and maintenance services and product suppliers. Much more attention would be given to maintaining and restoring existing buildings than to demolishing and replacing them. There would also be a growing sense of heritage and tradition associated with such buildings, people would enjoy a stronger sense of place, and more attention would be given to creating beautiful buildings and universally useable design elements such as those described in Christopher Alexander's architectural classic *A Pattern Language* (1977, 1979). Alexander studied ancient buildings and cities to identify design elements that meet the perennial needs of human beings. From these, he distilled a set of design principles that represent historically long-standing and satisfying approaches to meeting these needs. So useful were his observations that they have been generalized far beyond the field of architecture and are now applied in diverse design disciplines.

A third approach is that represented by the emerging discipline of restorative architecture—still very much in its infancy. Here architecture is approached as a sort of life-science aimed at constructing buildings that integrate with, participate in, and effectively enrich and restore their natural environments, while also meeting human needs for built environments. Goals in this discipline include buildings that produce all the energy they need rather than drawing it from distant power grids, or buildings that recycle and reprocess their own waste products in closed-loop systems, or buildings that are "grown" rather than "constructed" using biotechnologically altered plants or plant-like building materials. We might also imagine building elements that are edible so as to integrate meeting the human needs for food and shelter within a single technology.

As attractive as such a prospect might be to some readers, at this writing, concepts like these reside closer to the realm of science fiction than demonstrable practice. We already know a great deal about how to build very long-lived structures from environmentally, relatively benign, materials like wood, stone, glass, and ceramics. Less likely, but not entirely impossible, are more biodegradable or recyclable buildings. The technologies necessary for a fully restorative approach to architecture still lay some way off in the future and may not be ready for large scale diffusion in time to mitigate the sustainability crisis that is already upon us. Regardless of how humanity decides to satisfy its need for shelter, the more general implications of simple living for the construction sector of the economy are considerable. A general move away from the single family house as the *sine qua non* of the good life would sharply reduce employment in residential house construction. A more localized economy would reduce the need for large scale industrial construction, building ports, and container shipping facilities, and probably also for transportation infrastructure—or at least a change in the character of such infrastructure. There might also be a reduced need for mega projects such as dams, tar sands extraction projects, highway systems, and commercial construction of many types.

Conversely, we might expect to see increased activity in construction of public buildings, small-scale and sustainable energy projects, organic/permaculture food production facilities, landscape restoration and "de-paving" programs to return more urban land to food production activities and recreation spaces for a population with more leisure time to spend. Construction, which presently services the interests of mostly automobiles, might later be replaced by projects that enhance active transportation infrastructure (cycling, walking routes), urban mass transit systems, and sustainable, high-speed inter-urban transit systems like high-speed rail powered by electricity or hydrogen fuel cell technologies.

3.3 *Transportation*

Donella Meadows, one of the original authors of *The Limits to Growth* simulation exercise of the 1970s, reported facilitating a visioning exercise with some German engineering students around a more sustainable community. The students could envision sustainable housing, and food production, and waste and water management systems, but try as they might, they couldn't imagine a sustainable transportation system. Certainly they could imagine one more sustainable than our present transportation technology, but not one which was truly sustainable in any absolute sense. Their conclusion was that people living sustainably would probably travel very little

(Meadows 1996). But this still doesn't address very adequately the need to transport materials, finished goods and commodities from areas where they are abundant to areas where they are scarce. Transportation is a major sector of the existing economy and while it must diminish in any future economy based on mindful sufficiency and local self-reliance rather than globalization, it will still hold a prominent place among human activities.

Consumer culture also finds itself in an interesting dilemma respecting transportation. The push for globalized trade, which has been going on since the eighteenth century but which only achieved significant realization since about 1980, depends utterly on cheap fossil fuel for transportation. Unless major discoveries of new oil deposits are made soon, however, there is a very high probability that diminishing oil supplies will rapidly increase the cost of transportation worldwide. This will be especially true when the use of oil for transport comes more directly into competition with its use for food production (Campbell & Laherrere 1998). This will effectively end the globalization experiment unless equally inexpensive transportation tech-nologies using renewable forms of energy can be developed and implemented very quickly—an unlikely eventuality. On the other hand, if major new deposits of oil *are* discovered, thus making the world safe for globalization, the net effect will be to aggravate climate change by increasing carbon emissions. Thus globalized regimes of consumer culture face the unpleasant choice between ending globalization or intensifying climate instability—or else undergoing fundamental change in its basic assumptions about the good life.

While it is not at all clear at this writing how this dilemma will eventually be resolved, we can say that the practice of mindful sufficiency implies a more active, environmentally sustainable approach to transportation. Thus we might expect to see many changes to how we currently meet our transportation needs. Many people are now recognizing that transportation systems that depend entirely on fossil fuels are collapsing due both to price increases and supply restrictions. It is obvious that our society must engage the process of transitioning to a less energy intensive transportation system as well as generally more locally self-reliant, diverse and regionalized economies.

Every modern society must move goods and materials from the regions where they are produced or in abundance to areas where they are consumed or are in scarcity. This will be no less true for a society of simple living. We might expect, however, a reduction in the *quantities* of goods and materials transported corresponding to the reduced consumption of such goods by the population generally. As the economy, particularly food production, becomes more localized and self-reliant, the need to transport food long distances would diminish. A more localized and self-reliant economy generally would participate less in a globalized economy requiring large ships and especially aircraft. It may even be that air travel becomes a rarity given a reduced need for speed and the environmental impacts of aircraft.[18]

Perhaps the chief impact to the transportation sector of the economy might be a large shift of the population away from the use of automobiles to more human-powered modes of transportation. No such shift is likely to occur on a large scale without a corresponding re-design of human settlements so as to make them more pedestrian friendly, compact, and better serviced by mass transit. But any decided shift in the direction of mindful sufficiency necessarily implies finding less complex, costly, and environmentally damaging transportation alternatives than the individual automobile whether those consist of walking, cycling, or other forms of active transportation. Such a shift would effectively contract much of the manufacturing, marketing, servicing, and secondary services and product industries currently serving automobiles. Some employment would likely shift toward jobs related to construction, servicing, and staffing of urban mass transit systems as well as serving the needs of cyclists—and of course the need would remain for cargo vehicles to move goods and materials from place to place.

As transportation technologies shifted toward active transportation, more urban mass transit, and a reduced use of aircraft and highways for inter-city transportation, there would be a corresponding change to the transportation infrastructure and amenities associated with it. We might see improved

---

[18] There are some immovable physical limits involved in the relationship between energy consumption and speed for any object moving through an atmosphere. While streamlining of car bodies and airframes can certainly help, regardless of the shape of an object moving through air, the air resistance is a cube function of the speed, meaning that the energy necessary to overcome air resistance increases dramatically as a function of speed. Going fast is energy intensive no matter what technologies are brought to bear on the problem. Sustainability of transportation using renewable energy sources therefore implies a slowing down of commerce, if not life in general, regardless of how we design transportation vehicles.

passenger train services and stations, fewer highways and parking lots, more bike stations and pedestrian walkways. All of this would employ people differently than is currently the case, as well as constructing (and demolishing) everything required for the transition.

3.4 *Manufacturing*

Manufacturing represents a diverse sector of the economy. In Canada, compared to other developed countries, it is also a relatively small sector, employing only 13% of the workforce (*Wikipedia* 2008), and 10.2% of the workforce in the United States (Federal Reserve Bank of Boston - Bureau of Labor Statistics 2007). Manufacturing refers to any industrial operation that transforms the products of primary production into usable goods for sale.

Considered from a simple living perspective, which tends to value smaller scale economic activities, a re-localized economy, and greater emphasis on self-reliance, we might imagine manufacturing in such a society to move away from highly automated, capital intensive production of mass market goods and toward more craft, artisanal, and custom-built products. This is economically inefficient to be sure, but also depends in large measure on what we want an economy to do for us. This, in turn, depends on how we conceptualize the role of work.

In his classic book *Small Is Beautiful*, E. F. Schumacher (1973) proposed that to create a more sustainable and humane economy, we might consider the perspective of "Buddhist economics," including the idea that the main purpose of work is the perfection of human character, not generation of profit for its own sake. The economy should employ people using tools— devices designed to ease work and extend the creative process— rather than machines—devices designed to separate and alienate people from work. Work produces goods that fulfill real needs, and engages people in tasks that help us discover and express our interdependence and develop our capacities for spiritual liberation. Work becomes a means of meeting our material needs, to be sure, but also the crucible within which we perfect our character and learn to create communities of inter-dependence and common-wealth. But to achieve such goals would clearly require some measure of the de-automation of workplaces, not so as to re-immerse people in hazardous or onerous tasks—for those are the proper domains for automation—but rather to return people to a more holistic involvement in their work, and to allow for greater personal contributions to the products being manufactured. After all, even the Latin roots that comprise the word "manufacture"—*manus* (hand) and *facere* (to make)—means to "make by hand."

Manufacturing activities in a society oriented toward simple living would in part resemble those of the present day, but might differ in certain key respects. First, strong markets might be created for tools and other goods that assist people in the practice of self-reliance, such as gardening, and construction tools, equipment for the home processing and preservation of foods, a resurgence in clothes making activities, etc. We might also expect a decline in the manufacture of all sorts of disposable or single use products with a corresponding increase in products designed for easy recycling, operations which remanufacture or repair other products, and which use recycled materials to create new products. Commonly we would expect to see more and more products related to meeting authentic human needs and fewer and fewer items being brought to market purely because profits could be made by convincing people to want them.

Toxic to sustainable living is any form of design obsolescence, and we might expect that this practice could even be prohibited by statute. Design obsolescence occurs when science or technology are applied to the design of products in such a way as to assure that they will fail sooner than might otherwise be the case if the best of scientific and technical knowledge were applied to producing things that efficiently perform their intended purpose and last as long as possible. Designing products to "fail on time" is a widely used and effective method for increasing consumption. It forces consumers back into the marketplace for goods, which would not have failed so soon had they been better designed and manufactured in the first place. Another form of this same practice involves using marketing methods not to inform consumers about products, but to create fashion trends that promote the replacement of goods before they wear out, but instead because they are simply out of fashion. Another example of the same thing is designing information products such as computer software to include functionally trivial changes but which still require the user to purchase upgrades, or even equipment replacements "to keep up." The net effect is high corporate profit but at the cost of producing more wastes to landfill, the extraction of more resources, use of more energy, and of course, higher overall costs to the consumer. Anyone wishing to live on a lower income with fewer hours of paid work needed to support oneself must see design obsolescence as a particularly egregious form of economic oppression.

3.5 *Services*

The Service sector of the economy is very diverse, including retail sales, business services, such as financial services, real estate and communications, education, health services, tourism, and entertainment. It also includes the full spectrum of personal services such as legal and accounting services, child care, household maintenance, yard care, sex trade workers, personal attendants, and cleaning services. In Canada in 2007, 76% of the workforce was engaged in the service sector in one way or another (*Wikipedia* 2008), and 60.5% in the United States (Federal Reserve Bank of Boston - Bureau of Labor Statistics. 2007). By developed country standards, this is a very large fraction of the workforce, since in most other countries a larger share of the population is engaged in manufacturing.

Because of the very diversity of the service sector of the economy, the effects that a major social shift toward simpler living might have would be equally diverse. People adopting voluntary simplicity might choose to work less, which in turn might reduce the need for child care services, but could increase demand for recreational and leisure services. A more active lifestyle marked by a greater interest in holistic health practices and health maintenance products and services would hopefully dramatically reduce the need for medical services even as it increased the market for recreational services and teachers of disciplines like yoga and martial arts that contribute to overall wellness. The emphasis on self-reliance within voluntary simplicity might manifest as an increased interest in growing, preserving and preparing food at home, with a corresponding reduction in restaurant patrons, but perhaps a countervailing increase in attendance at cooking classes and gardening seminars.

As society becomes more focused on non-material understandings of the good life, we may witness a truly breath-taking renaissance in adult learning activities of all kinds. Teaching and learning art, storytelling, music, dance, languages, all variety of literary and performing arts, the arts, humanities and sciences in general, and all manner of training for self-reliance might witness a huge flowering. With expanded leisure time and reduced interest in purely instrumental learning, we might also see a greatly expanded interest in, and engagement with, the natural and social sciences, space exploration, and a renaissance of the human potential movement.

One service sector requirement which, sadly, will likely be increasing in demand in the future is toxic and degraded site restoration services. Consumer culture has left, and continues to create, a truly staggering legacy of depleted and degraded ecosystems and poisoned rivers, sea coasts, and landscapes. Earth cries out for re-afforestation, and a concerted program of wildlife habitat restoration. We have also to face the business of removing and dismantling objects of human physical culture that should never have existed in the first place—land mines, munitions dumps, nuclear reactors that require de-commissioning and demolition, and hundreds of thousands of hectares of military facilities, practice grounds, and test sites that require reclamation and rehabilitation. Left unattended, all of this detritus of fear represents a ticking bomb for future generations and other species. If we take up the challenge of righting the wrongs of the past, however, it is obvious that much employment potential exists here for very meaningful service.

No less pressing than restoration of the natural environment is rehabilitation of our built environments. At this writing the suburban landscapes of North America are poised to collapse under the triple crises of neglect, lack of access to mortgage credit, and soaring fossil fuel prices. As market economies continue to plunge past peak oil into uncharted territory, one of the few certainties available to us is that the future will not much resemble the past. It could be the case that the great North American suburbs will in a decade or two, be as hollowed out as the inner cities were by the flight to the suburbs in the latter part of the twentieth century. In any case, given the new realities of our collective sustainability challenge, we must reinvent our cities and towns from the ground up for the relocalized, solar-based societies of the future. This will require a great deal of reconstruction of city neighbourhoods, probably with more multi-family residential buildings using more materials recycled from the existing building stock. The most costly element in any construction project is labour. In the simple living society of the future, it may be that more people will choose to spend more of their leisure time working with some greener and more environmentally conscious descendent of organizations like Habitat for Humanity—literally reconstructing our settlements with volunteer labour and reclaimed materials.

If mindful sufficiency finds expression as more people earning less money, we might see lower overall rates of capital formation (savings). A smaller pool of capital available for credit purposes might place upward pressure on interest rates, in turn making credit more expensive and potentially reducing the use of credit even further. From a simple living perspective, this is a good thing, as "credit" is not viewed as the royal road to a good life, but rather, as a synonym for debt-slavery. Much of what passes today for financial services are in fact, very creative and subtle forms of such debt-slavery or else outright financial parasitism. As the need and the desire to seek the good life through over-consumption and the over-spending needed to sustain it decreases, we might see a corresponding contraction in financial services as a consequence.

4. Farther Down the Rabbit Hole

In this postscript, I mean to risk my credentials to being an amateur economist and ask some very fundamental questions which seem to be entirely taken for granted by people better trained and more experienced in economics than I am. I want to return to the intersection of simple living and economics and examine again the whole system we've made and whether it might be remade on a different plan. I realize what an outlandish suggestion this is, but my only defense is that we live in outlandish times and such speculations may be justified.

It seems to me that we currently live with a hideous level of social and economic complexity and effort and suffering. We also support an enormous amount of financial parasitism, exploitation, and speculation in pursuit of profit, which is to say the accumulation of money. All things related to money seem to dominate the consumer culture consciousness and I think it is the money system we need to address if we are truly to liberate ourselves into a simpler, freer way of life.

Money is a proxy for value. Price, which is a measure of the money being demanded for a good or service, is a quantitative expression of value. Today it's common to hear talk of prices as signals that people use to assess the abundance or scarcity of goods and services, and hence to making decisions about production and consumption.

The question that this raises for me is why we need money? And why do we need prices for that matter? It seems that what human beings need is the production of necessary goods and services and their delivery where and when they are needed. To achieve this end, what we need is information about scarcity and abundance which can be used to control production and distribution. So far, money and prices have served this function in society, but they are prone to obvious abuses partly because of the reification of money and its tendency to be manipulated as a thing which itself has value. This leads in turn to a myriad of *meta* activities having to do with money per se, apart from its use as an information system.

What we need is a simple system that allows people to signal when they have a deficiency or sufficiency of any needed good or service. This signal then needs to be sent back into a production system that adjusts its activities accordingly. But there is no *a priori* reason why this signal system must use money or prices. All that is required is a way of placing an order for a needed item, which today can be easily mediated by information technologies. The number and nature of orders received is a measure of demand for any given item and the magnitude of demand should substitute sufficiently for what is now reflected in prices.

Imagine then a society where every citizen by right of birth is entitled to sufficient means of material livelihood. All have access to the same menu of goods and services on offer at no monetary cost but subject to consumption limits. All are also obliged to work to help produce needed goods. Everyone orders what they need from a centralized production and distribution system and everyone contributes labour to the same system to produce what is needed. Information, not money, is what would make this system work, and it comes from the expressed needs of the population, not the hyper-stimulation of markets by advertising, planned obsolescence, or other extraneous pressures. Consumption limits for any good or service would be determined partly by the ecological carrying capacity limit for that good—how much of it can be sustainably supplied by the earth—and also by equity considerations, namely, that every person has an equal entitlement to the good in question. The equity principle would be especially effective in helping to limit human population as the fewer mouths there are to feed, the better everyone eats, so to speak.

I don't underestimate the challenges that would be involved in establishing such a system. What I find very appealing about it, however, is the possibility that if such a system could be established, it would essentially eliminate the need for wholesalers, the entire retail marketing sector, all financial services, banks, stock markets, and nearly all legal services as the vast majority of legal work now surrounds matters of private property and disputes over money, all taxation, a vast reduction in the scale of government, a huge potential reduction in social and economic injustice and hence conflict. Since money has been eliminated from the system, all the machinations that now surround all the things we do with money would disappear. People would have to work honestly for their living, but that entire process would be far simpler, more secure, and probably less demanding of time and effort. Property crimes would be substantially reduced because differences in material wealth would be smaller in a society that prized equity and assured adequate means of livelihood to all its members. The stage would finally be set for a shift among human beings from obsessive anxiety over material security to discovering instead the realm of intrinsic rewards. We might also discover how to liberate ourselves from the grip of money as the single proxy for nearly everything else in life that makes for well-being. We could pursue instead the host of psychological, social, and spiritual values that can also motivate human activity, express social admiration, and recognize real contributions to the human experiment. Life would become simpler for everyone and mostly in ways that many people might embrace quite happily.

Lest this proposal sound completely utopian, I hasten to point out that such systems have thrived for centuries in monastic settings that practice a "community of goods." In such communities, individuals take vows of poverty whereby they essentially surrender their right to *personal* property. In exchange, the community as a whole pledges to provide for that individual for the rest of his or her life. By relinquishing the claim to personal property, the monk nevertheless comes into possession of all the property shared by the community by virtue of his or her membership in it. While I'm not advocating that everyone adopt a monastic life—far from it!—I nevertheless find it instructive that this system of structuring our material relations with each other and with the natural world has persisted in some regions for several thousands of years, which is a far more impressive track record than can be claimed for capitalism. In any case, it is a real-world possibility for human beings, which has already been lived out in history.

Clearly, any major transition toward a culture of mindful sufficiency would have momentous economic implications, but not necessarily catastrophic or destructive ones. Any transformation of the economy would probably be gradual and preceded, or at least accompanied, by a much more general cultural change toward simpler living. Presumably, the economy would shift not abruptly as it does now in response to geopolitical crises, rampant greed, or catastrophic failure of one of these subsystems, but rather by evolving to fulfill the changing needs and desires of a more enlightened population.

Given the sustainability challenges that society faces, it is also reasonable to suppose that reducing the human population, preferably by choice rather than succumbing to biological necessity, would also be part of any program for a sustainable and civilized existence. The global demographic dynamics already in play, which promise a large and aging population by 2050, portend major change in any case. A smaller global population with consumption expectations better aligned with Earth's actual carrying capacity is also essential to sustaining the human experiment. All of these factors will also have economic consequences.

While it is likely that a general shift to simpler living would affect every area of the economy in some way, the effects we might imagine are benign compared to what lays in wait for us if we continue to pursue the delusion that nine billion human beings can live as two billion lived for a little while in the late twentieth century on borrowed days of ancient sunlight.

7

TWENTY QUESTIONS: TECHNOLOGY AND SIMPLE LIVING

> The issues are clearly not related just to technology, but are deeply rooted in society and our philosophies, cultures, and traditions. Our technology and industrial development are not separate from our culture but are a necessary expression of it. Therefore we must further examine, understand, and change the societal under-pinnings that create the propensity to abuse the resources upon which we are so dependent. Failure to do so is simply treating the symptoms. (Dixon 2002, 419)

1. Bringing Mindfulness to Technology

When I was growing up in 1950s and '60s North America, technological optimism was rampant. We "boomers" were the first children of the Atomic Age, which promised "electricity too cheap to meter" (despite the ever-present cloud of nuclear annihilation hanging over our heads during the Cold War). We saw humans become a space-faring species, building enormous submarines, transplanting hearts, growing babies in dishes, and eventually building computers and televisions that could fit in the palm of your hand. We spliced genes, engineered the Green Revolution, and wove polymers tight enough to stop bullets. We've not only automated the production of automobiles and rubber duckies, we automated *everything*, from agriculture to sex toys. These accomplishments are as amazing as sometimes they are trivial. There is no doubt that our lives would be extremely different, and most people believe, much worse, if all this technology hadn't been invented. The litany of achievements is truly dazzling, and credit should be given where credit is due.

On the other hand, our success with inventing new machines and materials, new processes and products, has induced a sort of culture-wide enchantment. We're entranced with the work of our hands and perhaps this is why we so often refer to these achievements as magic or miracles (cures, drugs, sound systems, skin treatments, whatever). From our experience of the very considerable list of things that technology can do for and to us, we have come to believe, broadly speaking, that technology might be the answer to nearly everything. In particular, we look to it to solve the sustainability crisis. Very many people today are technological utopians. In secular circles anyway, belief in technology has superseded belief in God as the most likely source of solutions for our problems, if solutions exist at all. Indeed, we mark our progress as a species in terms of technical achievement rather than evolution of our physique or improvement of our character (Segal 1999, 119-158).

The popularity of looking for technical solutions to the sustainability crisis is evident in many places. Green consumerism has already been with us for a generation. It aims to deliver products and services that are less environmentally harmful—in themselves welcome additions to material culture. But green consumerism mostly doesn't question the fundamental narrative of consumer culture, that well-being is achievable through consumption, and even more so through *green* consumption.

Appeals for better technology as a solution to environmental abuse have been with us at least since the first Earth Summit in Stockholm in 1972, repeated in the World Conservation Strategy in 1980, the Brundtland Commission Report in 1987, the UNCED in Rio de Janeiro in 1992, and all the calls since the Brundtland Commission Report for a "factor ten economy" (a global economy that can sustain economic growth at 3%+ per annum, but this while using only 10% of current resource and energy demand). Technical advancement is also a perennial theme at The Rocky Mountain Institute in Colorado, and numerous other efficiency and conservation-oriented agencies, departments, and NGOs worldwide. Of course, better technology is essential and we can only say, bring it on! But rarely do these earnest proposals include any critical analysis of consumerism itself and just what sort of culture we should be striving more efficiently to sustain (Rapley 2002, 170).

Even a survey of Internet media devoted to reporting the most hopeful developments in meeting the sustainability challenge, Treehugger.com, Worldchanging.com, and Grist.org, all report mostly technical developments. Much less glamorous (and less frequent) are stories related to culture, politics, or individual transformation. Chris Turner's (2007) book, *The Geography of Hope*, offers almost exclusively examples of hopeful technical developments such as renewable energy systems, Earthships as sustainable housing, green building standards like LEED (Leadership in Energy and Environmental Design), new developments in electric cars, etc. Of course it's exciting to hear that the residents of the Danish island of Samso adopted renewable energy systems (wind energy and solar district heating) years ago, and have since made renewable energy a mainstay of the island economy. But what interests me far more is how did the residents of Samso come to a consensus to implement such policies? Turner's explanation of a couple of guys offering free Tuborg at a tavern while introducing the proposal to local residents with low key reverse psychology, charming as it is, just doesn't seem either adequate or replicable. I certainly have nothing against Tuborg, and Turner himself discusses more than just the technological aspects of Samso's story. Nevertheless, I came away thinking more about the gadgets that made for Samso's renewable energy revolution than about the complex of interacting attitude changes, "Aha!" moments, visionary public policies and tax incentives, and probably a host of other non-rational factors that must also have been at work making the transition a reality.

What role does technology play in consumer culture anyway? Is the consumer culture approach to technology adequate for meeting the sustainability challenge, even though it also plays an enormous role in creating that challenge? And what role might technology play in a culture oriented toward mindful sufficiency and simple living?

2. Technology in Consumer Culture

The role of technology in consumer culture is parallel to its role in capitalism as a powerful driver of economic growth. The goal of capitalism is the expansion, accumulation, and concentration of profit. The purpose of technology under capitalism is to secure competitive advantages that increase profits. Any technology that increases profits and is not illegal, or that can even temporarily be fit into a loophole in the law, tends to get developed.

Unprofitable technologies, or those which might compromise existing patterns of profit-taking, no matter how beneficial they might be, are generally not developed. Even most "pure" scientific research tends to be biased toward problems which may hold future profit potential.

Subordinate, but clearly linked, to the profit motive as a driver of technical development are its other goals in consumer culture: social and environmental control; comfort and convenience; entertainment; and obsolescence.

Next to profit, military and security technologies are of major importance in consumer cultures—the social control focus for technical development. Indeed, the partnership is close to perfect, since military and security-related technologies are also immensely profitable, quickly become obsolete, and when used in war to destroy more important infrastructure become a means for multiplying profit even more as rebuilding follows conflict. Since capitalism is an inherently paranoid economic system,[19] it is prone to become obsessed with security issues. Since capitalism appropriates an ever-increasing fraction of resources and carrying capacity in order to fuel growth, it is continually in danger of over-shooting the carrying capacity of the Earth (Wackernagel & Rees 1996, 97-98). And since the extraction of resources can create resource scarcities and inequities, it can spark both regional and international conflict (Homer-Dixon 1996, 359-365). Finally, it has been estimated that worldwide, as much as 35% of all research and development funding, capital investment, and scientists and engineers, are engaged in military or security-related industries (Renner 1990). In fact, so entrenched is military research and production in the economies of developed countries that, in the unlikely event that people actually did "give peace a chance," it would cost hundreds of

---

[19] While it may sound like over-statement to suggest that capitalism is "paranoid" it's instructive to note that one symptom of paranoia is the belief that others are out to get you, and sometimes also by delusions of grandeur, i.e., that the reason others are out to get you is because you are really someone special, with special powers or insights or knowledge. While not a formally recognized diagnostic category, capitalism nevertheless bears marked similarities to paranoia, except under capitalism, others really are out to get you. They are your business competitors. Moreover, what makes you special and a worthy focus for their nefarious designs is your profit margin, your market share, and most of all, your patented technology, i.e., that special knowledge that makes your firm, under regimes of capitalism, a target not a neighbour in the same community.

billions of dollars to demilitarize them (Renner 1995). Clearly, if war, the preparation for war, and operation of peacetime security establishments can be considered examples of social control, then the technology necessary for these tasks must be an important priority in consumer culture to command such a large fraction of its creative talent and investment capital (*Wikipedia* (a) 2012).

Parallel with the control of people is technology for the control of nature. In its pleasanter forms most of us can recognize technology at work in our home heating systems, refrigerators, and automobiles. These technologies shelter (some would say isolate) us from, or moderate the effects of climate, obliterate distance and modify the experience of time in our daily activities. If the normal changes occurring in an environment make us uncomfortable or present an inconvenience, we use technology to change them. So we heat our houses in winter, chill our food all year round, and almost everywhere use technology to protect ourselves from the elements. The level of comfort and convenience we now enjoy is shared by more people in more different ways than at any previous time in history, even though it is mostly made possible because of cheap fossil fuels and the truly remarkable levels of power they place in the hands of individuals.

Environmental control technologies can also be applied at much larger scales. Examples include damming or diverting rivers, applying pesticides or herbicides to control pests or defoliate landscapes, modifying watersheds to make them more congenial for agriculture and most recently, modifying even the genomes of living things so as to bring the processes of evolution under human control. Biotechnology, while offering considerable promise to improve human welfare in many respects, has so far been used largely to consolidate corporate control over Earth's genetic resources and expand corporate profits through the patenting of life forms (King & Stabinski 1999, 73-89; Mooney 1999, 21; Shiva 1991, 231-264). Many biotech innovations have arisen not from popular demand for a product like Roundup-Ready™ canola seed, but apparently from a desire to increase corporate profits at the expense of farmers and consumers, especially in developing countries. So far, such innovations appear to offer only marginal increases in yields or improvements in the nutritional characteristics of crops, but they are very effective at establishing corporate monopolies on the use of seeds.[20]

One could hardly offer an account of technology in consumer culture without mentioning its role in providing comfort and convenience. The last century saw an enormous bloom of gadgets intended to take over, or at least reduce and speed up, many tasks of daily living like cooking, cleaning, shopping, and communication. This process reached what could easily be considered a stage of over-development where the applications of technology reflect less a real need for something and more an obsession to mechanize everything that can be mechanized, even if it requires creation of an artificial market. Electric carving knives, battery powered tooth brushes, leaf blowers, foot spas, electric blankets, heated water beds, and cooking appliances designed for only one food like popcorn poppers, waffle irons, bagel toasters, wiener heaters—the list is practically endless. While everyone needs a bed to sleep in, one might under-standably ask whether, in a world where millions of people have not even one bed, how North Americans can justify vibro-massage, automated self-adjusting, heated beds, or refrigerators with liquid crystal screens on their doors allowing Internet access while looking for the pickles. Our culture of entitlement leads us to think that because we work hard we're entitled to high incomes, and high incomes entitle us to whatever nonsensical

---

[20] A signal example of this came to my attention some years ago during a conference on the future of agriculture being held in Saskatoon, Saskatchewan, Canada, at which I was a co-presenter. I listened with interest to a rep-resentative from a major cereal grains company telling those assembled that the future of growing cereal grains on the Prairies of Canada was in boutique specialty crops. The example he offered was of General Mills, a major US multinational food manufacturer, who offered contracts to growers of oats for genetically engineered varieties of this grain custom tailored not for greater nutritional value, or productivity per hectare, or taste, or disease resistance, but rather, because this variety of oats was specially designed not to stick in their Cheerio®-making machines. It seems that unless the doughy precursor of Cheerios® is just the right consistency, it can gum up the dies that make the little Os round. When this happens, the whole production line has to be shut down for an entire day until the dough could be cleaned out of the dies to restart the machines. Growing specialty oats for this sort of use was the future of agriculture, the expert advised us, not growing the generic varieties farmers were used to and, incidentally, for which they could save their own seeds. No. The new reality was growing specialty crops using specialty seeds and all under corporate control.

excesses we can afford, simply because we can afford them. Riches become self-justifying and marketing marginally useful products to gullible consumers is just considered good business. This practice is particularly questionable on the grounds that psychologists are now discovering that the very multiplication of "choice" can itself diminish our quality of life (Schwartz 2004).

While there's certainly nothing morally wrong with being comfortable, the pursuit of comfort and convenience can create a momentum all its own that can lead to an inversion of values. Eating chocolate may be comforting and innocent enough as a simple pleasure. But the pleasure is neither simple nor innocent when the cocoa was harvested by child slaves in West Africa (Robins 2003). Oppression can even be found closer to home when one considers carefully the full cost of many of the gadgets that are flogged day and night as guaranteed to save us time and labour—which we hope to spend with our families and neighbours or engaged in other good works—only to discover that the time we need to earn the money to pay for these conveniences can sometimes leave us with less free time to enjoy them than we had without them. Moreover, it has been a perennial insight in the literature of voluntary simplicity that what is necessary to a decent life is relatively easy to obtain at little cost in time, money, or labour. But luxury consumption is often provided only through excessive toil, dangerous enterprise, or exploitation of one form or another (Woolman 1991).

Consumer culture also invests heavily in the technology of entertainment. When the daily round of one's activity loses most connection to the actual work of getting a living, then all that remains is to seek amusement. Home entertainment electronics and the vast communications infrastructure needed to support it is one of the fastest growing sectors of the economy. It is also certainly one of the fields that is most completely enmeshed with technical development. Middle class North Americans invest billions of dollars in computer systems, communication devices and services, and home theatre systems, to say nothing of the thousands of hours spent playing computer games and watching television (*Inside Facebook* 2009). This technology has enabled a head-long plunge by an entire generation into various virtual realities that taken together can only be considered an electronically mediated mass fantasy. One young man of my acquaintance proudly described the hundreds of pages of detailed maps he had compiled while playing *Ages of Camelot*, a popular online computer game. He knew every nook and cranny of this imaginary kingdom and all its denizens. But he was embarrassed to admit that he probably could not locate Sierra Leone or Myanmar on a world map. Even living in an officially bilingual country, he speaks more Klingon than French, and knows more about the history of Myst® than of the Canadian Federation. In essence, despite being intellectually gifted, he inhabits an imaginary world at precisely the time when his abilities are desperately needed in the real one.

Finally, we develop technology which itself is intended to increase consumption (and hence profits), namely: the science and techniques of design obsolescence on the one hand, and mass marketing on the other. Planned obsolescence has already been well documented but, inexplicably, most people in consumer cultures just shrug and accept rank exploitation of their time and incomes as part of normal living. I won't re-till this soil here, but only wish to point out that a great deal of product design and development effort is applied to assure that products which could last much longer don't. This forces us back into the marketplace to replace goods that have now become waste and which could have been designed for much longer and more efficient service.

One example of misapplied engineering that I find particularly odious is the efforts of truck manufacturers to "tune" engine designs to make sounds that potential buyers recognize as powerful, capable, and rugged. Engine efficiency, durability, and perhaps even safety are in the balance over against the impression the manufacturer wants to make on potential buyers.

In the same category is the enormous effort, expense, and ingenuity invested in marketing goods and services, including over-packaging, excessive and uninformative advertising, and the whole machinery of public relations that promotes consumerism. All of this is especially egregious when the technology concerned is approaching the limits of efficiency that are theoretically possible. For example, we can now manufacture home furnaces that are 94% efficient in converting natural gas to heat. With this level of performance available, why are such devices being manufactured to last only about 10 years when we could design them to last 100 years? Could this really be because consumers demand the right to replace their furnace often? What is to be gained by unnecessarily replacing a furnace nine times except increased waste and corporate profit?

The development of technology in consumer culture has been criticized on a number of fronts including the tendency of technology, when linked to a capitalist economy, to outrun its resource base (Wackernagel *et al.* 2002, 9266-9271). It happens that in some quarters, people not only admit the damage that technology can do, but continue to look to even more technology to fix it (Homer-Dixon 2001). Yes, it is generally agreed, consumerism as a way of life has polluted large expanses of the Earth, but nanotechnology and biotechnology will lead to machines and organisms that will safely dispose of the wastes from previous rounds of over-consumption. How soon we forget that one of the key reasons automotive technology was embraced so enthusiastically was that it helped eliminate solid waste and health problems associated with wide use of horses in urban areas—thus ultimately trading a manure problem for climate change, traffic congestion, and the highway death toll.

Herman Daly has pointed out that, while it is hazardous to underestimate human ingenuity and technical innovation, there are few historical examples of new technologies offered as answers to old problems which have not also brought their own new problems and risks in the bargain (Daly 1995, 180-194). Cars speed up long distance travel but incur serious casualties and are a major source of air pollution. Nuclear fission promised energy "too cheap to meter," but incurred highly toxic waste handling challenges and major security issues. Antibiotics initially cured serious diseases but have now given rise to even more virulent antibiotic-resistant pathogens. Jet air travel allowed circumnavigation of the planet in a few hours but now presents a significant terrorist threat, a conveyor belt for pandemics, and a high altitude contribution to climate change and a threat to the ozone layer. Daly also asserts, no matter how much ingenuity we have on hand, every idea requires high quality resources and available waste sinks before it can actually be built and used. If the current growth-oriented lifestyle of over-consumption runs its course, it may be that high quality resources will be so scarce that new ideas cannot take material form as economic goods and services, no matter what their merits might be (Beriault 2005).

Yet another consideration is the seldom mentioned time lag between the invention of a new technology in the lab and actually getting it into the homes of billions of people. Technological optimists are anxious to announce every new innovation or gadget as if merely to have thought of it makes it so. But every entrepreneur knows in his or her bones the many hurdles yet to cross between the geniuses in the lab and the customers in the marketplace. Taking a technology from concept to production poses a whole range of challenges. These include procuring adequate supplies of appropriate materials, obtaining the necessary licenses, studies, and approvals before production can begin, securing financing, scaling a process up from demonstration to actual production, meeting whatever challenges might be encountered in transport and distribution of the new widget, and then convincing the public to buy it, even if it does represent a real improvement over existing ways of meeting the same need. And all of this has to be achieved at a competitive price in the marketplace. This is not a short process even with expert leadership under ideal conditions. Conditions are seldom ideal.

Another concern that was pointed out over a generation ago by E. F. Schumacher is the fact that under capitalism, new technology tends to be labour-replacing (Schumacher 1973). Since labour is a cost of production, reducing this cost will increase profit. Work is therefore "bad," and if machines can be built that replace human labour, there are powerful incentives to do so. Thus, the advance of technology tends also to increase unemployment with all the negative social and personal consequences that follow from it. It is ironic that a society that celebrates high incomes and the consumption of material things as defining the good life tolerates an economic system that grows unemployment even as it grows profits, thus assuring that fewer and fewer people can participate in the good life it promises. One way to obscure this unpleasant reality is to try to grow the economy so fast that jobs lost in one industry are replaced by jobs created in another, thus making it appear that "employment" is growing. But one "job" is not necessarily interchangeable with every other job. Jobs may be created in an economy without this necessarily translating into employment for flesh and blood human beings. Job numbers look fine, but there may still be many people who cannot find a way to make a living without sacrificing other important determinates of quality of life—friends, rootedness in place, community, a mortgage-free home, etc. Finally, the cost of retraining workers in order to apply for new jobs is a cost of business which is externalized to workers or to society generally, not a costs paid by potential employers to be included in the price of products.

Research and development costs money. Under capitalism, money tends to be appropriated by capitalists (shareholders). This implies a concentration of control over technology, because it is corporations who have the most funds to develop new technologies that are then patented to limit access to and secure control over them. As technical development moves forward, control over the technology tends to become more centralized and more privatized. This isn't necessarily the most favourable arrangement for people who have well-being in mind rather than profit. It is mainly the profitability of a technology (constrained only by whatever regulatory formalities are in place) and not its contribution to overall well-being that determine what we eventually see in the marketplace.[21] The development of new technologies are seldom if ever subject to public review. Lobbyists are paid large fees to ensure that new technologies escape as many regulatory screens as possible.

Suffice it then to note that the purpose of technology in consumer culture is, first and foremost, the generation of profit, but also social and environmental control, comfort and convenience, entertainment, and design obsolescence and marketing that stoke further rounds of consumption, hence making the system self-perpetuating. The development and implementation of technology tends to be capital-intensive, concentrated under corporate control, labour replacing rather than job-creating, and relatively unmindful of the promotion of overall well-being when compared to its prime directive of generating profits. In this context, should we be looking to technology itself for the solution to the sustainability challenge?

3. Why Technology Isn't Enough

> In 1905 in Kansas City, Missouri, there were only two privately owned automobiles. In July of that year, they succeeded in achieving the first recorded head-on collision. (Mooney 1999)

Our confidence in technology as an instrument for meeting the sustainability challenge has considerable historical justification.

---

[21] A particularly disturbing example of this has been the relative neglect by big pharma of the discovery and production of new antibiotics in favour of lifestyle drugs like erection enhancers, cholesterol medications, obesity treatments, etc., because these drugs are used continually and are therefore a secure profit centre whereas antibiotics are only used occasionally to cure real illnesses. The net effect has been to contribute greatly to the current crisis in availability of effective antibiotics and the development of antibiotic resistance by many common pathogens.

Technology has made possible things that were previously thought to be impossible. Therefore, we perhaps feel justified in thinking that this will always continue and that technology will provide an escape hatch from the dilemma of immovable limits confronting limitless desires. In addition, since technology seems to be creating many of our sustainability problems, isn't it reasonable to expect that the solutions will simply be better technology? Sometimes missing from this confidence, however, is an appropriate appreciation for the role that fossil fuels have played in the triumph of technology, and how very dependent many of those triumphs still are on continuing, secure, and inexpensive supplies of these fuels—something that nearly everyone now recognizes as an unsustainable dependency.

I have already argued that a great deal depends on where we point consciousness, how we perceive our reality and what motivates our actions. Technology is just tools and know-how. Technology develops along lines that we set out for it, based on values, desires, and aspirations that don't themselves arise from technological or scientific considerations. While technology is extremely helpful in achieving our goals, it doesn't set our goals for us, nor does it contain any goals of its own. The world we see around us, the world of ecological decay and interpersonal violence, is largely the world delivered to us by a technology we specifically designed to achieve the goals of a consciousness oriented in a certain way. Change the orientation of consciousness and our goals would change, and a new technology could evolve to serve it. In my view, technology as we currently deploy it is, taken by itself, a vain hope for resolving the sustainability crisis for the following reasons:

First, we have already argued that current technology serves the values of consumer culture. It aims to deliver mass material affluence, the very meaning of which implies waste, so as to generate profits which must continually grow. Consumption is the opposite of conservation, and growth without limits is the opposite of a steady-state economy that might have a hope of persisting over the long term. It is logically impossible that any technology can conserve and consume its resource and energy endowments at the same time. It's also logically impossible for any technology to deliver sustainable affluence when the very meaning of affluence implies generating ever-increasing mountains of indigestible wastes. The very definition of sustainable development framed by the Brundtland Commission (meeting the needs of the current generation without compromising the ability of future generations to meet their own needs), while certainly appealing to our wish fulfillment fantasies of being able to have our cake while eating it too, doesn't seem achievable with any presently imaginable technology and our current understanding of the laws of nature. We will not be investing in conservation technologies as long as our economy is oriented toward consumption instead, except, that is, when conservation can be shown to reduce production costs and hence increase profits. But this sort of conservation applies only to inputs which can be priced and generally entirely ignores externalized costs. Small won't be beautiful until we really believe it is. And more will be better as long as we continue to conflate quality of life with quantity of consumption.

Technical development in consumer culture is generally driven by capitalist markets. The operative motive then is greed, not planetary sustainability. In practice this means that technologies that might be environmentally restorative but which have little or no profit potential tend not to be developed or implemented, no matter what their merits. Conversely, technologies that have large profit potential, tend to be implemented no matter how disastrous their environmental or social impacts. For example, technology has been proposed to construct artificial trees to scrub carbon dioxide from the atmosphere (as if living trees just aren't up to the challenge) so as to mitigate climate change, but it is not at all clear where the "profit centre" would be for such a technology, except perhaps from industries hoping to offset their carbon emissions by paying for artificial trees. On the other hand, all lights are green for the further exploitation of Alberta's Athabasca tar sands, which is an environmental disaster from beginning to end, but immensely profitable nevertheless (CBC-TV, *Tipping Point*, 2011).

Third, technology has limits inherent in the laws of nature. No technology can arbitrarily reverse the laws of thermodynamics, for example, or the law of conservation of matter and energy. It is precisely because natural laws operate with ironclad consistency that marvelous things can be done which appear to violate those laws. Powered flight of heavier than air craft that appear to defy gravity, for example, is possible only because of the laws of aerodynamics. Therefore, unless and until scientists discover a way of making water flow uphill, creating matter out of energy, arbitrarily changing the properties of chemical elements or increasing their quantities, we must find a way of fashioning a good life on the planet we have, with the resources available, and within the general conditions needed to sustain a productive community of other living things. Such limits, while we often aren't entirely sure precisely where they are, are immovable whenever we hit them (Robert *et al.* 2002, 197-214).

Fourth, no technology ever solves just one problem without creating other problems of its own (Tenner 1996). This is probably because every technological introduction is being made within an already hugely complex and interdependent system of pre-existing relationships which can result in consequences that are difficult to foresee. An example of this mixed-bag principle can be found in the construction of large scale hydro-electric dams. Dam building projects are often sold by appealing to the many advantages they can bring to people including elect-rification, flood control, providing recreational water in dam back-bays, water for irrigation and drought mitigation, and jobs both during construction and following commissioning. But such projects also have their downsides. It's impossible, for example, to optimize a dam to deliver all of its potential benefits at the same time. If we want maximum power generation then water retention will be compromised. If we want maximum irrigation water available, we may have to reduce power generation and take a loss on power revenues. If we want to maximize tourism and recreational potential, then both irrigation withdrawals and flow-through for power generation must be curtailed. While large dams operating at design efficiency can indeed generate cheap electricity, they have very high capital costs that must be serviced whether or not the dam is operating at peak output, and the availability of cheap energy may attract other industries into the area, which can have other unwelcome consequences for both human and non-human inhabitants. On top of all these trade-offs are a myriad of potential negative effects such as changes in downstream water ecology due to damming the river in the first place, flooding of back bays with possible displacement of pre-existing natural and human communities (the Three Gorges Dam project in China, for example, has displaced nearly 3 million people from their homes and traditional livelihoods), back bay siltation that eventually renders the dam useless, land subsidence and increased seismic risks due to the weight of water behind the dam, and of course, the potential for dam collapse with downstream flooding and loss of life. The larger the scale at which any technology is implemented, the larger the scale of both its potential benefits and its damages.

While technological mega-projects can certainly produce mega-problems, the mixed bag principle operates at small scales as well. For example, 70% of the contestants in Paralympics events are road accident victims. Low-nicotine tobacco has doubled the consumption of cigarettes. Motorists who have airbags and seat belts drive on average 20% faster than other motorists. More highways create more traffic; more lanes on the roads cause more queues. Crosswalks lead to more accidents involving pedestrians. To prevent the destruction of police cameras by speed demons, cameras have been installed to keep an eye on the speed cameras. The sturdier the chassis of a car, the harder it is to free the causalities trapped inside. Air conditioning affects the ozone layer, and contributes to the greenhouse effect. The cooling of offices, in other words, contributes to the heating of the atmosphere. Mad cows are the result of recycled butchers' waste. The consumption of paper in offices has increased since the introduction of computers. The development of cushioned jogging shoes intended to protect the knees has increased wear and tear on the hips. Filters for purifying tap water have proved an ideal breeding ground for bacteria. Suntan lotion is now suspected to cause skin cancer (von Boxsel 2004).

I'm not arguing that technology must be abandoned in order to have a good or sustainable life. Far from it. I only mean to highlight that technology is a mixed bag, and sometimes a lethal bag. Since there are now very many humans trying to share the same earth, and we have already made a large and ever-growing footprint, and we tend to gravitate, for economic reasons, toward large scale technologies, and many of our technologies are highly toxic to living things—all of these facts plead for bringing more mindfulness to our relationship with technology. And this must begin with an assessment of whether we need a given technology in the first place—not simply its profit potential.

Fifth, while it is certainly possible to imagine better technology than we now have for addressing many human needs, it's hard to imagine any technology that would have no environmental impacts at all. Every technology is a process by which human beings convert natural resources and energy into other forms we find useful or amusing. No matter how efficient or "green" this process may be, it will always create some waste, some expenditure of energy, some imprint left by extracting the resources needed to construct the product, in short, some change in the world. If we understand having a good life as limitless expansion of consumption, then no matter how green our technology, the human footprint on earth will inexorably expand. Better technology slows the pace at which this degradation occurs, but only replacing the consumer culture narrative of the good life promises to limit such damage definitively.

Next, we can see a curious paradox connected with the use of almost any green or conserving technology. This is the "Jevons' Paradox" named for the nineteenth-century British economist William Stanley Jevons (Alcott 2005, 9-12). Jevons observed that technological advances that increased the efficiency with which a particular resource was used (in his case, coal) resulted in increased consumption of the resource. It is probably a slight variant of this same paradox that can find even dedicated sustainability advocates making heroic efforts to reduce their consumption of certain resources like energy, only to take the savings they enjoy and spend them on more consumption. The tenacity of this paradox is evidence of how deeply rooted consumerist values can be in that when we want to reward ourselves for conserving choices, the first thing that comes to mind is something consumptive. An example of this is an acquaintance of mine whose concern for the environment is beyond doubt and who was thrilled to hear from me various measures she could take to reduce consumption of resources in her household. She then said, "Well, if I do all those things, I could probably save enough in a year to go visit my family in Britain!"—a trip which would have required air travel that would pretty much offset all the gains she achieved by her other household efficiencies. Thus it appears to be the case that as long as a consumerist worldview remains in place, developing and implementing more sustainable technologies may only shift consumption activities onto other classes of goods and services, perhaps with even higher environmental impacts than before.

Finally, every technology creates vested economic interests that once in place can become perverse to further progress on sustainability. The vested interests represented by oil companies and auto manufacturers are examples well known to everyone. But I encountered another instance of vested interest when I was invited to deliver a keynote presentation to a regional environmental industry association. While the 500 or so people in the room described themselves as the "environment industry," they were mostly owners and CEOs of waste handling and toxic clean-up firms. I was supposed to deliver an inspirational message about the importance of waste management and recycling to a sustainable economy as well as point out opportunities for development of their industry. I said, however, that if we were really serious about sustainability, every company in the room needed to start planning to transform itself into something completely different—maybe materials supply and reprocessing businesses, or something of the sort. When all the faces looked blank, I realized what they wanted to hear were ideas about new markets for their present businesses. What I told them was that their businesses currently depend on a steady supply of wastes and toxins that no sustainable society of the future could ever generate. Surely we would recycle materials. But the long caravans of compactor trucks heading for the landfills must become a thing of the past. If they wanted to thrive in the future, they must find a way of making themselves obsolete but stay in business in the process. My message was not well received. Nevertheless, we can find many examples of businesses, some of them quite large, that depend for their profitability on the continuation of problems we need to eliminate (Orr 1999). In so far as they represent vested economic interests and voter constituencies, they can also be roadblocks to a more sustainable way of life.

4. Separating the Wheat from the Chaff: Technology and Mindful Sufficiency

> If you would set to work creating the new technology, abandon all complex tools. They are misconceptions. All the brilliant discoveries and inventions of our times will be made with our minds and hands and senses, aided by simple tools and concepts. (Williams 1973, 139)

In taking up the topic of how the role of technology might change in a culture oriented toward voluntary simplicity, it is of course tempting to spool off a list of present technologies that would disappear (cars, fossil fuels, etc.) and the alternative technologies that might supplement or replace them (bicycles, solar energy, etc.). The problem with this approach is that it can get us tangled up in debates about the leaves on the tree without giving any attention to the roots and the trunk. In any culture, the specific technical innovations that emerge will largely be determined by the values and consciousness guiding development of them. So for our purposes, I would like to focus attention on these higher level issues and leave debates about the relative merits of different technical devices to those qualified to discuss them.

Certainly, any culture of mindful sufficiency would embrace technology as the powerful adaptive asset that it is. But I think it is also essential that technology would be subordinated to mindfulness and not allowed to run rampant as it does in consumer culture. Part of this subordination (i.e., to assign something a lower place) involves continuous and clear mindfulness of technology as a means to an end, and not an end in itself. Moreover, the end that technology exists to serve is the well-being of the whole life system of the Earth, not mere comfort, or mere profit, or dominance and oppression of others, or pleasure heedless of its consequences for others. Finally, a guiding value would be that of *sufficiency*; that technology is something we use to make sufficient provision for legitimate needs, not to maximize consumption for its own sake.

But just how, in a practical sense, might we subordinate technology to mindfulness and the requirements of a way of life expressing sufficiency rather than affluence? This implies bringing some measure of mindful discernment to each new technological enterprise, whether that is a decision to develop a new technology, to adopt one already developed, or to continue to maintain something already in place. We envision here an unhurried, deeply introspective "holding" of a proposal, idea, or project in awareness so that the full range of our perceptions and intuitions can arise in response to it. We need to take time to consider as many of its relationships, implications, and possible consequences as we can foresee. The process of holding a technology in mindful awareness, together with interrogating the technology in terms of certain principles and values, I will call *discernment*. So let's address the question of subordinating technology to mindfulness in two parts: (a) what principles and values might we use to interrogate technological development in order to subordinate it to mindful sufficiency, and (b) who has authority to perform this task of discernment and implement the results?

One way of structuring our consideration of technology is first to identify three levels at which we can bring mindfulness to technology. I use the word *levels* deliberately, because they represent what I see as a non-negotiable hierarchy of dependencies that arises from the nature of how things work on our planet. Levels cannot be substituted and they cannot be arbitrarily re-arranged. Moreover, the levels cannot be *balanced* as some models of sustainability now try to do, because they are not competing political constituencies who can be satisfied through skillful compromises where every party "gives a little." A technology contributes to a culture of simple living and mindful sufficiency when it passes various tests of discernment at all levels. If it violates any of the tests at any level, the technology is more or less toxic to sustainability. I make no claim that the criteria I am proposing are exhaustive. My aim in identifying these criteria for discernment is to keep them as simple, and few in number as possible while also assuring that they have substantial scientific and ethical coherence. Moreover, I am not aiming to create any sort of quantitative (protocol that can be applied mechanically to the evaluation of technologies, but rather a framework or sort of check list that can holistically enrich and inform intuitive discernment as to what is or isn't good for us and the planet.

Most readers of the sustainability literature will be familiar with the customary appeal to ecological, economic, and social dimensions of sustainability. I'm happy to adopt these as the three levels at which we interrogate technology, but with the following proviso—which is not always customary: In a sustainable culture, the economy is a system which synergistically resides *within* society just the way a cell organelle might reside synergistically within a cell, or a cell reside synergistically within an organ or larger body. Correspondingly, human society resides synergistically within the ecosphere, the community of all life on Earth. I want to stress that the nested relationship of these systems, the ecosphere being the largest and most independent, with human society carried within it, and the economy within our society, is non-arbitrary and non-negotiable. Should economic activities in any way contradict the requirements of human social well-being, then they become toxic (oppressive, prejudicial, inequitable, unhealthy) to sustainability and seal both their own demise and perhaps that of the society within which they subsist. I say "perhaps" because a toxic economy might, in a society that can subordinate its economy to mindfulness, be replaced with a differently structured economic system that is less toxic. Likewise, certain aspects of culture (the complex of functions, beliefs, etc., that define a society) can be toxic to the long-term relationship between people and the ecosphere. These toxic aspects of culture may be expressed through the society's economic system, but they could be expressed in other ways as well. Evidence suggests that Easter

Island society nearly extinguished itself by depleting island resources, not in pursuit of material affluence, but through religious and possibly social competition for status expressed through statue building. In the end, it came to the same thing—decimation of the island's ecosystems and the dramatic collapse of its human population.

So I'm suggesting that we interrogate technology at three levels: the ecological, social, and economic. But what questions shall we pose? There have been a great number of principles, guidelines, and requirements suggested for a sustainable culture by a variety of proponents for at least forty years. It is beyond the scope of this chapter to review and debate them all. My aim is more modest. I hope to offer an approach with representative criteria of how this discernment process might work. We must fully appreciate that if serious action is taken on this proposal, it will probably entail a protracted process of discovery and trial and error construction of a more definitive and well-documented list of discernment criteria. Nevertheless, we must make a start to get the idea. As a general principle, it would seem beneficial to seek the fewest number criteria at the highest level of generality and applicability as possible. Many sustainability criteria that have been proposed over the years have been variations on the same fundamental themes. Our aim will be always, in this present exercise and afterward, to seek out the simplest and most universally applicable themes so as to yield the shortest and most lucid list of discernment criteria.[22]

---

[22] I fully appreciate that this topic overlaps the traditional field of sustainability indicators with all of the complications this involves. But I'm hoping to frame this discussion not in terms of the technical aspects of the metrics involved in measuring sustainability performance or environmental damage, but rather taking a step back to the level where the discussion has more to do with what we value than how we measure it. This approach assumes that the decision to undertake or abandon any technical development consists of at least two parts: (a) the matter of whether or not such a development should be undertaken, that it's something we want, that it's something that will advance the core values and aims of our way of life, and then (b) how specifically do we measure the impacts of this or that technology (the indicator question per se).

4.1 *Ecological criteria*

The ecological criteria for sustainability are much easier to specify than to implement. They are essentially based on laws of chemistry, physics, and ecology that represent non-negotiable limits on human activities within a living and productive ecosphere. One of the most succinct and well-documented statements of these principles is available in The Natural Step system conditions (Robert et al. 2002, 197-214). I am paraphrasing the first three system conditions that directly relate to ecological sustainability, to put them in the form of questions that we might ask ourselves about any given proposed or existing technology in order to discern its consistency with a culture of mindfulness and sufficiency.

Will this technology systematically increase concentrations in the ecosphere of substances from the Earth's crust?

"Substances from the Earth's crust" consist of any minerals that can be mined from the crust of the Earth including fossil fuels. The concern is that as people extract these materials and concentrate them at the surface of the Earth without recycling them, or burn them and release their combustion products as is the case with fossil fuels, the concentrations of these materials will accumulate in the ecosphere until they reach some point, often unknown, when changes may occur to the ecosphere that threaten life in general, or human life in particular. We have only to look at the growing evidence for climate change driven by our use of fossil fuels for a prime example of this concern. But minerals yielding metals such as lead, mercury, cadmium, arsenic, and fissile materials like uranium all present risks of their own. Moreover, they are risks to all living things, not just humans.

But not only must we be concerned about minerals and metals that are toxic in their own right, non-toxic metals like iron, aluminum, tin, etc., require very energy-intensive refining processes thus representing high levels of what is called *embodied energy*—the energy needed to refine them from their parent ores. As these materials are manufactured into products for human use, they tend to be dispersed around the world in very small amounts, i.e., the waste represented by the worn out product which may not be recycled. An unsustainable economy is one that continually leaks materials derived from limited deposits of high grade ores to millions of small waste dumps, landfills, waste middens, and other locations around the world, none of which is large enough or close enough to a sizable market to qualify as a future high-grade deposit of that metal or material. The result is that future generations will have to invest even more time, labour, and energy to collect and re-concentrate these materials so that they are once again industrially useful. In many cases they will have been combined in alloys or composite materials so as to make them impossible to recycle at realistic levels of energy and labour investment.

Thus, the extraction of minerals from the Earth's crust represents a double threat: (a) the threat of direct toxicity due to the chemical properties of some substances themselves, and (b) the threat that all materials from the Earth's crust are being extracted and dispersed in the ecosphere in such small amounts or in such adulterated forms that they become economically lost to future generations. Minimizing these dual threats implies: (a) reducing our use of materials mined from the Earth's crust to such levels as can be replaced by the natural geophysical processes that concentrate such materials in the first place (regrettably, an extremely slow process), and/or (b) after mining and refining such materials, to use them only for essential applications and with the most scrupulous attention to conservation and recycling, and/or (c) developing substitutes whereby materials that are scarce, toxic, or energy intensive to procure from nature can be replaced by materials that are more abundant, less toxic, and less energy intensive to procure.

Does this technology contribute to systematic increases in the concentrations of substances in the ecosphere produced by society?

The technology developed and deployed by consumer culture is continually manufacturing things (substances like plastics, persistent pesticides, CFCs, PCBs, etc.) that persist in the ecosphere for long periods without biodegrading. Sometimes these materials are carcinogenic (cancer-causing), mutagenic (mutation-causing), or teratogenic (deformity-causing) on their own. Sometimes, as is the case with many plastics, manufacturing them is toxic, or else they simply break down in the environment into smaller and smaller particles until they are ingested or otherwise interfere with other plants and animals (e.g., as when birds, fish, or ocean mammals become entangled in plastic wrap, fishing nets or other detritus, or when birds, fish, and turtles ingest bits of plastic thinking they are food). The large-scale process of human beings converting materials derived from the ecosphere, even materials that are renewable like forest products, represents a gradual conversion of the living, biodegradable systems of the ecosphere to a gradually more artificial, non-living and non-biodegradable waste heap. The concern is that if this way of life continues, a way of life that conflates maximizing consumption of this sort as constituting the good life, these materials will reach concentrations, often unknown, when changes may occur to the ecosphere that threaten life in general, and human life in particular.

A culture of mindful sufficiency must orient its technology so as never to produce goods from human-made substances that are persistent in nature or impossible to recycle, and use instead materials that are abundant, biodegradable and/or recyclable. No matter what goods are produced for human use, we must use even renewable resources with scrupulous attention to conservation and efficiency, and to minimize the population of human-made artifacts absolutely, i.e., to live simply. By so doing, we leave the maximum possible share of the ecosphere in its pristine state upon which we depend like the rest of the living community of the Earth. Technologies which promise this result would pass this criterion of discernment.

Does this technology avoid systematic physical degradation of nature through over-harvesting, introductions, and other forms of modification?

In its greed to accumulate profit, consumer culture cuts a wide swath through ecosystems in search of what it's after. Commercial trawler fishing operations that capture every species of fish of any size in order to keep only the merchantable species and discard all the rest as "bi-catch" is one example. The use of herbicides that kill every green thing except a crop plant of interest such as RoundUp Ready Canola® is another example. Non-native species are introduced to ecosystems in attempts to control populations of other species considered to be pests such as the cane toads introduced to Australia in 1935 with the intention of controlling cane grubs threatening sugar cane crops. The toads themselves became a toxic plague on the landscape.

Perhaps some of the most significant introductions to ecosystems are estrogen mimickers—invisible chemical compounds that behave in the body (both of animals and humans) in ways similar to the hormone estrogen, feminizing the organisms ingesting them resulting in both increased cancer rates and impaired reproductive function (Biello 2007; *Environmental Health Perspectives* 2005). Introductions, over-harvesting (CBC-TV, *End of the Line* 2010) and other forms of modification such as genetic manipulations or radical and large scale alteration of habitats are all ways that human beings change or reduce the ability of ecosystems to reproduce and also to maintain both their genetic and species diversity. This implies that over time, ecosystems are becoming less diverse, less resilient, and therefore more at risk of catastrophic collapse when subjected to either human-caused or natural stresses. No ecosystem can be maintained if its ability to reproduce itself and maintain its diversity and variety is being systematically destroyed by human beings. The concern is that if the consumer culture way of life continues, human-caused degradation of ecosystems, introductions and over-harvesting of resources will reach some critical level, often unknown, when changes may occur to the ecosphere that threaten life in general, and human life in particular. A culture of mindful sufficiency must thus orient its technology in such a way as not to systematically reduce the productivity of ecosystems, their genetic and species diversity, nor to introduce exotic species or toxic substances that dramatically impact the ability of such systems to replicate themselves.

Will this technology operate at such a scale as to appropriate global carrying capacity which is prejudicial to the interests of other species?

Not present among The Natural Step criteria for ecological sustainability is any mention of the proportion of carrying capacity appropriated by human beings compared to the resources which are left available for the needs of other species. This concern, that the criteria we use to interrogate technology reflect only the value we place on human life and not also value other species, is an issue that bridges ecological and social (equity) criteria. I mention it here because we must be concerned with the overall scale of the technology we use lest we more or less satisfy the first three criteria above and in the end still turn the Earth into a great human plantation. Mindfulness practice reveals to us that we are members of a vast living web of interdependent beings the majority of whom are not human. The scale of human activity on the Earth facilitated by technology is already large compared to the ecosphere itself. A culture of mindful sufficiency would therefore likely be concerned to interrogate its technology respecting its scale and the implications that large scale technologies would have for the well-being of the whole (Berry 1987).

Meeting these four criteria of ecological sustainability is extremely challenging. Almost no existing technology satisfies them all. We can buy time, in particular respecting renewable resources, by reducing the overall human population, adopting strong forms of voluntary simplicity, and then reducing the scale of the economy relative to the ecosphere. But our aim must be to fashion a culture that lives harmoniously within these four criteria. We have no choice. Each criterion represents one or another non-negotiable law of nature. We cannot defy them any more than we can cancel gravity. Therefore, any technology, new or existing, that we bring into the discernment process of our mindfulness practice must satisfy these four ecological criteria for sustainability or it will not pass the test for inclusion in a culture of mindful sufficiency. Realistically, it is probably impossible to conserve the advantages of an advanced civilization without compromising these criteria to some degree. But our aim must always be to work hard to find the least damaging compromise and always to replace the compromise with a less damaging one as soon as better technology becomes available. And we must always remain conscious of the fact that with each compromise we make, we push against immovable laws of nature which always has consequences (effects), sometimes unforeseeable, and sometimes even difficult for humans to perceive given our natural and technical equipment for registering change in the world.

A significant contribution in this regard has been made by the Union of Concerned Scientists to the issue of how individual consumption choices can contribute to, or help reduce, ecological impact, and with it, a variety of related health and well-being consequences (Brower & Leon 1999). While Brower and Leon

(1999) specifically discount voluntary simplicity as a viable socio-cultural alternative to consumerism, they go on to do the simplicity movement a great service by helping to establish an empirical basis for ranking which human activities have the most impact on ecological footprint. Their research indicates three clear areas where the "technology" of simplicity should concentrate its developmental efforts: (a) transportation, (b) food production, (c) household operations and community planning. Clearly, there are linkages among these three areas, but based on their research, the *ecological* practice of simple living would imply a mostly pedestrian or mass transit solution to transportation needs, an organic, locally produced vegetarian or vegan diet, and a much more intensive and efficient approach to urban design than is current today—probably something closer to the leading edge work being done by Paolo Soleri at Arcosanti (Soleri accessed 2012). The Arcosanti experiment has demonstrated that by changing settlement designs, the need for transportation can be drastically reduced or eliminated and food production can be partly integrated with housing and manufacturing activities. This more integrated approach to human settlements also happily results in a slower-paced life which is simpler and highly conducive to mindfulness. Our current approach to settlement design, and particularly the persistence of suburbs, virtually assures a rushed, automobile-dependent, and high consumption way of life—things which simply won't be sustainable in a carbon-constrained future. Thus one important step in the direction of simpler living will be not to fan out into rural areas seeking a renewal of nineteenth-century agrarian culture, but just the reverse: the construction of high density, compact, and automobile free urban centres that are beautiful, healthy, self-reliant, and rewarding places to live.

4.2 *Social criteria*

Taking up the question of what might be the social criteria that a technology would have to satisfy in a culture of mindful sufficiency is a more complicated and contentious question than that of ecological sustainability. Regardless of what they are, however, we must remain ever aware of the fact that a sustainable culture must *in every way* satisfy the criteria of ecological sustainability in order to thrive. Consumer culture violates ecological sustainability mainly through its economy because it's an intensely materialistic and growth-oriented way of life. But as mentioned above in the Easter Island example, even if we forego the pursuit of affluence in favour of something else—wisdom, say, or happiness—we must always pursue these using technology which conforms within the ecological limits available to us. When our technological aspirations contradict planetary limits, it's the desires that must evolve, not indulging the delusion that we can somehow ignore planetary limits.

There seems to be *some* consensus on *some* of the social criteria that a technology serving a culture of mindful sufficiency would need to meet. I will review these first. Following are some miscellaneous criteria which I think are equally important, but less often mentioned in the sustainability literature.

How will this technology affect meeting human needs (economic, social, intellectual, material, aesthetic, spiritual) more equitably within and between countries, human generations, and species?

The concept of *equity* is complex but suffice it that equity is not exactly the same thing as direct equivalency since equity recognizes differences in needs whereas equivalency does not. But there is a general recognition that substantial equality of incomes can reduce both social conflict and ill health (Smith 1996). Equity strengthens the cooperative engagement of everyone in society needed to meet truly momentous collective challenges. Greater equity in sharing the primary productive capacity of the planet between human beings and other species would assure their access to the resources they need to sustain their own lives with possible long-term benefits for people as well (Wackernagel *et al.* 2002, 9266-9271). A more equitable level of consumption practiced by the current generation can help future generations avoid unacceptably high opportunity costs incurred because of their ancestors' over-consumption (Daly 1995). More equitable opportunities to participate in decision-making, including decisions respecting what technologies to adopt, can help avoid patterns of development that promote the interests or reflect the values of privileged elites while demoting and prejudicially marginalizing the values of the poor, women, and social minorities (Mies & Bennholdt-Thomsen 1999). Equity may sound like an altruistic luxury unaffordable for those who believe that life is pervaded by scarcity and competition. But behaving in equitable ways is the form that enlightened self-interest takes when our perception is transformed through mindfulness practice that reveals the deep interdependence and connectedness that pervades the universe. Technologies which, either by design or unintended consequence, systematically promote equity in the world also will systematically promote sustainability.

In what ways, if any, might this technology be perverse to maintaining the level of human population necessary for sustainability?

Many authorities on sustainability recognize that over-population is a key factor threatening the future of any civilized way of life. Clearly, consumption levels are inequitable within our current population. Growth in population promises only to aggravate both inequality and environmental impacts. There is also general agreement that it would be a good thing for the Earth's entire living community if the population of humans ceased growing and indeed, could achieve a substantial, non-violent and equitable reduction to a level around 1-1.5 billion worldwide—considerably below its current 7.0 billion. Population multiplied by the efficiency of prevailing Technology, multiplied by some measure of consumption expectations is seen as a function predictive of environmental load, or the demand being placed on the Earth's carrying capacity for our species (Wackernagel & Rees, 1995). Thus any technology being interrogated from the perspective of a culture of mindful sufficiency would need to demonstrate that its adoption would not be perverse in some way to promoting a sustainable level of human population.

In what ways are the effects this technology is likely to have consistent with or contrary to the promotion of holistic health?

Ever since Rachel Carson published *Silent Spring* in 1962, we have been sensitized to the potential impacts of industrial pollutants on human health as well as the health of other species. But by introducing this criterion, I mean to refer to *holistic health*, that is, wellness in its full array of meanings. This includes absence of physical disease or disability, to be sure, but also psychological, social, spiritual, intellectual, and economic well-being. A technical introduction should not make people or other beings sick—in any way. Technology should not be corrosive to the moral fabric of society.[23] Technology should not intensify social conflict and anxiety by promoting the welfare of some at the expense of others.[24] It should not addict us or socially isolate us or promote a sedentary lifestyle so extreme that it drives other physical and emotional disease processes (Alexander, Bruce K. 2001). It should not create benefits for us that are bought by externalizing the costs of the technology to other species or future generations.

How has this technology arisen from a participatory design and review process in which the interests of all parties affected by the technology have been represented and protected, including those of non-human species?

This criterion is formulated to reflect the broad concern that many technologies have been developed without due regard for their impact on others. This may take the form of inequitable sharing of benefits, or of risks, or of costs, or inequities in whose values are being promoted by the technology at the expense of someone else's values. The value of participation is multi-faceted in that it is believed often to contribute to better design solutions (Orr 1999), to help assure that technical introductions will be work-enhancing rather than labour-replacing (Schumacher 1973), that development promotes our collective interest in

---

[23] Among his "bio-physical and ethico-social limits to growth" economist Herman Daly has observed: "The desirability of growth is limited by the corrosive effects on moral capital of the very attitudes that foster growth, e.g., glorification of self-interest and the technocratic-reductionistic world view." (Herman Daly, *Steady State Economics* 2nd ed., [Washington, DC: Island Press, 1995], chapter 9).

[24] Also see Daly 1995: "The desirability of aggregate growth is limited by its self-canceling effects on individual welfare. i.e., aggregate growth cannot possibly make all people richer than all other people. Relative improvement is a zero sum game in the aggregate." (Herman Daly, *Steady State Economics* 2nd ed., [Washington, DC: Island Press, 1995], chapter 9).

preserving the global commons (Wackernagel & Rees 1995), and that technologies help promote retention of local control over the means of subsistence as well as enhancing synergies among people and between people and nature (Mies & Bennholdt-Thomsen 1999). Implementing technical innovations without a participatory process not only leaves significant parts of the community feeling bypassed and therefore alienated from the development, it may fail to include potentially game-changing input based on local knowledge of opportunities and constraints that might help assure the success of the introduction. Therefore, any technology being interrogated from the perspective of mindful sufficiency must arise from or be subject to a participatory development and evaluation process, about which I will say more below.

So far, I have proposed four key tests that any technology needs to pass if it is likely to contribute to a culture of mindful sufficiency: (a) equity; (b) promoting population control; (c) promoting holistic health; and (d) arising from a participatory design process. In addition to these, I would like to introduce a somewhat longer list of other criteria, but with less documentation and explanation than the previous four. I hope that their relevance to a technical evaluation process from the perspective of mindfulness is self-evident:

How will this technology promote non-violence?

Clearly, any culture which places mindfulness of interdependence among its most central guiding insights will be anxious to promote technologies that are non-violent to the greatest practicable degree. Humans by nature are heterotrophs, meaning that we must consume other organisms to sustain our lives. While we are not free with respect to needing to consumer to live, we are most decidedly free not to live to consume. We may therefore impose on our technology the ineluctable requirement to minimize elective violence whenever we can. Of course this principle has special application to any technology being developed primarily for a military purpose.

How will this technology promote development and maintenance of mindfulness, or at least not be perverse to the cultivation of mindfulness?

Clearly, any culture that values mindfulness would want to configure its technology as much as possible so as to promote mindfulness, and to offer as few distractions as possible from a mindful way of life.

How will this technology introduce more beauty in society and/or promote the conservation of beauty?

Many of the technical artifacts of consumer culture are hideously ugly. Some of this defacement of the planet is unavoidable. But beauty is essential to a healthy soul and a humane existence. In consumer culture, beauty is reserved for the gated enclaves and private preserves of the wealthy. In a culture broadly committed to sustainability however, efforts would be made to design beautiful things for everyone to use and enjoy. This does not necessarily entail the use of exotic or expensive materials, because beauty is not simply a function of decoration or elaborate display. Quite the contrary: Beauty arises from good design and good design is almost always consistent with sustainability.

How will this technology promote the development of intellectual wealth broadly in society, or is it likely to sequester information under the control of a few?

In consumer culture and regimes of globalized corporate ownership, a growing proportion of human knowledge is proprietary and legally protected by intellectual property statutes and treaties. This arrangement is broadly beneficial to corporate interests in that it can enhance profits by depriving others of access to technical information. But it violates the original intent behind the invention of patent law—generally to help assure a reasonable level of protection to individual inventors of their livelihoods whose innovations were routinely stolen in the eighteenth and nineteenth centuries. Today, intellectual property rights regulations slow the pace of research and discovery, contribute to monopoly capitalism, vastly increase the cost of health care by making patented medicines inaccessible for decades, and allow agro-chemical companies to marginalize organic producers and independent farmers from saving and sharing their own seeds. Such practices are prejudicial to the discovery of new knowledge, to social and economic equity, and to local self-reliance, all of which are essential for a sustainable culture.

How does this technology fulfill an authentic human need without inflaming desire or generating additional needs for people? Is it something that requires the creation of a market by artificial means or additional effort to be economically viable?

In other discussions about mindfulness, I've tried to demonstrate that it is not trying to satiate desires that promotes human well-being, but reducing desire itself. Any culture intent on sustainability and the promotion of human well-being would find it highly irrational to deliberately develop technology that inflames desire, creates artificial needs or fosters addictions when we have enough of a challenge managing the desires we're born with. It makes perfect sense to create markets for goods no one really needs if your aim is generating profits. It is an irrational and self-defeating occupation if your aim is sustainability and happiness.

How is this technology worthy of the trust that our ancestors placed in us to continue the human experiment?

This criterion encourages us to bear in mind the trust we carry from the past as well as the responsibility we have for the future. What would great-grandma think if we build this thing? Is this technology leading toward a society of the sort our ancestors fought and died and suffered and sacrificed for us to live in? While many are today cynical enough to scoff at the notion that we might ever be answerable to our ancestors for the decisions we make, the insights arising from mindfulness practice reveal a different sort of universe. Nothing is lost; nothing forgotten. Our relationships with others cross time just as they do space. The voices and dreams of our ancestors are inwardly present and available to us. Anyone who takes the time to listen steadily with inward directed attention will hear them.

I've proposed ten social criteria we can use to interrogate technology concerning its consistency with a culture of mindful sufficiency. There are probably many more which I will leave to the efforts of others to identify and discuss. I noted above that no culture of mindful sufficiency could flourish using technology that violates the essential requirements for ecological sustainability. Likewise, I would suggest that no culture of mindful sufficiency can thrive if its technology violates the social criteria I've outlined as well. Admittedly, it's easier to imagine a culture tearing itself apart because of inequity than it is if the same culture is pictured betraying the historical trust of its ancestors. So some of these criteria probably make a more directly causal contribution to a sustainable culture than others. I hope that what is and isn't most essential to the vision I'm trying to share here will, through considered debate and discussion, eventually become clear. For now, we should take up the question of the economic criteria that a technology should meet to satisfy the requirements of a culture of mindful sufficiency.

4.3 Economic criteria

The economy is a system that must operate within *both* the parameters set by the laws of nature and by the ecosphere, *and* by social criteria for sustainability. While every society must have an economy of some sort, there is no reason to believe that a market capitalist economy of the sort that now dominates the world is the penultimate development. Market capitalism gets rave reviews from economists and the affluent minorities of developed countries, i.e., from those whom the system currently benefits. Its global dominance may be attributed at least as much to the fact that it is the last system standing after the Cold War slug-fest of the 1950s-1980s as to any intrinsic virtues of its own. But market capitalism with its ravenous growth dynamics and the glaring income inequities it creates is clearly neither ecologically nor socially sustainable over the long run. Moreover, in any economy of mindful sufficiency, economics serves society, and no attempt would be made as is currently popular, to use economic principles to manage either society or the ecosphere. This would be like trying to force all the functions of the human body to conform to the rules governing a liver or a kidney. Even if such rules were perfectly well understood, a claim we can scarcely make for economics, they would still be inadequate for the management of much larger and clearly superordinate systems, the cultural and environmental ecology of human society.

It's also necessary to assure that we are framing the following discussion properly. We are searching for economic criteria by which we can interrogate technology for its consistency with a culture of mindful sufficiency. This is a somewhat limited project and doesn't amount to an attempt to design an alternate economic system, no matter how desirable that might be.

Herman Daly (1995) has already pointed out that for an economy to be sustainable, it must be subject to two sets of constraints which do not arise from any of the self-regulating mechanisms of markets. Limits on the *scale* of the economy must be established based on scientific observation of the ecosphere. Limits on *distribution of benefits* produced by the economy must be established according to socio-ethical norms. The same might be said for technology. With the exception of the proportion of the resources, space and net primary production which should be left available for the use of other species, limits on scale have already been effectively addressed by the ecological criteria mentioned above. What remains are the socio-ethical considerations arising from mindfulness and valuing sufficiency that may have relevance to technology.

How will this technology help to meet real needs while incurring a reduced demand for resources, energy, and human labour?

This criterion is intended to reflect the value of leisure, that leisure is required for the cultivation and maintenance of mindfulness, and to pursue the intrinsic sources of well-being which are given priority in a mindful way of life. It also reflects the desire for ecological efficiency in meeting human material needs. The purpose of technology within such a culture thus becomes that of making the economy more efficient in delivering what is needed for a life of mindful sufficiency, but always at a diminishing demand for resources, energy, and human labour. The purpose of the economy under such a regime is to provision material needs, not generate monetary riches for shareholders in the first instance. Technology in such a system is intended to liberate both people and the ecosphere from excessive through-put of materials and energy in meeting the material needs of society. Work is more driven by motives that arise from mindfulness and is less driven by material needs or the compulsive pursuit of profit.

How will this technology enhance human well-being, and particularly, the quality of the work experience of the people using it?

I have drawn heavily on E. F. Schumacher's insightful work *Small Is Beautiful* in writing this essay and want to reference him one more time in relation to the role technology plays in work. Schumacher proposes that work has three purposes: "...to give a [person] a chance to utilize and develop [his/her] faculties; to enable [him/her] to overcome [his/her] ego-centeredness by joining with other people in a common task; and to bring forth the goods and services needed for a becoming existence (Schumacher 1973, 39)." From this perspective, work is an activity that promotes community, development of character, and sustenance of livelihood, not solely or primarily profit. While production enterprises must be profitable to be sustainable (must create more ecological and social value than they destroy), this is not the same thing as supposing that profit is the single bottom line in relation to which every other value must find its relative place or can be sacrificed. On the contrary, if work is a means of personal and community development, then it can never be eliminated without also eliminating these ways of perfecting oneself as a person and a neighbour. Well-designed *tools* make the activities of work safer, easier, and more pleasant. Automated machinery, by replacing human workers and over simplifying the tasks of those who cannot be replaced, essentially destroys these values. Since the development of character, the skills necessary for a healthy self-reliance, and community solidarity and cooperation are all values prized in a culture of mindful sufficiency, technology that enhances these values would be adopted and technologies that undermine them would probably be avoided or discarded.

Can this technology operate on current sunlight?

It's now generally recognized even by the petroleum industry itself that our endowment of fossil fuels is limited and will eventually be exhausted, probably sooner rather than later. Even burning remaining proven reserves promises to contribute to climate changes the effects of which are already impacting human societies. Unless a breakthrough is achieved in fusion technology (which seems to have been "40 years away" for at least the last fifty years), we face equally inflexible limits in the supply of uranium for fission reactors as well—enough to meet world energy demand for only a few decades if uranium became the primary fuel for the global economy (*Wikipedia* 2011). As is often pointed out, the only reliable long-term source of energy is the sun and any culture aiming to sustain itself over the long-term must be powered by current solar energy.

How does this technology return a real benefit to the material economy (well-being) or is it something that generates only a monetary increase (riches)?

A number of thinkers and social commentators have noted our deplorable tendency to mistake a symbol representing something for the thing itself (Daly 1995; Dominguez & Robin 1992; Raven 1995, 46-48). Nowhere in consumer culture is this more common than in relation to money. A culture of mindful sufficiency would include exercises that help people toward clear awareness of the difference between a hand full of money and actual food, or shelter, or clothing, or a transportation service. So mesmerized are we by the conflation of money with the material things it can be exchanged for, that we look to money for security rather than look to intact and productive ecosystems; we look to money for a good life rather than look to the quality of our friendships and family relations; we also think an increase in our portfolio values will secure our future more surely than cultivating equitable relationships in society. Money is an extremely useful instrument for lubricating commerce and can help effect economic transactions far more easily than was the case when pure barter and trade were our only options. Money is a psychological abstraction, an idea, rather similar to say, a centimeter. Centimeters are useful for measuring things and without them, it is fairly difficult (though not entirely impossible) to build a house. We create difficulties for ourselves however, when we let ideas become more real to us than physical realities. It makes perfect sense to most people to say, "I couldn't build a house because a bank wouldn't give me a loan." But this makes about as much sense as saying, "I need a house; lumber and carpenters are available; we have the land; but we couldn't get any centimeters (Watts d. 1973)." The insights and clarity of consciousness that is cultivated during mindfulness practice can help disentangle illusions like this and liberate us from their almost hypnotic influence.

Sustainability requires that we notice different things about our experience. Governments and businesses are obsessed with the price of things to the prejudice of noticing what is happening to them in physical reality. The Earth notices physical realities. Earth really doesn't care how much we spend on anything, but she certainly cares and notices how much material and energy is being cycled through the human economy. It is these "through-puts" of energy and matter that we need to attend to if sustainability is our aim. Having money is just as useful as having centimeters, depending on what we want to do. But Earth cares about the lumber we're buying and measuring and how many trees died to provide it. A culture of mindful sufficiency would pay attention to this too and assure that all its technology could pass a similar test.

How will this technology contribute to local / regional self-reliance and self-provisioning, or does it encourage dependency on transportation and distant sources of supply?

This criterion posits that despite the economic advantages of globalization and the technology that supports it, such an economy may not be socially or ecologically efficient. If our concern is sufficiency, not affluence, and strengthening networks of local, face-to-face relationships, minimizing the environmental impacts of transportation, and keeping principles of equity and economic justice in view because we want to honour the interdependencies we perceive, then a more locally self-reliant economy is preferable to a globalized one. Technologies that are useful to a more localized economy would probably be more consistent with a culture of mindful sufficiency. Such a choice will not maximize economic efficiency, but as I pointed out above, the economy now tends to confuse what is monetarily profitable with efficient provision of "use values." An economy that attended more closely to use values (the material reality of things and how much use they are to us), might be less monetarily profitable, but it could serve real human needs much more efficiently and in greater synergy with the ecosphere.

It is likely that more economic criteria for evaluation of technology could be framed, but the five I have already mentioned should be sufficient to illustrate the principle. Thus, I envision an essentially contemplative process that would compare the characteristics and claims made by proponents of a new or existing technology against the criteria we have been discussing to discern their alignment with the values and worldview of a culture of mindful sufficiency. There remains the question of just how this process might work, and who would carry it out?

5. Who Dreamed up this Thing Anyway?

I'm sure that all readers can think of many examples from their own experience of having to purchase or adapt to technological devices, upgrades and improvements they never asked for or even wanted. Progress, far from being a steady improvement in our well-being, has become a dizzying and increasingly involuntary experience of adjusting to changes that seem to be hatched in the shadows like Orcs in caves. Who dreams this stuff up anyway, and who is watch-dogging them?

The worldview of consumer culture, heavily influenced by laissez-faire capitalism, favours the fantasy that innovations are brought to us by backyard inventors who hatch ideas and bring them to market in pursuit of the Horatio Alger myth of the self-made millionaire. This is true in just enough cases to keep the myth alive. But the vast majority of new technology these days is invented by teams of scientists and engineers working for corporations. The technology they develop is mostly shrouded in proprietary secrecy until designs are submitted for patents and products are unveiled for sale to the public. Apart from minimalist licensing and safety testing requirements, the creators of technical innovations are accountable to no one except the market. Which technologies get adopted and which disappear is something decided in a process of natural selection that would have made Darwin proud. The actual agent of selection is the individual consumer. The entire system operates on the assumption that individual consumers are sovereign in their consumption choices and as little as possible should be done to constrain that freedom, though corporations certainly aim to influence those decisions through advertising and other incentives. What people want is inferred from what they are willing to buy, but this is always a *post hoc* process often following the introduction of things no one has asked for. Thus we conclude that what people wanted is what they bought, and therefore the technology they will buy is the technology that *should* exist. Of course missing from this minuet is any comparison of what the market likes with the superordinate criteria of what the planet can stand to have around. Mindfulness of the life of the whole gets lost in the fog of individuals in hot pursuit of pleasure and prestige.

I have already suggested that a culture of mindful sufficiency might include some organ, probably institutional, that could apply to decisions about the development or retention of technologies a process of mindful discernment guided by the evaluation criteria I proposed above. I imagine this process happening well in advance of the introduction of such technologies to the open market. To some, this will sound like a "socialist" plot to subordinate consumer choice to a hidden green agenda. To this, I can only say my agenda is definitely green, but it is not hidden. In fact, all of our consumer choices are already subordinated to the corporate agendas of profit and consumption maximization through designed obsolescence. Libertarians who think consumer culture offers them the freedom to purchase whatever they like should just try to purchase foods free of chemical additives and genetically modified ingredients, or non-polluting forms of transportation, or environmentally-safe cleaning products, or affordable access to natural places which offer silence and solitude, or homes with enough privacy to allow having sex on the patio without your picture winding up on Google Earth.

I have participated in several public consultation processes over the years related to various real estate or corporate developments which sometimes involve the introduction of new technology to the community or bioregion. In every single case, these consultations have been *post hoc* exercises. It is very clear that the proposed development has been planned and discussed behind closed doors far in advance of any consultation with the community. Licensing processes and hearings are often staged in such a way as to present development projects in such small parts that few reasonable objections can be raised to the parts individually, but the entire project and all its implications are never brought before the public. Such consultations are neither really public nor consultative because the community is not really being offered a veto over a project it feels will be damaging to its well-being. Rather such exercises tend to be public information sessions to satisfy the requirement of political correctness that "you be consulted." The introduction of new products to the marketplace including prior review by focus groups and product testing groups is no different.

I propose an alternative to this that I think is more in alignment with the values and worldview of a culture of mindful sufficiency. Since most technical development currently occurs under corporate control and is considered proprietary, the decisions to launch new ventures are largely taken in private and do not come under public scrutiny, if at all, until licenses must be obtained to implement the technology. Yet technology has such profound impacts on overall human well-being that this sort of approach can be justified only when profit is valued more than anything else. In any society oriented around the pursuit of overall well-being, proposals to develop technologies would be subject to a meaningful multi-step public review process from the proposal stage forward.

I want to stress that this process would be engaged *before* technical development is undertaken, or very soon after an invention is created. There needs to be some mechanism for community review of an *idea* before it attracts a vested interest of venture capitalists and technical enthusiasts and paranoid security experts and intellectual property lawyers. Communities need a way of saying, ". . . we don't even want this idea to exist...," and the basis for taking such a position can legitimately be sourced from values other than quantitative cost-benefit analysis. We can see here a basis for communities to defend themselves against technological introductions that might promise to be very profitable, but not necessarily contributive to the community's well-being. Well-being is constituted from more ingredients than just financial prosperity.

I envision for this process the creation of community-based Development Review Panels charged with reviewing development proposals of all sorts, but in this case technical development. Positioning the authority of these panels at the level of communities avoids the possibly narrow or selectively informed biases we would encounter from individual expert reviewers. It also conserves the collective memory and knowledge of local place which is often absent from centralized authorities like national governments who try to apply one-size-fits-all policies to the diversity of local situations, ecological conditions, and cultural heritages characteristic of real-life communities. Large nation-state scale entities might nevertheless provide a useful information, research, and support function to local communities as they carry out their review activities.

The Development Review Panels would be authorized to issue licenses to developers of technological and other projects, as well as declining permission to proceed. The scope of these licenses would be relatively restricted to bioregions or sub-regions within them, because a technology that may not pass the tests of mindful sufficiency in one location or cultural context might pass it in another. Over the long-term, this would promote regional diversification in technologies designed specifically for their bioregions and adapted to their unique conditions and opportunities—an ecologically efficient outcome. It would, of course, militate against the economies of scale that are offered as apologies for enormous manufacturing operations designed to provide uniform goods for mass market consumption.

Proponents of technical development will object that such a process would slow technical progress and even if it didn't, the general public is not competent or knowledgeable enough to foresee the potential benefits or judge the potential risks associated with a proposed technology.

Conversely it might be argued that technology has been evolving faster than society's ability to soberly assess its real value and to skillfully assimilate it to other important values. With the possible exception of medical innovations, most technical development is not a matter of life or death, but rather is driven by the frenzy surrounding who will profit first and most from its introduction. Slowing this process down to some degree is not likely to harm anyone. The sun will still rise in the morning whether we make one million today or two.

The aptitude of the general populace to assess the merits of proposed technical development 39represents some concern, though perhaps more directly related to the number of potential innovations to be reviewed as much as their associated scientific mysteries. Special commissions could be established to review particularly challenging proposals if necessary. Technical experts would certainly play significant roles in every review. Equally important however, is not only the scientific or technical knowledge that ordinary citizens may bring to such activities but precisely their *lack* of it. That is to say, scientific considerations are not the only important ones in living. It is exactly the power of a wider discourse here to bring into play the diversity of human feelings, intuitions, memories, and commitments that may be our best guardians of overall well-being. Those who share a technical worldview very often lack a "view of the world"—as we all do. It is therefore vitally important that we consult with each other about what we plan to do, what we hope to achieve, what we may be risking, and how this particular gadget or recipe or process contributes to or may undermine all of the conditions we know to be necessary to well-being. To liberally paraphrase the philosopher David Hume, if an idea can't be explained to a barmaid, it's not a very good idea.

Correspondingly, we need to inquire to what extent cultivating well-being requires technology at all. I'm not refuting here the fact that technology, expressed in material culture, is humanity's principal means of adapting to environmental conditions, as well as transmitting culture itself. But what I do think the practice of simple living entails is mindfulness concerning whether a particular aspect of technology actually does contribute to well-being or whether its adoption and use arises merely from the enormous psychological momentum that technology seems to have in popular culture. *Some* applications of technology improve the human situation. But it would be invalid to then conclude that since a little technology is good thing, more of it is better in every way. I would imagine that any future society oriented toward a simpler, more sustainable way of life, would probably employ less technology overall, and *different* technology in many applications.

In most respects, the transition to a culture of simple and sustainable living requires no new technology *at all*. To think so is the conceit of consumer culture's technocrats and venture capitalists. Certainly, improvements in particular technologies such as renewable energy, organic permaculture, multi-century building designs would make welcome contributions. But in general, the transition to a culture of simple living doesn't require any new inventions. Mostly what we need is less of almost everything except mindfulness, and *more* only of the wisdom to selectively adopt what really ennobles human existence rather than simply expanding profit. When the object of human life becomes the development of consciousness toward ever increasing well-being rather than the mere expansion of material cravings, we will find grounds enough to decide on what to keep and what to let go.

MARK A. BURCH

8

SIMPLICITY, SUSTAINABILITY, AND HUMAN RIGHTS

1. Introduction[25]

I don't claim any professional credentials or special expertise with respect to human rights. My perspective is that of a layperson, not a jurist, or human rights specialist. What I can bring to the conversation, however, is my perspective on simple living. About simple living I know a little, I love a great deal, I have tried to practice nearly my entire life, and which I believe to have central relevance to sustaining and extending human rights.

I also confess to certain feelings of irony. I've been talking about voluntary simplicity to anyone who will listen for almost twenty years. I've written seven books on the topic. I've given scores of workshops and taught a university undergraduate course about simple living to packed classrooms twenty-one times. I've been on television and radio and podcasts, in newspaper columns and on the Internet. I've done this because I'm utterly convinced that the broad voluntary adoption of a mindful way of life in pursuit of sufficiency rather than the semi-conscious pursuit of affluence would, if not completely cure, then dramatically reduce much of what ails humanity, including violations of human rights. What I have to say is not hard to understand. It costs nothing to do. It requires no one else's permission, and no new apps. After hearing about what voluntary simplicity is, many people wind up agreeing with me that, yes, adopting a simpler life probably would make everything a lot better. Now the irony here is that I think most of my listeners return to their familiar daily round of stress, over-work,

---

[25] A Keynote presentation delivered to the Manitoba Association of School Superintendents, Sustainability: Educating for Action Conference, November 15, 2012.

haggling, competition, debt slavery, conflict, suffering, and insecurity, now and then punctuated by weekends at the lake that only partly compensate these afflictions. So here we are: We have in our own hands all the skillful means we need to live well, but most of us don't seem able or willing to employ them. Is this not ironic? Is this not so? So please consider, if only for an hour, how you might bend all your considerable creative talents to the task of learning how to live simply and well—rather than how to live more consumptively. It's our last best hope of conserving human rights, which I aim presently to demonstrate.

My thesis is this: Environmental issues are human rights issues. We cannot hope to conserve human rights without also protecting the ecological and biophysical integrity of the Earth. Since consumer culture and its associated economic and technical developments are the prime drivers of ecological destruction, the active promotion of a culture of voluntary simplicity is essential to conserving the ecosphere, and with it, human rights.

Beliefs, ideologies, and the general run of humanity's inhumanity to itself are perennial threats to human rights. They are mainly the issues we feature in our museums and public rhetoric. But the newest and most serious threat to human rights is the changes wrought in the ecosphere by consumer culture and its obsession with economic growth. This presents a paradox for advocates of human rights since many of the entitlements we claim as human rights consist of guarantees of participation in consumer culture—the same culture that is undermining the very basis of human rights. Again ironically, this amounts to claiming the right to participate in species suicide.

2. The Universal Declaration of Human Rights

I warned you that I am a layperson in these matters, so I must start this discussion with the *UN Universal Declaration of Human Rights* (UNUDHR, 1948). I do so in the hope that this document is generally recognized as a useful touchstone for understanding what we mean by human rights. I want to begin by making the following observations:

First, the UDHR consists of 30 articles that by my reading fall into three categories:

Articles 1 and 2 consist of affirmations that we hold to be true for everyone: that we are born with rights, reason, and conscience, and that everyone is equally entitled to enjoy these rights without limitation or qualification based on race, nationality, gender, etc.

A much larger group of articles, twenty in all (Articles 3-13, 15, 16, 18-21 28-30) consists of declarations that people should be free from certain forms of abuse or oppression such as slavery, arbitrary restriction of their freedoms, threats to life and property, and the right to conditions of life that assure human dignity. I assume that this declaration applies equally to relationships between individuals, and between individuals and states. Taken together I think they express the universal human aspiration to live without suffering violence or inflicting it on others. We might think that these rights to freedom and dignity of the person would be relatively easy to secure insofar as they call on us simply to refrain from doing bad things to each other. But there is a very real ecological dimension to the these rights.

The very first item in this second group of rights affirms everyone's right to life, liberty, and security of person. But for those whose consciousness has grown to include an ecological awareness of the world, this is a rather limited view. It's all about us, human beings. But in the connected world of nature, there is no "us" without "them" also. Human life is possible only in synergy with all life on Earth. Therefore *our* right to life and whatever we think makes for liberty and security of person, must be nuanced with what assures the lives, freedom, and security of all life on Earth. We must hang together to flourish or surely we will hang separately, disappearing one species at a time. Humans are not exempt from this.

The third group of articles, eight of them (Articles 14, 17, 22-27), consist of claims to rights that imply material entitlements, or which are contingent on consumption, access to consumables, economic benefits, etc. These rights depend much more on intact ecosystems and making a transition away from consumer culture toward a steady-state economy with equitable sharing of economic benefits and risks.

In my view, in addition to its considerable and often trumpeted material benefits, consumer culture constitutes a system of oppression which paradoxically undermines both categories of rights I have just mentioned—those pertaining to the affirmation of human freedom and dignity on the one hand— and those relating to material security and well-being on the other. It seems very frequently the case that it is our pursuit of material affluence which inclines us to treat each other badly. I think this is far more often the case than the abuses that arise purely for ideological reasons. The benefits conferred by consumer culture are the velvet glove that covers the iron fist of its systemic violence.

That human rights are constantly under threat is nothing new. But what I find puzzling and paradoxical in our current approach to securing rights is that we believe it consists mostly of getting admission for all the world's people to consumer culture's pursuit of material affluence. This is peculiar because it is precisely the pursuit of affluence which is most undermining human rights. Voluntary simplicity interrogates all these fundamental beliefs of consumer culture in the most radical way.

3. Key Threats to Human Rights

Issues of human rights are being reframed worldwide by the fact that exercising these rights no longer amounts to equalizing access to an ever-growing material pie. Rather, it means equalizing the consequences of energy descent and the transition to a zero-carbon economy amidst sovereign budgetary constraint, economic contraction, and social polarization.

I see the most urgent threats to human rights today as arising from four sources:

3.1 *Traditional threats to human rights arising from ideological differences between groups*

We have lots of historical examples of these from the last century alone when European cultural arrogance fueled human rights abuses in numerous colonized territories; when Nazism threatened the extinction of Jews; when Stalinism ended the lives of millions of Ukrainians; when the Cultural Revolution in China claimed the lives of millions more; when free market fundamentalism in the United States and its allies operated through the CIA to subvert democratic elections in Central and Latin American countries; and most recently when the ideology of international jihad has cost millions of lives in the Middle East and elsewhere. It is not likely that people will soon come to a consensus on what constitutes the good life so that these sorts of threats to human rights disappear. Moreover, they would continue to constitute threats even in a world where simple living was broadly adopted. But a very convincing case has been made by Amy Chua in her book *World on Fire: How Exporting Free Market Democracy Breeds Ethnic Hatred and Global Instability* (2002), that underlying economic inequity is very often the source of what later manifests as ideological conflict when one group has made life intolerable for another and ideology merely provides the rationale for violence. To the degree that simple living can reduce economic inequity by shifting the conversation about what really contributes to well-being—while it could never eliminate ideological disagreement—might still reduce its more virulent manifestations.

As the famous British economist and philosopher E. F. Schumacher (1973, 146) observed:

> Simplicity and nonviolence are obviously closely related. As physical resources are everywhere limited, people satisfying their needs by means of a modest use of resources are obviously less likely to be at each other's throats than people depending upon a high rate of use. Nonrenewable goods must be used only if they are indispensable, and then only with the greatest care and the most meticulous concern for conservation. To use them heedlessly or extravagantly is an act of violence, and while complete nonviolence may not be attainable on this earth, there is nonetheless an ineluctable duty on [us] to aim at the ideal of nonviolence in all [that we] do.

3.2 *The threat posed to democracy by consumer culture itself*

If human rights includes an entitlement to democracy—and most of us think it does—and even if there was no extinction event staring us in the face—democracy doesn't mix very well with consumerism. If democracy is casting a ballot once every five years, then we should all be able to spare time for that. But voter participation data show nearly half of us don't even bother to do that much. Participation in democratic activities seems to be inversely proportional to national prosperity. Democracies in the world that show the highest voter turnout rates are states that have legally mandated voting.

But if democracy means election of public officials by an informed and engaged citizenry who *stay* engaged with the political process *especially* between elections—then this sort of democracy takes time and energy. Citizens must study issues, organize around common concerns, represent their views to policy makers, counterbalance the power of corporations, persist in the face of resistance. This takes more than half an hour every five years. In the current reality, it's nearly impossible to sustain a democracy of involved citizens and run the treadmill of consumerism faster and faster at the same time. People who are running harder and harder just to stay in place are not likely to afford what they must perceive as the luxury of personal engagement in the issues of the day.

Relevant to the question of human rights is the likelihood that people who live simply will have more leisure. Having more leisure, they will have more time and energy for participation in democratic governance. They will be more available for community-based projects that contribute to economic equity, social inclusion, and protection of human rights. They would also be more available to contribute to Transition Town projects at the local level. These would set down the real foundation for economic and physical security. Such a way of life takes control back from globalized corporations, financial institutions and their government cronies who have created an economic system heart-stoppingly vulnerable to peak oil and disruption by the corrupt, the incompetent, and the fanatical.

3.3 *The collapse of consumer culture under the triple stresses of ecological, economic, and social dislocation*

Not only do human beings continue to find new and ingenious reasons to hate and abuse each other, the very biophysical basis for consumer culture is being exploited well beyond sustainable levels. This in turn threatens any possibility of actually exercising the right to various forms of material provision and economic participation mentioned in the UDHR. The Transition Towns movement has focused on four factors that have particular significance:

3.3.1 *Peak oil*

Peak oil is a major issue for us since virtually our whole transportation system runs on petroleum as does the plastics industry, construction of civic infrastructure, the rubber industry, much of our food production, and a significant share of textile manufacturing. Despite steadily rising demand, global oil production has not increased since 2006 (Heinberg 2011, 107). Discovery of new reserves peaked globally in 1965 and we discover less than 25% of our current annual consumption in new reserves every year. There have been no large new oil deposits (500,000 bbls or more) discovered since 2003. There is no more spare production capacity in the world oil supply. Spare capacity peaked in 1985 at 25%, but by 2004 it was down to less than 2%. In September 2012, Saudi Arabia announced it now has no spare production capacity, meaning that the Saudis have reached peak, which means the world has reached peak. Finally, estimates of total reserves are probably inflated because OPEC countries may have exaggerated their reported reserves. In 1986-87, *all* OPEC countries, including Saudi Arabia, revised their estimated reserves upward nearly 100% (Beriault 2005). It strains credulity that all OPEC countries suddenly discovered they had twice as much oil as they thought. Not only have we very likely reached peak oil, we have or will soon reach peak for a lot of other things including water, world grain production (peaked in 1984 at 342 kg/cap) (Heinberg 2011, 133), many metals and rare earth minerals, as well as peak Phosphorous essential for fertilizers (Heinberg 2011, 124-143).

In the last few years, particularly in North America, the petroleum industry and its loyal consumers have been seized with elation over the promise of hydraulic fracturing (fracking). This is a method of petroleum production that uses sand, chemicals, and enormous quantities of high pressure water to fracture sub-surface formations of oil and gas-bearing shales to recover the resource. There are very large shale formations in many regions of the world promising an enormous increase in oil deposits which now become commercially accessible. In the bi-polar world of commodity trading, this new technology is leading to extremely grandiose predictions of energy independence for North America as well as an indefinite prolongation of the age of fossil fuels for the whole world. Less well-publicized is the incredibly low EROEI (Energy Return on Energy Invested) ratio for fracking, which I will explain below, the enormous drain on capital markets that recovering oil in this manner is causing (Ahmed 2013), the generally short production life of fracked wells (Hughes 2013), and record breaking amounts of methane "blow-by" that occurs during drilling and extraction. Also unmentioned is the contribution to climate changing green house gas emissions, of which methane is a particularly potent one, that will occur if all this new-found fuel is actually burned.

Despite how much debate swirls around the world's total oil reserves, however, the amount of oil left in the ground is largely irrelevant. Far more relevant is what is called the EROEI ratio, or the ratio that expresses the energy returned by exploiting a given deposit compared to the energy that must be invested to achieve that return. If it takes more than a barrel of oil energy equivalent to retrieve a barrel of new oil, there is very little point in developing the deposit, no matter how much oil might be present. It's exactly like deciding to drive to a gas station to fill up your car knowing full well you don't have enough gas to get there. Over the past several decades, the EROEI ratio has been trending downward for many major oil deposits. EROEI pre-1950 was 100:1 in areas like Texas and Saudi Arabia. By the 1970s, this ratio had plummeted to 30:1. In 2005, it was 10:1. The EROEI for tar sands development in the Athabasca region of Canada, one of the world's largest and as yet mostly undeveloped petroleum plays, is 4:1 (maximum) and some authorities estimate as low as 2:1. At the end of the day, many of these extraction operations will be shut down long before their oil is completely gone because more energy will be needed to bring the oil to market than is contained in the oil itself. This is simply the Second Law of Thermodynamics at work, a law of nature far less flexible than those of economics.

To illustrate just one of the many potential consequences of peak oil, consider the connection between slavery and fossil fuels. Prior to about 1750, nearly all large public works projects were constructed by slaves and animals that were worked like slaves. Fifty years later, it seems that humanity made a moral quantum leap. We recognized the evil of slavery. Within a couple of generations, it practically disappeared worldwide. Or did we make that quantum leap after all? Is it just coincidence that also around 1750, fossil fuels came into wide use to power agricultural, construction, and manufacturing machinery? Why employ slaves who get sick, get tired, and sometimes rebel, when the same work could be done with less expense and more reliability by fossil fueled machines? Note also that in areas of the world where slavery or near slavery is still in vogue such as West Africa, parts of Asia, and Latin America, it is most prevalent where fossil fuel supplies are expensive, scarce, or non-existent or the work the slaves are doing cannot be easily automated. What might happen then, in a world that has not conserved these precious energy resources? Who will do the heavy lifting in a carbon-constrained future?

3.3.2 *Climate change*

Climate change is another dramatic challenge facing humanity. Ironically, it has been our profligate over-use of fossil fuels such as oil that is now stoking the planet to what, by mid-century, will be truly torrid temperatures not seen here since the Paleozoic 60 million years ago. Of course, in the entire history of the Earth, such temperatures are not without precedent; but they *are* without precedent since the human species has been around. We have no idea how to live in such a world.

Munich Re, the insurance company that insures insurance companies, reports that weather related disasters have tripled since 1980. The US National Oceanographic and Atmospheric Administration reported that average temperatures in June 2012 in the U.S. were a full 2°C higher than the twentieth-century average. Meanwhile up north, the extent of summer sea ice in the Arctic was measured in 2012 to be only 24% of its former extent, 4% less than the lowest year on record which was 2007. Scientists expect the Arctic to be ice free within three or four years with truly momentous effects on global weather patterns and food production. Climate change is already costing the global economy an estimated US$1.2 trillion and 1.6% of GDP growth, plus contributing to an estimated 400,000 excess deaths annually (Reguly 2012).

If Munich Re is right and weather-related catastrophes are becoming more frequent due to climate change, then events like Hurricane Katrina and the floods in Pakistan help us see that one of the first casualties in such situations can be our human rights. As authorities struggle with the operational collapse of most services and institutions during these disasters, they can also become pretty heavy handed in what they call "re-establishing civil order." That may call for pretty rough and tumble tactics and some extra-judicial killings here and there. Maybe Americans watch too many of their own disaster movies. So, when it came to a real disaster like Katrina, they got trigger happy. But maybe not. In both the New Orleans and Pakistani events, help was available both from within and outside the affected regions. What will happen if, in a world more broadly and frequently impacted by climate change, there is no "outside" where help can come from?

I hope it's obvious that if society broadly embraced simple living, a way of life that focused on well-being rather than material affluence, there would be less consumption, and hence less production, and hence less extraction and degradation of resources, and hence less environmental impact, including the drivers of climate change. More fuels would be conserved for future generations and also to help make the transition to a renewable energy economy.

3.3.3 Economic contraction

Economic contraction is also a staple of the daily news. Economic growth worldwide is grinding to a halt. In October 2012, the IMF released a report predicting that global economic growth would be less than 2% in both 2013 and 2014, well below the 3.5% required to absorb new workers into the economy and alleviate poverty (CBC-TV Newsworld, Business Report, 9 October 2012). Everywhere governments are priming economic pumps, trying to induce householders to square the circle by consuming but at the same time avoiding increasing their personal debts, which now in many Canadian households exceeds 150% of annual income. The entire European Union teeters on financial collapse as its more profligate members threaten to drag the frugal and the prudent into the abyss of financial ruin along with them. In some European countries like Greece and Spain, GDP has already turned negative, their economies are actually contracting, and social services and benefits are being curtailed with all the social unrest we might expect. Economic recovery from the 2008 debacle in the US continues to be sluggish and uneven. Even the great engines of the world economy, China and India, are now showing declining rates of growth. In a debt-based monetary system that uses fractional reserve lending continuous growth is imperative. Moreover, doing what we need to do to reduce our use of fossil fuels and forestall even worse climate change would likely further slow the economy. So consumer culture demands ever expanding consumption that neither the planet nor households can afford.

Needless to say that in economies that are shedding jobs, suffocating from both sovereign and personal debt, and suffering real losses from environmental mismanagement, it's rather hard to see how the economic "right" to gain entry to, and participate in, a consumer culture lifestyle will ever be realized by the majority of humanity. In consumer culture money is so central that access to it can literally constitute rights, as described by Raj Patel (2009, 112-113):

> The late Oxford philosopher Jerry Cohen conceived a thought experiment that helps us to understand how money works, and the way that it intersects with the liberty offered by free markets. When the market rations goods on the basis of money, he argued, there's reason to quarrel with the idea that markets make freedom. Imagine that we live in a world where we have little tickets distributed at random. On these tickets are rights—the right to go visit your sick mother, the right to cross a particular road, the right to live somewhere, the right to eat a steak, the right to treatment for a disease and so on. You don't *have* to do what's written on any given ticket—they simply limit the extent of your freedoms. If you try to do something for which you do not have a ticket, the law intervenes. The tickets map out the degree to which you are free (or not free) to do something—they are a complete accounting of your liberties. The more tickets you have, the freer you are.
>
> So here's the twist: Money is just like these tickets. What, after all, does money offer in a market society if not the ability to buy liberty, to afford health care, decent food, housing, the security of not working in retirement, insurance against accident or unemployment? Those without money are as unfree as those without tickets. Without cash in a market society, you're free to do nothing, to have very little and to die young. In other words, under capitalism, *money is the right to have rights.* (italics in original)

So I suggest that peak oil, climate change, and economic contraction are all direct threats to human rights in and of themselves. If conserving human rights matters to us, then it requires taking steps to reduce our use of fossil fuels and transition away from using them altogether. We need to do what we can to mitigate climate change even though it is now impossible to escape it. We also need to move immediately toward a lower consumption steady-state economy that demotes growth and promotes sharing more equitably the resources Earth can sustainably provide. All of these steps must be accompanied by a very comprehensive and deliberate effort to evolve our values and desires and consciousness toward understandings of the good life which give less emphasis to accumulation and consumption and more emphasis to non-material sources of reward in life.

3.3.4   *Elite panic*

The final key threat to human rights that I want to mention is what Rebecca Solnit (2009) has aptly called *elite panic*.

Elite panic includes fear of social disorder; fear of the poor, minorities and immigrants; obsession with looting and property crime; tendency to conflate looting (theft) with emergency requisitioning of materials and supplies; willingness to resort to deadly force without due process; actions taken on the basis of rumor; belief that in disasters the general population degenerates into a mob and that only the elites using armed force can re-establish social order. What distinguishes elite panic from regular panic is that it is largely driven by the deep-seated fear that *Others* will panic unless restrained by force. Elites, however, are in positions of power and can martial deadly force to do their bidding whereas ordinary citizens cannot. As Solnit (2009, 152-153) has described this:

> In the absence of governments, people govern themselves. Everyone from Hobbes to Hollywood filmmakers has assumed this means 'law of the jungle' chaos. What in fact takes place is another kind of anarchy, where the citizenry by and large organize and care for themselves. In the immediate aftermath of disaster, government fails as if it had been overthrown and civil society succeeds as though it has revolted: the task of government, usually described as 're-establishing order,' is to take back the city and the power to govern it....So the more long-term aftermath of disaster is often in some sense a counterrevolution, with varying degrees of success. The possibility that they have been overthrown or, more accurately, rendered irrelevant is a very good reason for elite panic if not for the sometimes vicious acts that ensue.

To the extent that our society is impacted by climate change-driven natural disasters in the future, and our capacity to respond to and rebuild from these disasters is seriously curtailed by peak everything, I'm concerned that elite panic will become more common as well. We already see many signs of this with the hugely amplified emphasis on "security" in the face of global terrorism, with the effect that many human rights have already been eroded or extinguished.

As natural disasters become more frequent and intense, the best way to conserve human rights is by organizing and empowering communities, e.g., the Transition Towns initiatives, rather than investing in systems that maintain order and security and elite privilege at the expense of human rights. We need to prepare society at the grassroots level to be resilient in the face of crisis and change, not merely obedient to authority. In all past natural disasters, your first responders are your neighbours and there's no reason to think this will be different in the future. Again, ironically, in the future consumer culture offers us, governments, and security institutions, the very institutions charged with protecting human rights, may become one of the greatest threats to them.

4. Voluntary Simplicity Protects and Promotes Human Rights

4.1 *Voluntary simplicity is strongly oriented to nonviolence*

The orientation of simple living toward nonviolence is most relevant to human rights that call for changes in social relations such as refraining from imposing slavery or discrimination or systematic abuse of each other. Consumer culture aims to consume more and more with the result that both people and other species are oppressed by violence.

One way of thinking of the relationship between consumption and violence is to consider the following distinctions: Violence can be characterized as *direct* or *structural*. When violence is direct, then we as individual actors inflict violence on other people, other species or physical objects. If I punch someone in the nose, I am inflicting direct violence on them.

In the case of structural violence, however, some harm is being inflicted on our behalf and usually at a distance, and as a result of the structures that characterize our economic arrange-ments. I perpetrate structural violence when I consume chocolate confections made with cocoa harvested by child slaves in West Africa. I am not inflicting this violence directly, but rather indirectly through the structural economic arrangements that inflict this violence on my behalf because I consume the product harvested by the slaves. I can inflict structural violence every day and still think of myself as a fine, upstanding fellow, because mostly this violence occurs far away and to other people. Out of sight and out of mind is the motto of consumer culture.

To this distinction between direct and structural violence we also need to add the distinction between *necessary* and *elective* violence. It happens in the current state of things that almost all consumption incurs violence of some sort because human beings are *heterotrophs*. We must consume other beings in order to live because we cannot produce our food in our own tissues as plants do. So the consumption which is inescapably required to support our lives also necessarily implies killing, dismembering, grinding and digesting at least plants and often other animals as well. Several spiritual traditions such as Buddhism, Hinduism, and Jainism have been particularly sensitive to this issue and have endeavoured, by mandating vegetarian diets for their followers, to reduce the suffering of sentient beings, living things clearly capable of experiencing pain and suffering. In any case, the violence we inflict on other beings probably cannot be much reduced below what is inescapably required to support our own lives. Happily, this can be a very low level.

Contrasted with necessary violence, however, is the *elective* violence we inflict when we orient our way of life around the consumption of luxuries. All production of luxury goods also incurs violence through the harvesting of resources and the killing of animals to procure the materials needed for luxury manufactures or the destruction of habitat needed by other species. It also tends to subject other human beings to working in conditions that are toxic or hazardous since many luxury goods acquire their status as luxuries simply by being scarce or difficult to procure. Since these products and services *are* luxuries and by definition unnecessary to supporting our livelihood, their consumption is clearly unnecessary and the violence inflicted is therefore clearly elective.

These fundamental distinctions can be arranged as a two by two grid that helps us classify most forms of violence as being (a) necessary and direct (e.g., acts of violence inflicted on others in self-defense), (b) elective and direct (e.g., acts of violence inflicted on others as recreation, such as participation in martial arts tournaments or boxing matches), (c) necessary and structural (e.g., the provision through the general economy of basic food stuffs and clothing) and (d) elective and structural (the entire realm of consumer luxury consumption including such ordinary indulgences as meat, coffee, gold, liquor, tobacco, chocolate, tea, etc.).

The case of violence has been of special concern among practitioners of simple living, both today and throughout its history. It is often observed that what people actually *need* for a good life is easy to provide, rarely pushes ecological limits, minimizes the suffering inflicted on other beings, and is of such a scale that equity of provision can be realistically achieved among all people. But of *luxury* consumption there appears to be no limit as to what people can learn to want. The same can be said about the pursuit of monetary gain for its own sake. And it is the pursuit of luxuries and monetary gain which has called people to the most dangerous, exotic, toxic, and precarious sorts of enterprises, overworking both people and animals, exploiting and oppressing both nature and human communities. Consumer culture is nothing if not a full on effort to continually develop new varieties of luxury consumption and bring them to market in pursuit of monetary gain. In demoting the importance of luxury consumption in particular, and the spirit of commerce in general, voluntary simplicity aims to counteract these fruitful sources of violence and abuse of human rights. In consumer culture, people live to consume; in living simply, we consume to live.

One further observation might be worth making at this point: Voluntary simplicity might be considered an exercise in what Gandhi called *satyagraha*, nonviolent social change driven by "spirit force." Every campaign of satyagraha consists of two simultaneous movements. First, we withdraw our cooperation from a system of oppression by refusing to participate in it, and often actively opposing it by nonviolent means. At the same time, we set about establishing new social and economic arrangements that meet the same needs but do so in ways that respect human rights and ecological limits. I believe voluntary simplicity is a campaign of satyagraha to replace consumer culture since non-consumption, especially of luxuries, is definitely a form of nonviolent non-cooperation with consumer culture. To the extent that practitioners of simple living withdraw their energies and imagination from consumer culture and apply them elsewhere to create alternate institutions and economic arrangements that honour human rights, we are also constructing an alternate positive system to replace the system of oppression now in place.

Apart from, but related to, the question of violence is the fact that in consumer culture there is also a strong belief in corporations to provide a better life. But it has been convincingly demonstrated that corporations are unaccountable tyrannies that in many respects behave like psychopaths (Anchon *et al.* 2002). It is unlikely that institutions with no conscience and no capacity for empathy will treat human rights as anything other than "externalities" to production. Any institution that automatically treats every humane value as an externality of its operations must on that account alone be considered violent. A glaring example of this is noted by Raj Patel (2009, 54):

> [To make cellphones, Nokia] uses minerals extracted from bloody conflict in the Congo, where 70 percent of the world's reserves of coltan are found. Coltan is the source of niobium and tantalum, used to make the capacitors at the heart of most portable electronic gadgetry. In patrolling access to these resources, military units in the Congo have raped, tortured, enslaved and killed. Women struggling to bring up children in the Congo have a life expectancy of forty-seven years, continue to suffer through the world's worst rape epidemic and earn just over half what men do—$191 per year.

4.2 *Voluntary simplicity reduces material consumption and re-orients human motivations*

The practice of mindfulness within a lifestyle of voluntary simplicity helps to reorient human motivations toward intrinsic, nonmaterial rewards, thus conserving resources and ecosystem integrity that are the sources of the material means we need for well-being. It is also the basis for any future claims to material entitlements as human rights. As the American farmer and philosopher Wendell Berry has so poetically observed:

> The world that environs us, that is around us, is also within us. We are made of it; we eat, drink, and breathe it; it is bone of our bone and flesh of our flesh. It is also a Creation, a holy mystery, made for, and to some extent by, creatures, some but by no means all of whom are human. This world, this Creation, belongs in a limited sense to us, for we may rightfully require certain things of it—the things necessary to keep us

fully alive as the kind of creature we are; but we also belong to it and it makes certain rightful claims upon us: that we leave it undiminished, not just to our children, but to all the creatures who will live in it after us. [Wendell Berry, source / date unknown.]

4.3 *Voluntary simplicity promotes personal and community self-reliance*

Personal and community self-reliance are seen within the simplicity movement as effective approaches to providing for security, e.g., alternate "investing" in community and production for own consumption to meet essential life needs. The value of self-reliance also promotes security by disengaging from the systemic violence of consumer culture, e.g., Gulf Wars, terrorism, etc. It is our addictions to oil and opiates that drive wars, terrorism, and abuse of human rights as much as ideological differences.

6. Conclusion

I've tried to present the relationship between voluntary simplicity and human rights first by distinguishing human rights that have to do with maintaining the dignity and freedom of persons from those which imply claims to material entitlements. If we destroy the basis for material entitlements through over-population, over-consumption, and waste, then this will rebound not only as expanded conditions of material poverty, but also elite panic which will undermine human dignity and freedom.

When I parse this issue as deeply as I can, I see consumer culture not as the path to realizing our human rights, but rather as a thoroughgoing threat to human rights. I truly believe that we can live justly and honourably in relation to each other, and sustainably in relation to nature, only if we live simply.

Our dreams matter. Our beliefs about what the real world is like and how to do well in it matter. Different dreams and assumptions can be carried within us, but they never stay contained. They seep out of us like a vapor that our kids inhale from the very air they breathe. Do we gas them with frenzy and structure and self-centeredness and mindless obsession with technology for its own sake? Or can we refresh them with mindfulness, calm, gentleness, appreciation for what is simply here and simply ordinary? Are we in touch with these things ourselves? Do we believe the future needs more of what we've already got, or is it time for a change?

References

Adbusters: *A Journal of the Mental Environment.* http://www.adbusters.org

Ahmed, Nafeez Mosaddeq. 2013. The great oil swindle. *Le Monde Diplomatique* (March). http://mondediplo.com/2013/03/09gaz (accessed August 28, 2013).

Alcott, B. 2005. Jevons' paradox. *Ecological Economics* 54, no. 1:9–21. http://www.sciencedirect.com/science/article/pii/S0921800905 001084 (accessed August 28, 2013).

Alexander, Bruce. 2000. *The roots of addiction in free market society.* Vancouver: Canadian Centre for Policy Alternatives. This very process is partly what is meant by "psycho-social dislocation" as described by Alexander, Bruce (2000). As we lose rootedness and a sense of place in our own culture, we fall prey to increased risk of all sorts of addictions and their associated threats to personal and community health. This comes about mainly because of the intense psychological pain that accompanies psycho-social dislocation and the efforts sufferers make to escape it in any way they can, usually through a substance addiction or else a behavioral addiction, such as shopping, over-work, sex, etc.

Alexander, Christopher. 1977. *A pattern language: Towns, buildings, construction.* New York: Oxford University Press.

Alexander, Christopher. 1979. *The timeless way of building.* New York, NY: Oxford University Press.

Alexander, Samuel. 2012. Living better on less? Toward an economics of sufficiency. *Simplicity Institute Report* 12c, 2012.

"Alternative energies: oil shales/oil sands." *Alternative Energies.* http://altenergysources.webs.com/oilshaletarsands.htm (accessed January 10, 2011).

Andrews, Cecile. 1997. *The circle of simplicity.* New York: HarperPerennial.

Arntz, W. and B. Chase. *Down the Rabbit Hole (What the Bleep Do We Know?).* Produced by W. Arntz and B. Chase and Directed by William Arntz, Betsy Chase and Mark Vicente. 300 min. Lord of the Wind Films, 2004. DVD.

AtKisson, Alan. 2010. The Lagom solution. In *Less is more: Embracing simplicity for a healthy planet, a caring economy and lasting happiness*, eds. Cecile Andrews and Wanda Urbanska, 101-106. Gabriola Island, BC: New Society Publishers.

Bakan, Joel. 2002. *The Corporation.* Produced and Directed by Mark Achbar and Jennifer Abbot. Big Picture Media Corporation, DVD?

Ban Breathnach, Sarah. 1995. *Simple abundance: A daybook of comfort and joy*. New York: Warner Books.

Bellis, Mary. 2013. *The history of money*. http://inventors.about.com/od/mstartinventions/a/money.html (accessed July 24, 2013).

Bender, Sue. 1989. *Plain and simple: A woman's journey to the Amish*. New York: HarperCollins, 1989. An excellent memoir of this sort of immersion learning experience.

Beriault, R. 2005. *Peak oil and the fate of humanity*. www.peakoilandhumanity.com (accessed June 28, 2005).

One particularly telling example of this process is the changing ratio of the "Energy Return on Energy Invested" in oil production, or the EROEI ratio. As oil deposits located near markets and close to the surface are depleted over time, oil companies must seek deeper deposits of lower grade oils located farther from markets. As the resource is degraded, more units of energy must be invested to bring each unit of oil to market. The trend in EROEI ratios over time is: pre-1950, 100:1; 1970s, 30:1; 2005, 10:1; Tar sands efficiency is 4:1 (maximum) and some authorities estimate as low as 2:1.

Bernstein, Henry. 2000. Colonialism, capitalism, development. In *Poverty and development into the 21st century*, eds. Tim Allen and Alan Thomas, 241-270. Oxford: Oxford University Press.

Berry, Wendell. 1970. A continuous harmony. In *Less is more: An anthology of ancient and modern voices raised in praise of simplicity*, ed. Goldian VandenBroeck, 287. Rochester, VT: Inner Traditions.

———. 1981. *The gift of good land*. San Francisco: North Point Press.

———. 1987. Does community have value? In *Home economics*, 179-192. San Francisco: North Point Press.

———. 1987. *Home economics*. San Francisco: North Point Press.

Wendell Berry has on more than one occasion noted that human beings are tinkerers. We are also fallible, and therefore, when we tinker, we must always be mindful of our fallibility and tinker at small scales, saving all the parts in case we forget something, which we certainly will, and eschewing giantism in our tinkering in favor of screwing up in limited ways rather than letting our errors become huge disasters. This is wisdom that should be pondered by the emerging madness of geo-engineering.

Biello, D. 2007. *Bringing cancer to the dinner table: Breast cancer cells grow under influence of fish flesh*. Scientific American, April 17.

Brower, Michael and Warren Leon. 1999. *The consumer's guide to effective environmental choices: Practical advice from the Union of*

Concerned Scientists. New York: Three Rivers Press.

Buckley, Chris and Matt Spetalnick. 2011. Obama presses China's Hu on currency, rights. Reuters, January 19, 2011, http://www.reuters.com/article/idUSTRE70H07Z20110119, (accessed August 28, 2013).

Burch, Mark A. 2009. *The simplicity study circle II: Tools for participation.* Winnipeg: Simplicity Practice and Resource Centre.

————. 2012. Mindfulness: The doorway to simple living. Melbourne, Australia: The Simplicity Institute.

————. 2012. *The simplicity exercises: A sourcebook for simplicity educators.* Melbourne: The Simplicity Institute.

Burke, Monte. 1995. *The Four Basic Arguments for a National TV-Turnoff Week.* Washington: TV-Free America.

————. 1996. *Television and Health.* Washington: TV Free America.

Campbell, Colin J. and Jean H. Laherrere. 1998. The end of cheap oil. *Scientific American*, March Issue.

Campbell, Greg. 2003. Blood diamonds. *Amnesty Now*, 2003, www.amnestyusa.org/amnestynow/diamonds.html (accessed August 28, 2013).

CBC-TV The Passionate Eye. *End of the Line.* Produced by Arcane Pictures, Calm Productions and Dartmouth Films. 60 min. CBC-TV, 2010. Television.

CBC News Network. *Who Killed the Electric Car?* Directed by Chris Paine. Produced by Jessie Deete. 60 min. CBC-TV, 2010. Web. www.cbc.ca/documentaries/passionateeyeshowcase/2009/electriccar

CBC-TV Doc Zone. 2010. *Are We Digital Dummies?* Broadcast November 18, 2010.

CBC-TV The Nature of Things. *Tipping Point: The Age of the Oil Sands.* Produced by Clearwater Documentary, Inc. 90 min. CBC-TV, 2011.

Chataway, Joanna and Les Levidow and Susan Carr. 2000. Genetic engineering of development? In *Poverty and development into the 21st century*, eds. Tim Allen and Alan Thomas, 469-484. Oxford: Oxford University Press.

Chatfield, Tom. 2010. Cataclysm coming... www.boingboing.net/2010/11/05/cataclysm.html (Review of new video game published online.)

Chittister, Joan. 1992. Qualifications of the Monastery cellarer. In: *The Rule of Benedict: Insights for the ages*, ed. Joan Chittister, 104-106. New York: Crossroad Publishing Company.

Chua, Amy. 2002. *World on fire: How exporting free market democracy breeds ethnic hatred and global instability.* New Haven: Yale Law School.

Cohen, Michael J. 1993. *Beyond meditation: An introduction to the pure science of speaking with Earth and its spirit.* Bangkok: World Peace University.

Cone, Marla. "Environmental health perspectives," *LA Times.* May 27, 2005, http://www.latimes.com/news/science/la-na-babies27may27,0,1746496.story?page=2&coll=la-home-headlines. (accessed 28 August 2013)

Curtis, Adam. *Century of the Self.* Produced and Directed by Curtis Adam. 235 min. BBC, 2002. Format (accessed from vimeo.com).

Daly, Herman. 1995. The steady-state economy: Alternative to growthmania." In: Herman Daly. *Steady state economics,* 2nd ed. Chapter 9. Washington, DC: Island Press.

David Suzuki Foundation. Aquaculture. (accessed at: http://www.davidsuzuki.org/oceans/aquaculture)

de la Rosa, Roman. (Thirteenth century) 1996. From Charles Dahlberg (trans.) from the French by Guillaume de Lorris and Jean de Meun. In *Less is more: An anthology of ancient & modern voices raised in praise of simplicity,* ed. Goldian VandenBroeck Rochester, VT: Inner Traditions.

DePalma, Anthony. 2001. *NAFTA's powerful little secret.* New York Times, March 12, 2001.

Dixon, T. 2002. *Tools for environmental management: A practical introduction and guide.* Gabriola Island, BC: New Society Publishers.

Dominguez, Joe and Vicki Robin. 1992. *Your money or your life: Transforming your relationship with money and achieving financial independence.* New York, NY: Penguin Books.

Durning, Alan. 1992. *How much Is enough? The consumer society and the future of the earth.* New York: W. W. Norton & Co.

Eastabrooks, J. 2002. Christianity and voluntary simplicity. Unpublished paper; Menno Simons College, Winnipeg, Manitoba, Canada.

Edsall, Thomas B. 1995. TV tattered nation's social fabric, political scientist contends. *The Washington Post,* September 3, 1995.

Elgin, Duane. 2010. *Voluntary simplicity: Toward a way of life that is outwardly simple, inwardly rich.* New York: Harper.

Epicurus. 1996. "Epicurus." *Less is more: An anthology of ancient & modern voices raised in praise of simplicity,* edited by Goldian VandenBroeck, 101. Rochester: Inner Traditions.

Esteva, G. and M.S. Prakash. 1996. From global thinking to local thinking. In *The post-development reader,* ed. Majid Rahnema and

Vitoria Bawtree, 277-289. London: ZED Books. Fascinating discussion of the shifting meaning of global and parochial perspectives in a developmental context. During the heyday of international development thinking, taking a global perspective of the economy was considered more modern and progressive than the local, more parochial perspectives common in less developed societies. But over time, globalized thinking has become the new orthodoxy and parochial in its own way in as much as it is incapable of grasping the full ecological and social complexity of the Earth and all the cultures it supports. Indeed, the most ecologically sustainable ideas of development might, in fact, be rooted precisely in intimate local knowledge that globalized regimes of development are too large scale and too abstract to recognize. Thus, because of its inflexibility and dogmatic reliance on neo-conservative economic doctrines, globalization turns out to be the more "parochial," backward, inflexible, even superstitious worldview. Sustainability may in fact be found in global networks of local knowledge and development practice that can inform and inspire each other, but which don't seek a one-size-fits-all formula for improving human well-being.

Federal Reserve Bank of Boston - Bureau of Labor Statistics. 2007. *Nonagricultural employment by sector and industry in Massachusetts and the United States for 2007.* http://www.mass.gov/Aosc/docs/reports_audits/CAFR/2007/page_174.pdf (accessed August 28, 2013).

Freed, J. 2011. *The Trouble with Experts.* Produced by Josh Freed Production, and Directed by J. Freed. 60 min. Canadian Broadcasting Corporation, Toronto, Ontario, 2011. Network broadcast.

Freire, Paulo. 1995. *Pedagogy of the oppressed.* New York, NY: Continuum.

Fuller, A. 1994. *Psychology and religion: Eight points of view.* London: Rowman and Littlefield.

The Toronto Globe and Mail. "Report on business." *The Toronto Globe and Mail,* May 31, 2008.

Goddard, Dwight. 1938. The 118th Discourse. In *The Buddhist Bible*, ed. Dwight Goddard, 73-82. Boston: Beacon Press.

As contrasted with the variety of meanings assigned to mindfulness by Charles Tart, the classical Buddhist sources identify four objects of mindfulness practice: the body, mental states, emotions, and external phenomena (dharmas).

Greenspan, Miriam. 2003. Healing through the dark emotions: The wisdom of grief, fear, and despair. Boston: Shambhala.

Gregg, Richard. 1936. The value of voluntary simplicity. Wallingford, PA: Pendle Hill.

Gurdjieff, G. I. Date unknown; Source unknown.

Hanson, Jay. "Neurological effects of television." Personal communication. August 13, 1996.

Hawken, Paul. 2007. *Blessed unrest: How the largest social movement in history is restoring grace, justice, and beauty to the world.* New York: Penguin Books.

Heinberg, Richard. 2011. *The end of growth: Adapting to our new economic reality.* Gabriola Island, BC: New Society Publishers.

Homer-Dixon, Theodore. F. 1996. Environmental scarcity, mass violence, and the limits to ingenuity. *Current History* 95 no. 604 (1996): 359-365.

———. 2001. *The ingenuity gap: Facing the economic, environmental and other challenges of an increasingly complex and unpredictable world.* Toronto: Vintage Books.

One the world's technological optimists but nonetheless influential, Thomas Homer-Dixon considers the near future to be a race between gathering climate challenges and resource scarcity on the one hand, and human ingenuity on the other. He places his bet on ingenuity without seriously questioning the underlying values of consumer culture, even as his own examples suggest clearly that exponentially growing and interacting problems will soon swamp human ingenuity. Another truly delirious example of this worldview is that shared by geo-engineers who plan to counteract the effects of climate change by planetary scale interventions in processes like cloud formation, plankton growth in the oceans, and adjusting the levels of solar radiation reaching the Earth.

Hopkins, Rob. 2008. *The transition handbook: From oil dependency to local resilience.* White River Junction, VT: Chelsea Green Publishing Co.

———. 2011. *The transition companion.* White River Junction, VT: Chelsea Green Publishing.

Hubbert, M. King, 1956. Hubbert peak theory. https://en.wikipedia.org/wiki/Hubbert_peak_theory (accessed August 28, 2013).

Huber, Cheri. 1990. One less act of violence. In: *That which you are seeking is causing you to seek*, ed. Cheri Huber. Murphys, CA: Zen Meditation Centre.

Hughes, David J. 2013. *Drill, baby, drill: Can unconventional fuels usher in a new era of energy abundance?* Post Carbon Institute.

Ignatius of Loyola. 1521. *Spiritual exercises of St. Ignatius Loyola.* Christian Classics Ethereal Library, www.ccel.org/ccel/ignatius/exercises.html (accessed August 28, 2013).

Inside Facebook:
(accessed at: http://www.insidefacebook.com/2009/06/02/total-us-time-spent-on-facebook-up-700-in-the-last-year). It is estimated, for example, that in the US alone, and for the period from April 2008 to April 2009 alone, Facebook users spent 232 million hours and MySpace users 83 million hours in online socializing.

Irvine, William B. 2009. *A guide to the good life: The ancient art of Stoic joy.* Oxford, UK: Oxford University Press. In his survey of the philosophy of Stoicism, Irvine cites the practice recommended by Chrysippus (d. c. 206 BCE) and later Stoics of negative visualization. In this practice, one uses imagination to visualize the loss of relationships or possessions that one values, partly as a way of preparing the soul for such loss, which is inevitable, but also to heighten appreciation and enjoyment of them while we have them. As such, the technique sometimes referred to as "premeditation of evils" is another way of cultivating gratitude for what we have rather than focusing attention on what we don't have.

James, William. 1958. *Varieties of religious experience.* New York: New American Library.

Johnston, Timothy C. and Jay B. Burton. 2002. Voluntary simplicity: Popular definitions and major themes. *Academy of Marketing Studies Journal.* Conference presentation, April 19, 2002. http://www.docin.com/p-64508434.html (accessed August28, 2013).

Jung, C. G. 1961. *Memories, dreams, reflections,* ed. A. Jaffe. New York, NY: Bantam.

———. 1969. *The archetypes and the collective unconscious.* Vol. 9, Part 1. Princeton, NJ: Princeton University Press.

Kabat-Zinn, Jon. 1994. *Wherever you go there you are: Mindfulness meditation in everyday life.* New York, NY: Hyperion. An obvious example of this might be work already being done by Jon Kabat-Zinn, where mindfulness practice is being applied to the treatment of anxiety, depression, and obsessive-compulsive disorders. Less obvious appear to be applications where mindfulness-like meditation and centering practices have been used in the context of gardening and food production for a number of decades at the Findhorn Foundation in northern Scotland, http://www.findhorn.org.

Kasser, Tim and Kirk Warren Brown. 2010. A scientific approach to voluntary simplicity. In: *Less is more: Embracing simplicity for a healthy planet, a caring economy and lasting happiness*, eds. Cecile Andrews and Wanda Urbanska. Gabriola Island, BC: New Society Publishers.

Keating, Thomas. 1998. *Intimacy with God*. New York, NY: Crossroad Books.

King, Jonathon and Doreen Stabinsky. 1999. Biotechnology under globalization: The corporate expropriation of plant, animal and microbial species. *Race and Class* 40 (2/3):73-89.

Koestler, Arthur. 1967. *The ghost in the machine*. London, UK: Arkana.

Kuhn, Thomas S. 1962. *The structure of scientific revolutions*. Chicago, IL: University of Chicago Press.

Lovelock, James. 1990. *Ages of Gaia: A biography of our living Earth*. New York, NY: Bantam.

Lovitt, J. M. 2010. Beyond Beverly Hills and Rodeo Drive: Compulsive shopping triggered by dopamine levels. One 80 Center, August 3, 2010. http://one80center.com (accessed August 28, 2013).

MacLuhan, Marshall. 1962. *The Gutenberg galaxy: The making of typographic man*; 1st ed. Toronto, Ontario: University of Toronto Press.

———. 2001. *The medium is the massage: An inventory of effects*. 1st ed. New York, NY: Random House. Reissued by Gingko Press.

Macy, Joanna. 1983. *Despair and personal power in the nuclear age*. Gabriola Island, BC: New Society Publishers.

Macy, Joanna and Molly Young Brown. 1998. *Coming back to life: Practices to reconnect our lives, our world*. Gabriola Island, BC: New Society Publishers.

Maslow, Abraham. 1954. *Motivation and personality*, Third Edition. New York, NY: Harper and Row Publishers.

McGrane, Bernard. 1998. The Zen TV experiment. http://adbusters.org/Articles/zentv.html (accessed January 1998). A Zen-inspired look at how television shapes perception and carries people away from reality rather than connecting them to it. Includes exercises for cultivating greater awareness of the effects media have on us.

McGrew, Anthony. 2000. Sustainable globalization? The global politics of development and exclusion in the new world order. In *Poverty and development into the 21st century*, eds. Tim Allen and Alan Thomas. Oxford, UK: Oxford University Press.

McKenzie-Mohr, Doug. 1999. *Fostering more sustainable behavior*. Gabriola Island, British Columbia, Canada: New Society Publishers. After reviewing a considerable amount of empirical research on the factors that contribute to people adopting more sustainable behavior such as increasing their use of recycling facilities or participating in car pooling programs, McKenzie-Mohr concluded that taken in isolation, information and advertising campaigns were generally ineffective to spark sustainability-positive behavior change. Instead, what seems to be required is a multi-faceted approach that includes analyzing and removing barriers to the desired behavior, identifying effective motivators and rewards for the desired behavior, having role models (celebrities) model and endorse the behavior, incessant communication and reinforcement of the desired behavior, highly targeted advertising campaigns, information campaigns stressing the benefits and progress being made in establishing the desired behavior, creation of peer-pressure networks to reinforce and strengthen the behavior, publicized rewards for performing the behavior—and all this to establish extremely modest changes to our daily habits.

McLeod, Ian. 2001. Biotech companies seek to patent gene data: Free flow of knowledge at stake, experts say. *National Post*, April 5, 2001.

McMurtry, J. 2002. The life-ground, the civil commons and the corporate male gang. *Canadian Journal of Development Studies* 22: 840.

Meadows, Donella H. 1996. Envisioning a sustainable world. In: *Getting down to earth: Practical applications of ecological economics*, eds. Robert Costanza, Olman Segura, and Juan Martinez-Alier. Washington, DC: Island Press.

———. 2004. *Urban growth means lower taxes—and other myths*. Hartland, VT: Sustainability Institute.

Merkel, Jim. 2003. *Radical simplicity: Small footprints on a finite earth*. Gabriola Island, BC: New Society Publishers.

Mies, Maria and Veronika Bennholdt-Thomsen. 1999. *The subsistence perspective: Beyond the globalized economy*. London, UK: ZED Books.

Miller, Timothy. 1995. *How to want what you have: Discovering the magic and grandeur of ordinary existence*. New York, NY: Avon Books.

Mills, Stephanie. 2002. *Epicurean simplicity*. Washington, DC: Island Press.

Mollison, Bill. 1991. *Introduction to permaculture*. Tyalkgum, Australia: Tagari Publications.

Mooney, Patrick R. 1999. The ETC century: Erosion, technology transformation and corporate concentration in the 21st century. *Development Dialogue*, 1-2: 21.

Moore, Thomas. 1994. *Meditations: On the monk who dwells in daily life*. New York, NY: HarperCollins Publishers.

NBC/*Wall Street Journal*, 2009. NBC News Health Care Survey, August 2009.

Orr, David. 1999. The ecology of giving and consuming. In: *Consuming desires: Consumption, culture, and the pursuit of happiness*, ed. Roger Rosenblatt. Washington, D.C.: Island Press. Many businesses these days are involved in what David Orr has called changing the coefficients of sustainability problems without really addressing the systemic, structural, and design issues giving rise to them. The answer to the waste problem is not more garbage trucks and bigger landfill operations. It involves changing product designs, materials, transportation systems, and materials recovery activities.

Parker-Pope, Tara. 2005. This is your brain at the mall: Why shopping makes you feel so good. *Wall Street Journal*. December 6, 2005. www.mindfully.org/Health/2005/Shopping-Dopamine-Junkie6dec05.html.

Pascal, Blaise. Date unknown. Source unknown.

Patel, Raj. 2009. *The value of nothing: Why everything costs so much more than we think*. New York, NY: HarperCollins Publishers.

Pieper, Josef. 1996. Leisure, the basis of culture. In: *Less is more: An anthology of ancient & modern voices raised in praise of simplicity*, ed. Goldian VandenBroeck. Rochester, VT: Inner Traditions.

Pierce, Linda Breen. 2000. *Choosing simplicity: Real people finding peace and fulfillment in a complex world*. Carmel, CA: Gallagher Press.

Pimentel et al. 1973. Food production and the energy crisis. *Science*, November 2, 1973.

Progoff, Ira. 1969. *Depth psychology and modern man*. New York NY: Dialogue House Library.

———. 1973. *The symbolic and the real*. New York, NY: Dialogue House Library.

———. 1975. *At a journal workshop*. New York, NY: Dialogue House Associates. Some of the most creative and compelling sources on journaling are various works by Ira Progoff who developed the National Intensive Journaling Program. The journaling process he devised is based heavily on the depth psychology of C. G. Jung.

———. 1985. *The Dynamics of hope*. New York, NY: Dialogue House Associates. While non-rational psychological factors can be manipulated for corporate gain, they are also a natural part of how human beings tick, and the very basis for personal and social change. For as the twentieth-century depth psychologist Ira Progoff observed: ". . . societies . . . move forward in terms of dreams or visions of reality that carry the image of potentiality by which the meaning of a given society can be fulfilled. It may even be that human society as a whole has such an image implicit in the seed of its being, implicit in the social nature of [humanity]. It may be that this image has been dreamed imperfectly in the past, has been dreamed many times in the past, and that it needs to be dreamed again and again until it can become a reality of history." (25)

Pullela, Philip. 2008. Vatican lists 'new sins', including pollution. Reuters, March 10, 2008.

Rapley, John. 2002. *Understanding development: Theory and practice in the third world*. 2nd ed. Boulder, CO: Lynne Rienner Publishers. Such conversations also often fail to note questions as to the feasibility of seeking technical solutions in their own right. Rapley fundamentally questions the capacity of technology to deliver what it promises when he argues:

"Nevertheless, some optimists maintain that future technological developments, or even the widespread application of existing technologies, will resolve any future problems. . . . But if we apply that principle [extrapolation from past trends to the future] we see the sort of problems that lie ahead. Let us assume, for instance, that a combination of convergence and efficiency improvements applies. That is, first-world economic growth spills over into the third world, and brings with it efficiency gains that ultimately lead to the market solving, on a global scale, every environmental problem it has created. By the end of this century, it was postulated [by Julian Simon—a "cornucopian" theorist], the world would be uniformly rich, clean, and healthy. Does this vision stand to reason? We can do a simple test. If we assume that the economies of the first world will continue to grow at a 3 percent annual growth rate over the next century; that the global population will stabilize at around 10 billion by 2050, with the increase coming in the third world; and that the third world countries will grow at rates that enable them to more or less converge with the first world by the end of the century, the global economy will then end up roughly 140 times greater than it is today. Now let us extrapolate from past trends in efficiency gains. The efficiency of the car, thanks to improvements in engine efficiency and a lightening of the body, generally improved by roughly a factor of four in the second half of the twentieth century, measured by fuel consumption. Evidently, past trends in efficiency gains will clearly be outstripped—they have been so far—by output increases." (170)

Raven, John. 1995. The quantity of money. In: *The new wealth of nations*, ed. John Raven. Unionville, NY: Royal Fireworks Press.

Reguly, Eric, 2012. A world on thin ice, an economy in peril and a dose of perspective. *The Toronto Globe and Mail*, Toronto, Ontario, Saturday, September 29, 2012: B1-2.

Renner, M. 1990. Converting to a peaceful economy. In: *State of the world*, 1990: A Worldwatch Institute Report on progress toward a sustainable society, eds. Brown et al. New York, NY: W. W. Norton & Company.

———. 1995. Budgeting for disarmament. In: *State of the world*, 1995: A Worldwatch Institute Report on progress toward a sustainable society, eds. Brown et al. New York, NY: W. W. Norton & Company.

Riu, S. J. Environmentally regenerative/restorative architecture: The future of sustainable design. http://sooryu.files.wordpress.com/2008/09/regenerative-restorative-architecture.pdf (accessed May 21, 2012).

Robbins, J. 2003. Is there slavery in your chocolate? The food revolution. (accessed at: www.foodrevolution.org/slavery_chocolate.html.)

Robert, K-H et. al. 2002. Strategic sustainable development — selection, design and synergies of applied tools. *Journal of Cleaner Production* 2002, 10:197-214. A theoretical model of sustainability based on the laws of nature rather than politics can be found in the oddly named "Natural Step" formulated by Swedish oncologist Karl Henrik Robert. The Natural Step (TNS) postulates four, high level, "system conditions" which must be met for any human society or culture to be sustainable: "(1) Eliminate our contribution to systematic increases in concentrations of substances from the Earth's crust. This means substituting certain minerals that are scarce in nature with others that are more abundant, using all mined materials efficiently, and systematically reducing dependence on fossil fuels; (2) Eliminate our contribution to systematic increases in concentrations of substances produced by society. This means systematically substituting certain persistent and unnatural compounds with ones that are normally abundant or break down more easily in nature, and using all substances produced by society efficiently. (3) Eliminate our contribution to the systematic physical degradation of nature through over-harvesting, introductions and other forms of modification. This means drawing resources only from well-managed eco-systems, systematically pursuing the most productive and efficient use both of those resources and land, and exercising caution in all kinds of modification of nature. (4) Contribute as much as we can to the meeting of human needs in our society and worldwide, over and above all the substitution and dematerialization measures taken in meeting the first three objectives. This means using all of our resources efficiently, fairly and responsibly so that the needs of all people on whom we have an impact, and the future needs of people who are not yet born, stand the best chance of being met." These system conditions are essentially restatements in the language of sustainability of the laws of conservation of matter and energy, the second law of thermodynamics, and the conservation of biodiversity, genetic diversity, and bio-productivity in ecosystems.

Rubin, Jerry. 2009. *Why your world is about to get a whole lot smaller: Oil and the end of globalization.* Toronto, ON: Random House Canada. Rubin argues that peak oil essentially ensures that transportation costs will increase dramatically between now and mid-century, which will essentially be the death-nell of globalization. In its place, we will have to re-construct more self-reliant regional economies.

Ruskin, John. 1996. Morals and Religion. In: *Less is more: An anthology of ancient & modern voices raised in praise of simplicity*, ed. Goldian VandenBroeck. Rochester, VT: Inner Traditions.

Schor, Juliet B. 1992. *The overworked American: The unexpected decline of leisure*, New York: Basic Books.

Schumacher, E.F. 1973. *Small is beautiful: A study of economics as if people mattered*, ed. E. F. Schumacher. London, UK: Vintage.

―――. 1973. Buddhist Economics. In: *Small is beautiful: A study of economics as if people mattered*, ed. E. F. Schumacher. London, UK: Vintage Books.

―――. 1977. *A guide for the perplexed.* New York, NY: Harper & Row.

Schwartz, B. 2004. *The paradox of choice - Why more is less.* New York, NY: HarperPerennial. Schwartz argues that a key tenet of the good life in consumer culture is that freedom is essential to well-being. Increasing freedom amounts to increasing the choices we have among things to consume or experiences to enjoy. Thus having more choices should expand freedom, which in turn should increase well-being. In fact, however, increasing options is generally stressful for people if the number of options exceeds some unspecified threshold. This stress partly depends on how important it is to a person to make the best possible choice from among the options available which is progressively more difficult to do the more options are available. Second, when many options are available and a person makes a poor choice, it is not easy to blame the lack of choices for one's lack of satisfaction. Instead, we wind up blaming ourselves because, after all, so many choices were available that it must be our lack of skill in choice making that explains our dissatisfaction. Moreover, having made a choice, even one we are happy with, does not protect us from speculating about what we may have missed by making the selection we did, i.e., essentially obsessing about the opportunity-cost associated with the choice we made. Thus, even when we make good choices from a wide array of possibilities, the pleasure we feel is diminished when we are preoccupied by thinking about opportunity costs. Finally, liberal societies that allow a wide array of choices in all sorts of social situations rather than prescribing roles, duties, rules, and responsibilities more strictly, tend to evoke stress and depression because every situation during the day becomes a matter of choice and decision-making. This can be extremely fatiguing, contributes to depression, and feeds stress as well. Perhaps this is part of the appeal of fundamentalist movements of all sorts, especially religions, that offer strict rules of conduct for their members, hence relieving them of the stress of making all their decisions personally.

Segal, Jerome. 1999. *Graceful simplicity: The philosophy and politics of the alternative American dream.* Berkeley, CA: University of California Press. Segal outlines an interesting debate concerning the nature of progress that occurred in the eighteenth century and has continued in one form or another ever since. The central question was whether there is such a thing as human progress? It turns out that it is quite difficult to demonstrate that human character has improved over the centuries, or whether we can find examples of people who are any more morally or spiritually evolved today than were Jesus or Pericles, or Socrates, or Buddha. Moreover, even given the examples of these spiritual prodigies, there seems to be little evidence that human moral development is in any way cumulative. Each person must start over again to discover wisdom and cultivate personal integrity, as did the early masters, although their life stories and teachings are indeed helpful and inspiring.

Where we do seem to discern evidence of cumulative progress, however, is in the field of science and technology. Here discoveries accumulate that allow each succeeding generation to build on the insights and sacrifices of the previous generation to attain ever more impressive results. So while improvement in human character seems to be non-cumulative and no more widespread than in ancient times, it is possible to mark a very considerable record of material and technical progress from the past, which promises in principle to continue indefinitely.

The cultural effect of this conversation, however, has been essentially to abandon any serious discussion concerning the improvement of character, even in individual cases, and to focus nearly all our attention on the development of material technology. Of course individuals are here and there deeply interested and committed to self-improvement. But we must observe that this is not a major focus of attention in public discourses, political debates, or investment of public time and resources. There are publicly funded programs of scientific research and technical development, but few if any such programs of research and development into expanding human happiness, virtue, or well-being. There appears to be no such thing as a "Manhattan Project" project for the human soul. Thus our collective attention, concern, and commitment has come to be almost entirely usurped by the technological project, which has become entirely conflated with the human project.

Self-Storage Association. 2007. Self-Storage Association: 81% growth in number of US facilities since 2000. Business Wire, August 31, 2007.   http://www.allbusiness.com/construction/building-renovation/5268603-1.html. "New information released this week by the Alexandria, Virginia-based Self-Storage Association (SSA) indicates that the number of primary self-storage facilities in the United States has nearly doubled since the year 2000. At the end of 2006, 51,2000 primary self-storage facilities dotted the country with 23,075 of those facilities added between 2000 and 2006. This represents an 81% growth in the number of facilities during this period."

Sheldrake, Rupert. 1988. *The presence of the past: Morphic resonance and the habits of nature.* New York, NY: Times Books.

Shi, David E. 1985. *The simple life: Plain living and high thinking in American culture.* New York, NY: Oxford University Press.

Shiva, Vandana. 1991. The seed and the spinning wheel. In: *The violence of the green revolution: Third world agriculture, ecology and politics.* 231-257. London, UK: ZED Books.

Smith, G. D. 1996. Income inequality and mortality: Why are they related? British Medical Journal, 312:987-988. How does the gap between rich and poor harm the health of the poor? Evidently, the psychological hardship of being low down on the social ladder has detrimental effects on people[s' health], beyond whatever effects are produced by the substandard housing, nutrition, air quality, recreational opportunities, and medical care enjoyed by the poor.

Soleri, P. and the Consanti Foundation. www.arcosanti.org.

Solnit, Rebecca. 2009. *A paradise built in hell: The extraordinary communities that arise in disaster.* New York, NY: Penguin.

Spina, Anthony. 1998. Research shows new aspects of voluntary simplicity. The Simple Living Network. Spina conducted research on people who had made a decision to take up the practice of voluntary simplicity and their reasons for doing so. His research respondents consistently reported that succeeding in consumer culture carried them away from the values in life that mattered most to them. These values Spina called the "Life World" which included the day-to-day, face-to-face relationships and experiences that give our lives meaning. The Life World provides the signals we need to stay in touch with what matters to us and feeds our souls. Consumer culture, by contrast, was perceived as a source of noise that blurred or dimmed out signals from the Life World. This noise consisted of physical noise itself, but much more of a torrent of information, advertising, propaganda, and urgent messages of all sorts arising from governments and commercial interests. The result was that people eventually felt as though they were wandering in a data smog of information that lost relevance in direct proportion to its abundance. Escaping this milieu eventually became an urgent matter if staying connected with one's Life World was to be possible. Voluntary simplicity provided both the tools and the rationale for a transition out of consumer culture and its smog of information to recover the values and experiences of the Life World.

Stockholm International Water Institute, the UN Food and Agriculture Organization, and the International Water Management Institute. 2008. Saving water: From field to fork - Curbing losses and wastage in the food chain. *Environment News Service* (accessed August 22, 2008).

Tart, Charles. 1994. *Living the mindful life: A handbook for living in the present moment.* London, UK: Shambala. In popular culture, mindfulness can mean just paying attention to the details of a situation or decision and making responsible choices. It includes looking into the background of the question at hand, making an unhurried and considered decision, and including in that decision everything that should rightly be included. Being mindful is thus a sort of synonym for due diligence or being prudent in our decision-making.

Charles Tart, a twentieth-century cognitive psychologist, practitioner of Tibetan Buddhism, and pioneer in the study of changing states of consciousness, has also identified four other shades of meaning that define mindfulness:

Mindfulness can refer to a clear, lucid quality of awareness of the everyday experiences of life. The state of awareness is focused on actual happenings in the present moment, undistracted by fantasies of what has happened (memory) or fantasies of what might happen (imagination).

Mindfulness may refer to a clear quality of awareness as applied to deeper and more subtle processes of the mind. The capacity to distinguish among sensations, perceptions, memories, thoughts, imagination, etc., and how these arise and succeed each other and from where they originate.

Mindfulness can refer to awareness of being aware (witness consciousness). This is a form of self-consciousness which consists in not being totally identified or completely absorbed in the content of ongoing experience: some part of the mind, a neutral observer or "fair witness" remains aware, in a relatively objective way, of the nature of on-going experience as related immediately to here and now existence. This is "self-remembering"—being clearly aware of what is happening, and also aware of oneself as being aware of them.

Mindfulness can be a continuous and precise awareness of the process of being aware, such that a thought is recognized at the time as a thought, a perception as a perception, an emotion as an emotion, etc., rather than mistaking any of these for each other.

Tenner, E. 1996. *Why things bite back: Technology and the revenge of unintended consequences.* New York, NY: Alfred A. Knopf, Inc.

The Global Ecovillage Network, http://gen.ecovillage.org.

The Simplicity Forum, http://www.thesimplicityforum.org.

Thera, Soma. 1967. *The way of mindfulness: The Satipatthana Sutta and its commentary.* Kandy, Sri Lanka: Buddhist Publication Society. The authoritative classical text on mindfulness practice in the Buddhist tradition. Downloaded as .pdf from http://www.accesstoinsight.org/lib/authors/soma/wayof.html (accessed August 28, 2013).

Thoreau, Henry David. 1992. *Walden.* New York, NY: Alfred A. Knopf.

Toynbee, Arnold. 1947. *A study of history.* Vol. 1. New York, NY: Oxford University Press.

Tsunetomo, Yamamoto. 1716. *Hagakure: The book of the Samurai,* trans. William Scott Wilson. 1973. New York, NY: Kodansha International.

Turner, Chris. 2007. *The geography of hope: A tour of the world we need.* Toronto, ON: Vintage Canada.

United Nations. 1948. *Universal Declaration of Human Rights.* (accessed at: http://www.un.org/en/documents/udhr/index.html).

Von Boxsel, M. 2004. *The encyclopedia of stupidity.* London, UK: Reaktion Books.

Wackernagel, Mathis and William Rees. 1995. *Our ecological footprint: Reducing human impact on the earth.* Gabriola Island, BC: New Society Publishers.

Wackernagel, Mathis, et al. 2002. Tracking the ecological overshoot of the human economy. In *Proceedings of the National Academy of*

Sciences, 99 (14):9266-9271. The most recent measurements of the footprint of the human economy in the ecosphere clearly suggests that such activity already exceeds 120% of earth's capacity to sustain such activities. Previous ecological footprint exercises had postulated the ecological load that would be imposed if everyone on earth consumed as much as North Americans and concluded that at least three additional planets would be required to support such consumption. This scenario, however, was speculative, since everyone on earth does not in fact consume as much as North Americans, nor would this ever be the case as the footprints of people living in the tropics will be smaller due to climate factors. But until 2002, the question remained, what was the current ecological load of human activities? This has now, unfortunately, been answered.

Wagner, Charles. 1903. *The simple life*, trans. Mary Louise Hendee. New York, NY: McClure, Phillips & Co.

Walker, Brian, trans. 1995. *Hua Hu Ching*: Unknown teachings of Lao Tzu. New York, NY: HarperCollins.

Walters, Kerry. 2001. *Rufus Jones: Essential writings*. Maryknoll, NY: Orbis Books.

Watts, Alan (d. 1973) I am indebted to author, philosopher, and Zen roshi, Alan Watts for this example, though I'm afraid I cannot recall which of his many insightful books it may have appeared in.

Wheatley, Myron. J. and Margaret Kellner-Rogers. 1996. *A simple way*. San Francisco, CA: Berrett-Koehler Publishers.

Wikipedia. 2008. Economy of Canada. www.wikipedia.com (accessed June 9, 2008).

Wikipedia, (b) Peak uranium. http://en.wikipedia.org/wiki/Peak_uranium (accessed February 9, 2011). The question of exactly how much uranium is available worldwide, how much of it can be economically extracted and converted to energy, what proportion of total energy demand can be met from nuclear sources, and when, if ever, the world will encounter a "uranium peak" are all highly contentious questions. Some authorities believe world peak uranium production was achieved in 1980-81 and production has been declining ever since. Other authorities are far more optimistic and predict thousands of years of potential supply depending on how much we are prepared to pay for it and what level of risk society is prepared to accept. Many projected supply scenarios seem to compare known reserves to current consumption rates, thus making it appear as though many centuries of supply are available, but few scenarios seem to compare know reserves against total global demand for energy. Since energy from nuclear sources still only represents a small fraction of total energy when compared to consumption of fossil fuels, it is reasonable to infer that if nuclear energy became the world's dominant supply, reserves would be depleted far sooner than the most optimistic scenarios suggest.

Wikipedia. "Military budget of the United States." Wikipedia. http://en.wikipedia.org/wiki/Military_budget_of_the_United_State s (accessed May 31, 2012).

Wikipedia, (a) Military Budget of the United States, http://en.wikipedia.org/wiki/Military_budget_of_the_United_State s (accessed May 31, 2012). The military and military-related budgetary expenditures of the United States in FY 2010, for example, totaled somewhere between $1.01 and $1.35 trillion, and spending for the Department of Homeland Security totaled $56.4 billion for the same period (Wikipedia, "United States Department of Homeland Security", http://en.wikipedia.org/wiki/United_States_Department_of_Home land_Security (accessed May 31, 2012). These budgets exceed the total military spending for the rest of the world combined.

Wilber, Ken. 1998. *The essential Ken Wilber: An introductory reader.* Boston, MA: Shambhala:88-91.

Williams, Paul, 1973. *Das Energi*, New York, NY: Elektra Books.

Winnipeg Free Press. October 24, 1998. (Associated Press wire story).

Woolman, John. 1991. A Plea for the Poor or A Word of Remembrance and Caution to the Rich. In: *Moulton, The journal and major essays of John Woolman*, ed. P. Philips. Richmond, IN: Friends United Press. A classic example of concern for the impact of luxury consumption on human well-being is expressed by the eighteenth-century Quaker preacher John Woolman, who argued that what was necessary for a decent life could be easily and honestly obtained, but that craving for luxuries caused plantation owners and the managers of industrial firms and trading networks to work both their employees and their animals too hard, to undertake miserable and dangerous sea voyages to Europe merely to import superfluous fashion objects and luxuries, and most troubling of all to Woolman, to support the institution of slavery and appropriation of land from aboriginal peoples.

By only slight extension we can see these same dynamics at work today when children in China and other south Asian countries are engaged to dismantle the toxic materials present in electronic wastes imported from other parts of the world, and where the continual inducements of consumer advertising entice North American consumers to over-extend themselves in the use of credit—average individual consumer debt at this writing amounting to almost 1.5 times their average annual incomes.

World Public Opinion.org, 2010. Voters say election full of misleading and false information: Poll also finds voters were misinformed on key issues. http://www.worldpublicopinion.org/pipa/articles/brunitedstates canadara/671.php?nid=&id=&pnt=671&lb= (accessed December 9, 2010).

World Resources Institute. *A guide to world resources 2000-2001: People and ecosystems: The fraying web of life.* Washington: World Resources Institute, 2001.

Wright, Ronald. 2004. *A short history of progress.* Toronto: Anansi Press, 2004.

Young, Mildred Binns. 1939. *Functional poverty.* Wallingford, PA: Pendle Hill.

Young, William; Kumju Hwang; Seonaidh McDonald; Caroline Oates. 2004. Understanding individual decision-making for sustainable consumption. http://72.14.205.104/search?q=cache:8-UNTLU01J0J:homepages.see.leeds.ac.uk/~leckh/leeds04/2.5Young%2520et%2520al.pdf+public+attitudes+voluntary+simplicity&hl=en&ct=clnk&cd=27&gl=ca&client=firefox-a (accessed August 28, 2013).

ABOUT THE AUTHOR

Mark Burch is an author, educator, and group facilitator who has practiced simple living since the 1960s. Since 1995, he has offered presentations, workshops and courses on voluntary simplicity. In 2010, he retired as Director of the Campus Sustainability Office for The University of Winnipeg, and is currently a Faculty Member of The Simplicity Institute in Melbourne, Australia, Chair of Transition Winnipeg, a Director of Sustainable South Osborne Community Cooperative, and Clerk of the Peace and Social Action Committee of the Winnipeg Monthly Meeting of The Religious Society of Friends (Quakers). He has been a featured guest on CBC-TV Man Alive, and What On Earth?, CBC Radio Ideas, Vision TV's The Simple Way, and a radio columnist on Discovering Simplicity for CBC-Winnipeg. Other books by Mark A. Burch include:

Simplicity: Notes, Stories and Exercises for Discovering Unimaginable Wealth, New Society Publishers, 1995.

Simplicity Study Circles: A Step-by-step Guide, New Society Publishers, 1997.

Stepping Lightly: Simplicity for People and the Planet, New Society Publishers, 2000.

The Simplicity Circle: Tools for Participation, (Co-authored with Eszti Nagy), Simplicity Practice and Resource Centre, 2007.

De-Junking: A Tool for Clutter-Busting, The Simplicity Practice and Resource Centre, 2007.

The Simplicity Circle II: Tools for Participation, (Co-authored with Eszti Nagy and Kelly Janz) Simplicity Practice and Resource Centre, 2009.

The Simplicity Exercises: A Sourcebook for Educators in Simple Living, The Simplicity Institute, Melbourne, Australia, 2012.

CPSIA information can be obtained at www.ICGtesting.com
Printed in the USA
BVOW07s1729051214

377993BV00001B/5/P